TOP **10**
LONDON

ROGER WILLIAMS

DK
EYEWITNESS TRAVEL

Left **Old English Garden, Battersea Park** Right **Tower Bridge**

LONDON, NEW YORK,
MELBOURNE, MUNICH AND DELHI
www.dk.com

Colour reproduction by Colourscan, Singapore
Printed and bound in China by Leo Paper
Products Ltd
12 13 14 15 10 9 8 7 6 5 4 3 2 1

Published in the United States by DK Publishing,
375 Hudson Street, New York, New York 10014

**Copyright 2002, 2012
© Dorling Kindersley Limited
Reprinted with revisions
2004, 2005, 2006, 2007, 2008, 2009,
2010, 2011, 2012**

Published in Great Britain by
Dorling Kindersley Limited

A catalog record for this book is available from
the Library of Congress
ISSN 1479-344X
ISBN 978-0-7566-8449-5

Within each Top 10 list in this book, no hierarchy
of quality or popularity is implied. All 10 are, in the
editor's opinion, of roughly equal merit.

Floors are referred to throughout in accordance
with British usage; ie the "first floor" is the floor
above ground level.

MIX
Paper from
responsible sources
FSC™ C018179
www.fsc.org

Contents

London's Top 10

Cover: Front – **Alamy Images**: Roberto Herrett main. **DK Images** Steve Bere bl.
Spine – **DK Images** Stephen Oliver b. Back – **DK Images:** Philip Enticknap cl; Stephen Oliver cr;
Getty Images: Joe Cornish c.

Left **Houseboat, Regent's Canal** Right **Riverside Walk, Southbank**

Left **Lamb and Flag pub, Covent Garden** Right **View from Parliament Hill**

LONDON'S
TOP 10

🔟 London Highlights

A city of infinite colour and variety, London is both richly historic, tracing its roots back over 2000 years, and unceasingly modern, at the forefront of fashion, music and the arts. There is a fantastic amount to interest and entertain the visitor here: a selection of the best of the best is explored in the following chapter.

British Museum
The oldest museum in the world, it contains a rich collection of treasures and artifacts from every corner of the globe *(see pp8–11)*.

National Gallery and National Portrait Gallery
The nation's most important art collections are held here, including this 1581 miniature of Sir Francis Drake *(see pp12–15)*.

London Eye
The world's tallest cantilevered observation wheel sits in the heart of London opposite the Houses of Parliament, on the South Bank, and offers great views of the city *(see pp16–17)*.

Camden

Regent's Park

St. John's Wood

Maida Vale

Marylebone

Notting Hill

Paddington

Soho

Mayfair

Hyde Park

St James's

Kensington Gardens

Holland Park

Green Park

7

Knightsbridge

6
5

Kensington

Victoria

Chelsea

Pimlico

Tate Modern and Tate Britain
London's two Tate galleries house a superb collection of international art. Tate Modern focuses on contemporary work after 1900, and Tate Britain on art from 1500 to the present *(see pp18–21)*.

Natural History Museum
The enormous and varied collection here explores both the geology of the Earth and the incredible range of life it supports *(see pp22–3)*.

Science Museum
6 A huge museum with fascinating exhibits that demonstrate and explain the wonders of science *(see pp24–5)*.

Westminster Abbey and Parliament Square
8 This royal abbey has, since 1066, been the place where all Britain's monarchs have been crowned *(see pp32–5)*.

Buckingham Palace
7 The official home of the Queen, Buckingham Palace is one of the city's most recognizable landmarks, where the changing of the Queen's guard happens every day *(see pp26–7)*.

Tower of London
9 Steeped in bloody history, the Tower has been a royal palace, fortress and prison, and is the home of the Crown Jewels *(see pp36–9)*.

St Paul's Cathedral
10 Sir Christopher Wren's Baroque masterpiece, St Paul's still dominates the City skyline and has been the setting of many great ceremonial events *(see pp40–43)*.

⑩ British Museum

The world's oldest museum has no fewer than 6 million items spanning 1.8 million years of world civilization. The collection was started with the bequest of a physician and antiquarian, Sir Hans Sloane, in 1753. In the 18th and 19th centuries travellers and emissaries, such as Captain James Cook, Lord Elgin, Lord Curzon and Charles Townley, added treasures from around the world. The present, Classical style building was completed around 1850. The central courtyard is used as a public space, the Great Court (see p11).

The British Museum façade

● There are three cafés and one restaurant.

Picnics can be eaten in the forecourt by the main entrance.

◐ Highlights' tours give an introduction to the collection.

The British Museum shop sells reproduction artifacts.

• Great Russell Street WC1
• Map L1
• 020 7323 8000
• www.britishmuseum.org
• Open 10am–5:30pm Sat–Thu, 10am–8:30pm Fri. Great Court: Open 10am–5:30pm Sat–Thu, 10am–8:30pm Fri
• Guided tours at 10:30am, 1pm & 3pm daily

Top 10 Exhibits

1 Parthenon Sculptures
2 Mummified Cat
3 Ram in a Thicket
4 Mildenhall Treasure
5 Rosetta Stone
6 Portland Vase
7 Rameses II
8 Mixtec-Aztec Mosaic Mask
9 Kwakwaka'wakw
10 Amitabha Buddha

Parthenon Sculptures

This spectacular 5th-century BC frieze from the Parthenon *(below)* was made under Pericles and shows a procession in honour of the goddess Athena. It was obtained in 1779 by Lord Elgin, Ambassador to Constantinople.

Key to Floorplan

▨	Lower floor
▨	Ground floor
▨	Upper floor

Mummified Cat

Cats and sacred cows were mummified in Ancient Egypt. This cat comes from Abydos and dates from around 30 BC. Many Egyptian deities took on animal shapes, as seen on wall paintings and other artifacts.

Ram in a Thicket

Decorated with shells and gold leaf, this priceless ornament comes from Ur in Sumer, one of the world's earliest civilizations. Games and musical instruments are also displayed.

Mildenhall Treasure

Some of the greatest early English treasures are 34 silver plates from the 4th century, found at Mildenhall in Suffolk. Their lively decorations include sea nymphs, satyrs and Hercules.

Rosetta Stone

In 196 BC Egyptian priests wrote a decree on this tablet in both Greek and in Egyptian hieroglyphics. Found in 1799, it proved crucial in deciphering Egyptian pictorial writing.

Portland Vase

Sold by Britain's ambassador to Naples, Sir William Hamilton, to the Duchess of Portland, this exquisite 1st-century blue-and-opaque glass vase comes from a tomb in Rome, and was probably made by a Greek craftsman.

Rameses II

This is all that remains of the colossal granite statue of Rameses II (c1275 BC) from his memorial temple at Thebes. The statue was acquired in the late 18th century by Charles Townley, British ambassador to Rome.

Mixtec-Aztec Mosaic Mask

Made by Mixtec artisans for the Aztec royal court in Mexico, this mosaic mask *(below)* is believed to be of the god Quetzalcoatl, and dates from the 15th century.

Kwakwaka'wakw

The large, carved and painted wood thunderbird from North America was used as an anvil for breaking *coppers* (a form of currency) at *potlatches* (ceremonies of Pacific Coast peoples in which chiefs destroyed their worldly goods).

Amitabha Buddha

This impressive stoneware Buddha dates from around AD 585, during the Chinese Sui Dynasty, when Buddhism became the state religion.

Museum Guide

Free maps are available and guides are on sale at the information desk in the Great Court and shops. Otherwise start to the left of the main entrance with the Assyrian, Egyptian, Greek and Roman galleries. The North Wing ethnography and Asian galleries provide a change from Classical material, as do the early British, medieval and Renaissance collections on the east side.

For more London museums See pp48–9

Left **Classical colonnade, British Museum** Right **Lindow Man**

🔟 British Museum Collections

1 Middle East
Some 6,000 years of history start with the spectacular carved reliefs from the Assyrian palace of Nineveh.

2 Ancient Egyptian and Sudanese
Mummies and sarcophagi are among 70,000 objects in one of the world's greatest collections.

Ancient Greek vase

3 Greek and Roman Antiquities
Highlights from the Classical world (c.3000 BC to c.AD 400) include the Parthenon sculptures and exquisite Greek and Roman vases.

4 Japanese and Oriental Antiquities
Buddhist limestone reliefs from India, Chinese antiquities, Islamic pottery and a Japanese collection so large it has to be shown on a rotating basis.

Native Canadian gull mask

5 Ethnography
An incredible 350,000 objects from indigenous peoples around the world. The Africa gallery holds a fine array of art and artifacts.

6 Prehistory and Europe
Covering a long period from prehistoric cave dwellers to the

Floorplan

modern day, this collection includes Lindow Man, a 2,000-year-old body found preserved in a peat bog, the Sutton Hoo Ship Burial and some fine decorative arts including medieval jewellery and Renaissance clocks.

7 Coins and Medals
A comprehensive collection of more than 750,000 coins and medals dating from the 7th century BC to the present day.

8 Prints and Drawings
Priceless prints and drawings from the Renaissance form part of this rotating collection.

9 Enlightenment
This exhibition features the museum's 18th-century collections from around the world.

10 The Joseph Hotung Great Court Gallery
This small gallery is used for temporary exhibitions.

For more London museums **See pp48–9**

Top 10 Library Readers

1. Karl Marx (1818–83) German revolutionary
2. Mahatma Gandhi (1869–1948), Indian leader
3. Oscar Wilde (1854–1900), playwright and wit
4. Virginia Woolf (1882–1941), Bloomsbury novelist
5. WB Yeats (1865–1939), Irish poet and playwright
6. Thomas Hardy (1840–1928), English novelist
7. George Bernard Shaw (1856–1950), Irish playwright
8. EM Forster (1879–1970), English novelist
9. Rudyard Kipling (1865–1936) Poet, novelist and chronicler of Empire
10. Leon Trotsky (1879–1940), Russian revolutionary

The Great Court

A magnificent glass-roofed addition encloses the heart of the British Museum. Opened in December 2000, the Great Court was designed by architect Sir Norman Foster. In the centre of the Court is the domed Reading Room, built in 1857. Holding one of the world's most important collections of books and manuscripts, the Reading Room has been the workplace of some of London's greatest writers and is now being used to host major exhibitions. The Great Court is the capital's largest covered square and contains shops, cafés and the British Museum's main ticket and information desk, supplying visitors with everything they need for an informed visit.

Rooftop View of the Great Court
In the heart of the city, the top of the museum's Reading Room dome can be seen above the rooftops, protruding from the impressive glass roof of the Great Court.

The Reading Room at the centre of the Great Court

TOP 10 National Gallery

The National Gallery has around 2,300 pictures, from the early Renaissance to the Impressionists (1250–1900), forming one of the greatest collections in the world. Containing work by the most important painters of the main European schools, the collection was acquired by the government from John Julius Angerstein in 1824, and moved to the present building (also home to the National Portrait Gallery, see pp14–15) in 1838. The Sainsbury Wing, built in 1991, houses the excellent early Renaissance collection.

National Gallery façade

🍴 There is a café and a good restaurant.

📚 The Sainsbury Wing has an excellent art bookshop.

Guided tours and audio guides are available.

Explore the collection on screen with ArtStart, which is situated in the Sainsbury Wing.

- Trafalgar Square WC2
- Map L4
- 020 7747 2885
- www.nationalgallery. org.uk
- Open 10am–6pm Sat–Thu (10am–9pm Fri)
- Free
- Free guided tours at 11:30am and 2:30pm daily (also 7pm Fri)

Top 10 Paintings

1. The Virgin and Child with St Anne and St John the Baptist
2. The Arnolfini Portrait
3. The Ambassadors
4. The Wilton Diptych
5. The Rokeby Venus
6. Mystic Nativity
7. The Sunflowers
8. A Young Woman Standing at a Virginal
9. A Woman Bathing in a Stream
10. Bathers at La Grenouillière

1 The Virgin and Child with St Anne and St John the Baptist

This full-size drawing for a painting, known as a cartoon (from *cartone*, a large sheet of paper), is one of the masterpieces of the Renaissance, by Leonardo da Vinci (1452–1519).

2 The Arnolfini Portrait

One of the most famous paintings from the extensive Flemish collection is this unusual and masterly portrait of an Italian banker and his wife in Bruges *(above)*. Jan van Eyck (c.1385–1441) brought oil painting to a new and colourful height.

3 The Ambassadors

Symbols, such as the foreshortened skull foretelling death, abound in this painting by Hans Holbein (1533).

Sainsbury Wing entrance

Key to Floorplan

▨	13th–15th century
▨	16th century
▨	17th century
▨	18th–early 20th century

5 The Rokeby Venus
Painted in Rome to replace a lost Venetian painting, *The Rokeby Venus (left)* is the only nude by Diego Velázquez (1599–1660), court painter to Spain's Philip IV.

6 Mystic Nativity
Feminine grace has never been depicted better than by the painter Sandro Botticelli (1445–1510). Painted in a centennial year, *Mystic Nativity* reflects his own anxieties, with an inscription from *Revelation*.

9 A Woman Bathing in a Stream
This portrait by Rembrandt (1606–69) was painted when his technical powers were at their height, and shows his striking brushwork and mastery of earthy colours.

7 The Sunflowers
This work was painted in Arles in France during a period of rare optimism while Van Gogh (1853–90) was awaiting the arrival of his hero, the avant-garde painter Paul Gauguin.

Getty entrance

Trafalgar Square entrance

4 The Wilton Diptych
A highlight of Gothic art, this exquisite English royal painting *(below)*, by an unknown artist, shows Richard II being recommended to the Virgin by saints John the Baptist, Edward and Edmund.

8 A Young Woman Standing at a Virginal
Peace and calm rule the works of the Dutch painter Jan Vermeer (1632–75). Many of his interiors *(above)* were painted in his home in Delft, but it has never been possible to identify his models.

10 Bathers at La Grenouillière
Claude Monet (1840–1926), the original Impressionist, explored the effect of light on water at La Grenouillière *(above)*, a popular bathing spot on the Seine, where he worked alongside Auguste Renoir.

Gallery Guide
The gallery is divided into four areas. The Sainsbury Wing contains the Early Renaissance collection, with paintings from 1250 to 1500. The West Wing displays works from 1500 to 1600, the North Wing 1600–1700, and the East Wing 1700–1900. Although the main entrance is on Trafalgar Square, the Sainsbury Wing makes a more sensible starting point.

For more London galleries **See pp50–51**

🔟 National Portrait Gallery

This is one of the most unexpectedly pleasing galleries in London. Unrelated to the neighbouring National Gallery, it opened in 1856. Well-known names can be put to some not-so-well-known faces, and there are some fascinating paintings from Tudor times to the present day. Royalty is depicted from Richard II (1367–1400) to Queen Elizabeth II, and the collection also holds a 1554 miniature, the oldest self-portrait in oils in England. The displays are changed regularly so paintings from the collection are not always on view.

Royal coat of arms, main gallery entrance

🍴 **The Portrait Restaurant has great views across Trafalgar Square, down Whitehall to Parliament.**

🛍 **The Gallery bookshop stocks fashion, costume, history and biography titles.**

The ground-floor gift shop has good postcards.

A range of talks and free music events take place on Thursdays and Fridays.

• St Martin's Place WC2
• Map L3
• 020 7312 2463
• www.npg.org.uk
• Open 10am–6pm Sat–Wed, 10am–9pm Thu–Fri
• Free (separate charge for some exhibitions)

Top 10 Portraits

1. Queen Elizabeth I
2. William Shakespeare
3. The Brontës
4. The Whitehall Mural
5. George Gordon, 6th Lord Byron
6. Horatio Nelson
7. Charles II of England
8. Sir Walter Raleigh
9. Germaine Greer
10. Prince William and Prince Harry

2 William Shakespeare

This is the only portrait of Britain's famous playwright known with certainty to have been painted during his lifetime (1564–1616).

The Brontës 3

Found in a drawer in 1914, this portrait of the great literary sisters, Charlotte, Emily and Anne Brontë, from York-shire, was painted by their brother, Branwell. He appears as a faint image behind them.

1 Queen Elizabeth I

This anonymous portrait is one of several of Elizabeth I, who presided over England's Renaissance (1533–1603). The Tudor rooms are the most satisfying in the gallery, and they contain two cases of miniature paintings, a popular genre of the time.

Key to Floorplan

- Ground floor
- First floor
- Second floor

The Whitehall Mural

4 This cartoon of Henry VII and his son Henry VIII by Hans Holbein (1537) was drawn for a large mural in the Palace of Whitehall, lost when the palace burnt down in 1698.

George Gordon, 6th Lord Byron

5 This painting of Lord Byron (1788–1824), by Thomas Phillips, depicts the poet and champion of liberty in Albanian dress. He died fighting with Greek insurgents against the Turks.

Horatio Nelson

6 This 1799 portrait *(below)* by Guy Head depicts Nelson after the Battle of the Nile. Apart from Queen Victoria and the Duke of Wellington, he was painted more often than any other British figure in history.

Charles II of England

7 Produced around 1680 by English portrait painter Thomas Hawker, this painting depicts King Charles II towards the end of his life, looking rather lascivious and a little glum. The image is not a particularly attractive one but it is an important one.

Sir Walter Raleigh

8 This portrait was painted in 1602 when military and naval commander and writer Raleigh was at the height of his renewed favour with Queen Elizabeth I. The image, by an unknown artist, depicts Raleigh with his son.

Germaine Greer

9 The feminist author of *The Female Eunuch* is brilliantly captured *(below)* by Portuguese artist Paula Rego, the first artist-in-residence at the National Gallery.

Prince William and Prince Harry

10 Commissioned in 2009, this first double portrait of the princes was painted from life by Nicola Jane ("Nicky") Philipps. It shows the Princes wearing the dress uniform of the Household Cavalry (Blues and Royals).

Gallery Guide

The gallery's three floors are arranged chronologically. Take the escalator to the second floor and start with the Tudor and Stuart galleries (1–8). Men and women of arts, science and industry from the 18th and early 19th century are in galleries 9 to 20. The first floor has eminent Victorians and early photographs. The balcony and ground-floor galleries have 20th- and 21st-century works.

 For more London galleries **See pp50–51**

15

🔟 London Eye

An amazing feat of engineering, the world's tallest cantilevered observation wheel offers fascinating views over the whole of London. Towering over the Thames opposite the Houses of Parliament, it was built to celebrate the Millennium year, and has proved enormously popular. Its 32 enclosed capsules each hold 25 people and offer total visibility in all directions. A flight on the London Eye takes 30 minutes and, on a clear day, you can see up to 40 km (25 miles) across the capital and the south of England.

Observation capsule

🍽 There are two cafés in County Hall.

🎫 Tickets are available on the day but advanced booking is advisable, especially at weekends and in the school holidays.

Binoculars are rented out in the ticket hall.

After-dark flights make the city look romantic.

• South Bank SE1
• Map N5
• 0870 5000 600
• www.londoneye.com
• Open Oct–Apr: 10am–8pm daily; May–Sep: 10am–9pm daily (9:30pm Jul–Aug). Ticket office opens 9:30am daily. Closed 25 Dec and early Jan
• Prices vary. Reductions for children, the disabled and senior citizens
• Timed tickets on the hour and half-hour

Top 10 Sights

1. Houses of Parliament
2. Wren Churches
3. Canada Tower
4. The Shard
5. BT Tower
6. Windsor Castle
7. Heathrow
8. Alexandra Palace
9. Crystal Palace
10. Queen Elizabeth II Bridge

1 Houses of Parliament

The London Eye rises high above the Houses of Parliament *(see p34)* on the far side of the Thames. From here you can look down on Big Ben and see the Commons Terrace, where Members of Parliament and the House of Lords drink, dine and discuss policy by the river.

3 Canada Tower

With its distinctive pyramid roof, Canada Tower is located in the heart of Docklands, the East London business and finance centre. It stands in the middle of the Isle of Dogs, in an area formerly occupied by the West India Docks.

2 Wren Churches

The dome of St Paul's *(see pp40–43)* stands out as the star of the City churches. Pricking the sky around it are the spires of Wren's other 31 churches, such as St Bride's, the tallest, on which wedding cakes have been modelled.

The Shard
Designed by Renzo Piano, this 306-m (1,004-ft) glass spire rises from the South Bank at London Bridge and gives the city skyline a new defining point. There is an observation deck on the 72nd floor.

BT Tower
Built for the Post Office in 1961–5, this 190-m (620-ft) tower *(left)* is now a television, radio and telecommunications tower. It was given Grade II Listed Building status in 2003, meaning its now defunct antennas cannot be removed.

Crystal Palace
This BBC transmission mast to the south of the city *(below)* is near the site of the 1851 Great Exhibition "Crystal Palace" that was moved here in 1852 and burned down spectacularly in 1936.

Queen Elizabeth II Bridge
On a clear day you can just make out the lowest downstream crossing on the Thames, a huge suspension bridge at Dartford, some 32 km (20 miles) away. Traffic flows north in a tunnel under the river, south over the bridge.

Windsor Castle
Windsor Castle sits by the Thames to the west of London *(below)*. The largest occupied castle in the world, it is still a favourite residence of the royal family.

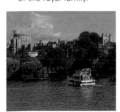

Heathrow
To the west of the city, London's main airport is one of the busiest international airports in the world. The Thames acts as a kind of runway, as planes line up overhead to begin their descent.

Alexandra Palace
The world's first high-definition television broadcasting service was transmitted by the BBC from Alexandra Palace on 2 November 1936. There are exhibition halls and an ice hockey rink here.

Millennium Legacy
The London Eye was one of a number of nationwide projects designed for the Millennium. The focus in London was on the enormous Millennium Dome, a spectacular structure built in Greenwich to house a national exhibition. Other projects were Tate Modern *(see pp18–19)* and the Millennium Bridge, the Waterloo Millennium Pier, the Great Court at the British Museum *(see pp8–11)* and the opening up of Somerset House *(see p99)*.

⑩ Tate Modern

Affiliated with Tate Britain (see pp20–21), one of London's most exciting galleries is housed within the old Bankside power station, on a prime riverside site opposite the City. Large enough for huge installations, its many galleries provide a light, airy space for the Tate's collection of international modern art. This includes works by Dalí, Picasso, Matisse, Rothko and Warhol as well as work by many acclaimed contemporary artists. The displays are changed frequently.

Three Dancers
Pablo Picasso (1881–1973) was noted for the different painting styles he mastered as he pushed the boundaries of Modern Art. *Three Dancers (above)* marks the beginning of a new major phase in his work.

Bankside power station, now home to Tate Modern

🍴 There is a great view from the restaurant on level 7. The Café on level 2 overlooks the gardens. The Espresso Bar on level 4 has a riverside balcony.

🛍 With more than 10,000 titles, the Turbine Hall bookshop claims to be the largest art bookshop in London.

Daily events of cinema, video, talks and tours are advertised in the main hall.

• Bankside SE1
• 020 7887 8888
• www.tate.org.uk
• Map R4
• Open 10am–6pm Mon–Thu, 10am–10pm Fri–Sun. Closed 24–26 Dec
• Free (admission charge for temporary exhibitions)
• A boat service connects with Tate Britain (see p20)

Top 10 Exhibits

1. The Snail
2. The Acrobat and His Partner
3. Whaam!
4. Three Dancers
5. Coffee
6. Suicide
7. Summertime No. 9A
8. The Reckless Sleeper
9. Fish
10. Spatial Concept "Waiting"

The Snail
This 1953 cutout is one of Henri Matisse's (1869–1954) final works, completed whilst bed-ridden. The paper spirals represent a snail's shell.

The Acrobat and His Partner
Fernand Léger (1881–1955) completed this painting *(above)* in 1948, months before attending a Communist-sponsored peace congress. The circus is portrayed as a symbol of energy.

Whaam!
This 1963 painting *(above)* by Roy Lichtenstein (1923–97) is based on an image from *All American Men of War*, published by DC Comics in 1962. He was inspired by comics or advertisements, presenting powerful scenes in an impersonal, detached way.

5 Coffee
Pierre Bonnard (1867–1947) frequently painted life at the dining table. In this 1915 canvas, the artist portrayed his wife Marthe sipping coffee with her pet dachshund by her side, suggesting an intimate domestic routine.

6 Suicide
This painting by George Grosz (1893–1959) reflects the artist's disillusionment with German society especially during World War I.

8 The Reckless Sleeper
René Magritte (1898–1967) painted this work (below) in 1928, during a period in which he explored Surrealism and Freudian symbolism. A man sleeps in an alcove above a dark sky and a tablet embedded with everyday objects, as if dreamed by the sleeper.

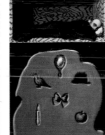

9 Fish
Constantin Brancusi (1876–1957) created Fish in 1926. This sculpture presents a bronze "fish" on a polished disc above a wooden base. Brancusi was known for his ability to capture the essential qualities of his subjects in elementary, abstract forms.

10 Spatial Concept "Waiting"
The Italian-Argentine artist Lucio Fontana (1899–1968) began to cut canvases in 1959. Although these cuts were carefully premeditated, they were executed in an instant. In this work, Spatial Concept "Waiting" (below), the cut erupts from the surface, giving the impression of a gesture towards the viewer in a way that is at once both energetic and threatening.

7 Summertime No. 9A
The American Jackson Pollock (1912–56) was the pioneer of Action Painting. He carried out his first "drip" painting in 1947, pouring paint on to huge canvases on the floor. Summertime No. 9A (below) dates from 1948.

Gallery Guide
The main entrance is down a ramp into the huge Turbine Hall below ground level, on level 1, where the coat check, information and main shop are. You can also enter the gallery on the ground floor, level 2, by the Café or by the Millennium Bridge. The main themed galleries are on level 3 (material gestures; poetry and dream) and level 5, which includes a learning zone. Temporary exhibitions are on level 4, and level 7 has a restaurant with great views of the Thames. As with many London galleries, Tate's works of art are sometimes moved temporarily, loaned out or removed for restoration.

For more London galleries See pp50–51

Tate Britain

Opened in 1897 as the national gallery of British art, the magnificent collection at London's first Tate gallery ranges from 1500 to the present day. Its founder was Henry Tate (1819–99) who made his fortune from sugar. The collection contains works by all Britain's major painters, and was greatly added to by J M W Turner. Paintings are often moved to Tate's other galleries, loaned out or removed for restoration. The works on these pages, therefore, may not always be on display.

Tate Britain's grand portico

🍴 Good basement café.

Excellent restaurant, with good wine list.

🎧 **Free guided tours daily, weekly talks and films shown monthly.**

Comprehensive art bookshop.

Free cloakroom.

- Millbank SW1
- Map E5
- 020 7887 8888
- www.tate.org.uk
- Open 10am–5:50pm daily. Late opening first Fri of the month until 10pm. Closed 24–26 Dec
- Free (admission charge for most temporary exhibitions)
- Tate-to-Tate boat service travels between Tate Britain and Tate Modern every 40 minutes from Millbank Pier outside Tate Britain

Top 10 Paintings

1. Norham Castle, Sunrise
2. The Deluge
3. Wooded Landscape with a Peasant Resting
4. Three Ladies Adorning a Term of Hymen
5. The Lady of Shalott
6. Elohim Creating Adam
7. Girl with a White Dog
8. Carnation, Lily, Lily, Rose
9. Pink and Green Sleepers
10. Three Studies for Figures at the Base of a Crucifixion

1 Norham Castle, Sunrise
J M W Turner (1775–1851) was the great genius of English landscape painting. This work typifies his use of abstraction and luminosity of colour.

2 The Deluge
Irish artist Francis Danby (1793–1861) moved to London from Bristol in 1824, where he painted large-scale biblical subjects as well as fantasy landscapes, such as this work.

3 Wooded Landscape with a Peasant Resting
Thomas Gainsborough (1727–88) was a portrait and landscape painter and a favourite of the Royal Family. His family groups in landscapes are among the finest "Conversation pieces" in English art. An artistic interpretation of his native Suffolk, this is one of his earliest landscapes, painted in 1747.

4 Three Ladies Adorning a Term of Hymen
Joshua Reynolds (1723–92) was the first president of the Royal Academy and a painter in the "Grand Manner" – as typified by this painting *(above)*. He raised the international status of British art.

5 The Lady of Shalott

Educated at the Royal Academy Schools in London, John William Waterhouse (1849–1917) famously revived the literary themes of the Pre-Raphaelites, as seen in this piece. Waterhouse's subject is taken from Lord Alfred Tennyson's tragic poem of the same name.

6 Elohim Creating Adam

Born in London and trained at the Royal Academy School, poet, mystic, illustrator and engraver William Blake (1757–1827) claimed to be guided by visions. *Elohim Creating Adam* is typical of his work, of which the Tate has a large collection.

7 Girl with a White Dog

This picture *(above)* by Lucian Freud (b1922) shows the artist's wife while pregnant. The style of the painting has roots in the linear portraiture of the 19th-century French painter Ingres.

8 Carnation, Lily, Lily, Rose

John Singer Sargent (1856–1925) moved to Britain from Paris in 1885 and adopted some of the Impressionist techniques established by his friend, Claude Monet. The title of this work is from a popular song of the time.

9 Pink and Green Sleepers

One of several 20th-century artists from Yorkshire, Henry Moore (1898–1986) was an outstanding sculptor whose work is on public display around London. This drawing by Moore shows two sleeping figures.

10 Three Studies for Figures at the Base of a Crucifixion

Leading light of the Soho arts scene, Francis Bacon (1910–1992) was uncompromising in his view of life. When first shown, this series of paintings caused an immediate sensation, shocking audiences with their savage imagery. They have become some of his best-known works *(below)*.

Gallery Guide

The permanent collection occupies three-quarters of the main floor. Starting in the northwest corner, it follows a broad chronological sweep from the 16th century to the present. The collection is arranged into rooms exploring historical themes interspersed with displays devoted to single major artists. Impressive loan exhibitions covering all manner of British art are installed in the remaining quarter of the main floor and in the six galleries on the lower floor. The Turner Bequest, some 300 oil paintings and about 20,000 watercolours by J M W Turner, is displayed in the adjoining Clore Gallery, with oil paintings and watercolours on view.

➜ *For more London galleries* **See pp50–51**

TOP 10 Natural History Museum

There are some 70 million specimens in the Natural History Museum's fascinating collections. Originally the repository for items brought home by Charles Darwin and Captain Cook's botanist, Joseph Banks, among others, the museum combines traditional displays with innovative, hands-on exhibits. With kid-pleasers such as the impressive dinosaur collection, it remains one of London's most popular museums. Still a hot-house of research, the museum employs 300 scientists and librarians.

Main entrance

🍴 Try the restaurant in the green zone, or the other two cafés and snack bars.

🎫 A number of different tours are available, including a visit to the outdoor Wildlife Garden. Details at the Central Hall information desk.

- *Cromwell Road SW7*
- *Map B5*
- *020 7942 5000*
- *www.nhm.ac.uk*
- *Open 10am–5:50pm daily. Last admission 5:30pm*
- *Closed 24–26 Dec*
- *Free*

Top 10 Exhibits

1 The Vault
2 Earthquake Simulator
3 Images of Nature Gallery
4 Attenborough Studio
5 Model Baby
6 Water Cycle Video Wall
7 Fossils
8 Blue Whale
9 Dinosaurs
10 Darwin Centre

1 The Vault

The museum's extensive collection of gemstones, rocks and minerals includes brilliant red Rhodochrosite from the USA. The displays of glittering and colourful stones and rocks include descriptions of how we depend on them.

2 Earthquake Simulator

The Power Within looks at volcanoes and earthquakes. Experience a simulation of the 1995 Kobe earthquake in a Japanese supermarket *(below)*.

3 Images of Nature Gallery

Opened in January 2011, this gallery showcases the museum's most beautiful historic artworks and modern images of nature. More than 110 exhibits span 350 years to the present day.

4 Attenborough Studio

On the ground floor of the Darwin Centre, the Attenborough Studio is a state-of-the-art audio-visual facility with 64 seats. The venue hosts events, films and talks covering all aspects of life on earth as well as scientific discovery.

Model Baby

5 A giant model of an unborn baby in the Human Biology galleries demonstrates sounds heard in the womb. Other hands-on exhibits test abilities and reactions and show how physical characteristics are inherited.

Water Cycle Video Wall

6 A semi-spherical video wall in the Ecology Gallery shows the water cycle and how it links all life on the planet. A walk-through leaf shows how plants make oxygen.

Dinosaurs

9 T. Rex, one of the museum's impressively life-like animatronic models, lurches and roars in this hugely popular gallery. More traditional exhibits of fossilized skeletons and eggs are also on display.

Darwin Centre

10 One of the centre's many attractions is Cocoon (left), a permanent exhibition where visitors can see incredible insect and plant specimens as well as world leading scientists at work.

Key to Floorplan

▨	Ground floor
▭	First floor
▨	Second floor

Blue Whale

8 The Mammal gallery houses this fascinating exhibit, where both modern mammals and their fossil relatives are dwarfed in comparison to the astounding life-sized model of a blue whale, the largest mammal in the world.

Fossils

7 Marine reptiles that lived at the time of the dinosaurs have survived in some remarkable fossils, such as the pregnant female *Ichthyosaur*, found in a Dorset garden, which lived 187–178 million years ago.

Museum Guide

The Natural History Museum is divided into four zones: the blue zone, which includes the dinosaur gallery and Images of Nature; the green zone , which includes the ecology and creepy-crawlies galleries; the orange zone, which includes a wildlife garden; and the red zone, incorporating the geological displays.

The ornately embellished Cromwell Road entrance leads to the imposing central hall with its grand staircase.

An additional entrance on Exhibition Road leads to the red zone.

Science Museum

Packed with exciting hands-on exhibits, this huge museum explores the fascinating world of science through centuries of scientific and technological development. It shows British inventiveness leading the world in the Industrial Revolution, with looms and steam engines, navigation and early flight. It also has displays on contemporary science, climate change and cutting-edge technologies, with many inter-active exhibits in the hi-tech Wellcome Wing.

Science Museum façade

❶ There is a restaurant, several cafés and a picnic area where you can eat your own food.

❷ Visitor information touch screens throughout the museum give details of exhibits.

The museum store is an excellent place to buy innovative gifts.

• Exhibition Road SW7
• Map B5
• 0870 870 4868
• www.science museum.org.uk
• Open 10am–6pm daily
• Closed 24–26 Dec
• Free (separate charge for special exhibitions, simulator rides and IMAX cinema)

Top 10 Exhibits

1. Exploring Space
2. The Secret Life of the Home
3. Apollo 10 Command Module
4. Harle Sykes Red Mill Engine
5. Puffing Billy
6. Babbage's Difference Engine
7. Who am I?
8. Launchpad
9. IMAX 3D Cinema
10. Pattern Pod

3 Apollo 10 Command Module

The Apollo 10 Command Module, which went around the moon in May 1969, is on display, as is a replica of the Apollo 11 Lunar Lander. Buzz Aldrin and Neil Armstrong stepped onto the moon from the original in July 1969.

1 Exploring Space

Rockets, satellites, space probes and landers can all be explored as well as learning about Sputnik, the world's first satellite, how we sent spacecrafts to other planets and walked on the moon.

2 The Secret Life of the Home

This gallery contains a wacky variety of house-hold gadgets and gizmos, from washing machines to burglar alarms.

4 Harle Sykes Red Mill Engine

This immaculate steam engine *(above)* can some-times be seen up and running. It's just one exhibit in the Energy Hall gallery, which includes one of James Watt's original 1788 rotative steam engines.

Puffing Billy
5 *Puffing Billy (left)* is the world's oldest remaining steam locomotive. It was built in England in 1813 and used to transport coal. George Stephenson's famous 1829 *Rocket*, the first locomotive engine to pull passenger carriages, is also on display.

Babbage's Difference Engine
6 The Computing and Mathematics galleries on the second floor display a model of the *Difference Engine No 2*. Designed by Charles Babbage (1791–1871), it was the forerunner of the modern computer.

IMAX 3D Cinema
9 The cinema shows 2D and 3D films on a screen higher than four double-decker buses. An impressive six-channel surround sound system will totally immerse you in the action.

Pattern Pod
10 Suitable for children under eight, this multi-sensory gallery introduces ideas about patterns in the world. The electronic kaleidoscope and interactive exhibits make science fun.

Who am I?
7 The upgraded Who am I? gallery presents the latest in brain science and genetics through a mixture of interactive exhibits and object-rich displays.

Key to Floorplan
▓	Basement
▓	Ground floor
▓	First floor
▓	Second floor
▓	Third floor
▓	Fourth floor
▓	Fifth floor
▓	Wellcome Wing

Launchpad
8 This hands-on gallery is aimed specifically at children. In this area *(left)*, friendly "explainers" make key science principles fun and easy to understand.

Museum Guide
The museum is spread over seven floors. Heavy machinery and large-scale museum highlights are on the ground floor. Tele-communications, measuring time, and agriculture and weather are on the first floor. The Energy Gallery and computing are on the second floor, and health and flight are on the third. The fourth and fifth floors are dedicated to medical history. At the west end of the building is the four-storey Wellcome Wing.

For more London museums **See pp48–9**

TOP 10 Buckingham Palace

London's most famous residence, and one of its best recognised landmarks, Buckingham Palace was built as a town house for the first Duke of Buckingham around 1705. In 1825, George IV commissioned John Nash to extend the house into a substantial palace. Completed in 1840, it was first occupied by Queen Victoria in 1837. The extensive front of the building was refaced by Sir Aston Webb in 1913. The Palace is now home to the present Queen and the State Rooms are open to the public during summer. Many royal parks and gardens in London are also accessible to the public (see pp28–9).

Decorative lock on Palace gates

Top 10 Highlights

1. Changing of the Guard
2. The Balcony
3. Queen's Gallery
4. Grand Staircase
5. Throne Room
6. Picture Gallery
7. State Ballroom
8. Royal Mews
9. Palace Garden
10. Brougham

Victoria Monument

⭐ Coincide your visit with the Changing of the Guard (see below).

• Buckingham Palace SW1
• Map J6 • 020 7766 7300 (booking line) • www. royalcollection.org.uk
• State Apartments: Open Aug–Sep: 9:45am–6pm daily (last adm 3:45pm). Admission: adults £17; students and over 60s £15.50; under 17s £9.75; family ticket £44; under 5s free
• Royal Mews: 020 7766 7302 Open Apr–Oct: 11am–4pm daily (last adm 3:15pm). Admission: adults £7.75; students and over 60s £7; under 17s £5; under 5s free
• Queen's Gallery: 020 7766 7301 Open 10am–5:30pm (last adm 4:30pm). Admission: adults £15; students and over 60s £13.50; under 17s £8.75; under 5s free

1 Changing of the Guard
The Palace guards, in their familiar red tunics and tall bearskin hats, are changed at 11:30am each morning (and alternate days Aug–Apr, weather permitting). The guards march to the Palace from the nearby Wellington Barracks.

2 The Balcony
On special occasions, the Queen and other members of the Royal Family step on to the Palace balcony to wave to the crowds gathered below.

3 Queen's Gallery
The gallery hosts a changing programme of exhibitions of the Royal Collection's masterpieces, including works by artists such as Johannes Vermeer and Leonardo da Vinci.

4 Grand Staircase
The Ambassadors' Entrance leads into the Grand Hall. From here the magnificent Grand Staircase, with gilded balustrades, rises to the first floor where the State Rooms are found.

5 Throne Room
This houses the thrones of Queen Elizabeth and Prince Philip used for the coronation. Designed by John Nash, the room has a highly ornamented ceiling and magnificent chandeliers.

6 Picture Gallery
One of the largest rooms in the Palace, it has a barrel-vaulted glass ceiling and a number of paintings from the Royal Collection, including works by Rembrandt *(above)*, Rubens and Van Dyck.

7 State Ballroom
Banquets for visiting heads of state are held here. The most glittering social event of the year is in November, when 1,200 members of the Diplomatic Corps arrive in full court dress.

8 Royal Mews
Caring for the Cleveland Bay and Windsor Grey horses that pull the royal coach on state occasions, these are the finest working stables in Britain. The collection of coaches, motorcars and carriages includes the magnificent Gold State Coach, which was built in c.1760.

10 Brougham
Every day a horse-drawn Brougham carriage sets out to collect and deliver royal packages around London, including the Palace's weekly copy of *Country Life*.

9 Palace Garden
The extensive Palace garden is an oasis for wildlife and includes a three-acre lake. There are at least three Royal garden parties each year, to which over 30,000 people attend *(below)*.

Palace Life
The official business of the monarchy takes place in the Palace, which has a staff of around 450. The Duke of Edinburgh, Duke of York, Prince Edward and the Princess Royal all have offices here. The most senior member of the Royal Household is the Lord Chamberlain. The Master of the Household and the Palace's domestic staff organise many functions every year, including Investitures for recipients of awards which are given by the Queen.

 For more on royal London **See pp54–5**

ＴＯＰ 10 Royal Parks and Gardens

Buckingham Palace overlooks two of London's most central Royal Parks – St James's and Green Park – and is just a short walk from Hyde Park and Kensington Gardens. Along with the other London parks, these provide year-round pleasure and an invaluable retreat for all who live, work and visit the city. Many offer facilities for tennis, riding and boating, as well as opportunities for other activities. Picnicking in the park while a band plays is one of London's greatest summer joys.

Statue of Peter Pan in Kensington Gardens

🌀 Most of the larger parks have a number of open-air cafés, restaurants and ice-cream stands.

Parks open at dawn and close at sunset (around 9:30pm in summer). Don't get caught in the middle of large parks just as the sun goes down.

Open-air concerts, festivals and other events are regularly held in Hyde Park, Regent's Park and St James's Park in the summer months.

• Royal Parks HQ, The Old Police House, Hyde Park, London W2
• Map C4
• 020 7298 2000
• www.royalparks.org.uk

Top 10 Green Spaces

1. Hyde Park
2. St James's Park
3. Kensington Gardens
4. Regent's Park
5. Green Park
6. Greenwich Park
7. Richmond Park
8. Primrose Hill
9. Bushy Park
10. Grosvenor Square

1 Hyde Park
One of the most popular features of this huge London park *(above)* *(see p74)* is its lake, the Serpentine, with boats for rent and a swimming area. Horses can be rented and ridden in the park. On Sundays at Speakers' Corner, near Marble Arch, you can get up on a soapbox and address the crowds who gather there.

2 St James's Park
London's most elegant park *(below)* was laid out in the 18th century by Capability Brown. Its lake is home to some 40 varieties of water-fowl. It has an attractive café and, in summer, lunchtime concerts are given on the bandstand *(see p113)*.

3 Kensington Gardens
A continuation of Hyde Park, Kensington Gardens was opened to the public in 1841. Since 2000, the magical Diana, Princess of Wales Memorial Play-ground *(below)* has proved a great hit with children.

Regent's Park
4 Home to London Zoo and an open-air theatre, Regent's Park *(above)* is surrounded by John Nash's Classical terraces. The fragrant Queen Mary's Rose Garden is a delight *(see p129)*.

Greenwich Park
6 The 0° longitude meridian passes through the Royal Observatory Greenwich, located on a hill in this leafy family park. There are great views of the Old Royal Naval College *(below)*, and over London *(see p147)*.

Richmond Park
7 Covering an area of 2,500 acres, this is by far the largest Royal Park. Herds of red and fallow deer *(below)* roam freely across the heath. In late spring, the Isabella Plantation is a blaze of colourful rhododendrons. The Royal Ballet School is based in the White Lodge, originally built for George II in 1727.

Bushy Park
9 Chestnut Sunday in May, when the trees' blossoms are out, is one of the best times to come to Bushy Park, near Hampton Court. Highlights include the Arethusa "Diana" Fountain and Chestnut Avenue.

Grosvenor Square
10 The hub of high society from the early 18th century until World War II, Grosvenor Square is the only London square that is owned by the Crown. On its west side stands the imposing American Embassy.

Green Park
5 Popular with office workers, this small park *(below)* has deckchairs for hire in summer. It was once part of the grounds of St James's Palace.

Primrose Hill
8 North of Regent's Park, Primrose Hill offers spectacular views of the city skyline from its 66-m (216-ft) summit. Once a popular venue for duels, this small park was saved from development in 1841 when it was taken over by the Crown Commissioners.

Sport for Kings

Much of the land of London's Royal Parks was taken from the Church by Henry VIII in the 1530s, during the Reformation. He was a passionate hunter and filled Hyde, Green and St James's parks with deer. Henry also hunted in Greenwich Park, London's oldest, having been founded in 1433.

From the late 17th century, parks were landscaped and gardens laid out. In 1689 William and Mary ordered the planting of Kensington Gardens. In 1811 the Prince Regent and Nash built the private estate that became Regent's Park.

Following pages **View from Trafalgar Square to Houses of Parliament**

Westminster Abbey

A glorious example of Medieval architecture on a truly grand scale, this former Benedictine abbey church stands on the south side of Parliament Square (see pp34–5). Founded in the 11th century by Edward the Confessor, it survived the Reformation and continued as a place of royal ceremonials. Queen Elizabeth II's coronation was held here in 1953 and Princess Diana's funeral in 1997. It was also the venue for the wedding of Prince William to Catherine Middleton in April 2011.

3 Poets' Corner
This corner of the transept contains memorials to many literary giants, including Shakespeare and Dickens.

The Abbey's north transept

🎵 Hear the choir sing at services at 5pm every weekday, 3pm on Saturdays and at the three Sunday services.

Listen to free organ recitals at 5:45pm every Sunday.

Guided tours and audio guides are available.

• Broad Sanctuary SW1
• Map L6
• 020 7222 5152
• www.westminster-abbey.org
• Abbey: open 9:30am–3:30pm Mon–Fri (to 6:30pm Wed), 9:30am–1:30pm Sat. Open Sun for worship only. Museum: open 10:30am–4pm daily. Pyx Chamber and Chapter House: open 10am–4pm daily
• Admission: adults £15; concessions £12; children 11–17 £6 (under 11s free); for family tickets see website

Top 10 Sights

1. St Edward's Chapel
2. Nave
3. Poets' Corner
4. Lady Chapel
5. Coronation Chair
6. Grave of Elizabeth I
7. The Choir
8. Grave of the Unknown Warrior
9. Chapter House
10. Cloisters

1 St Edward's Chapel
The shrine of Edward the Confessor (1003–66), last of the Anglo-Saxon kings, lies at the heart of the Abbey. He built London's first royal palace at Westminster, and founded the present Abbey.

2 Nave
At 32 m (102 ft), this is the tallest Gothic nave in England. Built by the great 14th-century architect Henry Yevele, it is supported externally by flying buttresses.

4 Lady Chapel
The fan vaulting above the nave of this eastern addition to the church is spectacular late Perpendicular *(above)*. Built for Henry VII (1457–1509), it includes two side aisles and five smaller chapels and is the home of the Order of the Bath *(see p36)*.

Preceding pages View of Big Ben from Trafalgar Square

5 Coronation Chair

This simple chair was made in 1301 for Edward I. It is placed in front of the high altar screen on the 13th-century mosaic pavement when used for coronations.

6 Tomb of Elizabeth I

England's great Protestant queen (1553–1603) is buried on one side of the Lady Chapel while the tomb of her Catholic rival, Mary Queen of Scots (beheaded in 1587), is on the other side. Mary's remains were brought to the abbey by James I in 1612.

7 The Choir

The all-boy Westminster Abbey Choir School, the only school in England devoted entirely to choristers, produces the choir which sings here every day. The present organ was installed in 1937 and first used at the coronation of George VI.

Abbey Floorplan

10 Cloisters

The cloisters were located at the heart of the former Benedictine monastery and would have been the monastery's busiest area. On the east side are the only remaining parts of the Norman church, the Pyx Chamber, where coinage was tested in medieval times, and the Undercroft, which contains a museum.

Abbey History

A Benedictine monastery was established by St Dunstan (AD 909–988) on what was the marshy Isle of Thorney. King Edward the Confessor re-endowed the monastery, and founded the present church in 1065. William the Conqueror was crowned here in 1066. Henry III's architect Henry of Reyns rebuilt much of the church in 1245. The nave was completed in 1376. The eastern end of the church was extended by Henry VII who had the Lady Chapel built. Finally, in 1734–45, the twin towers on the west front were completed by Nicholas Hawksmoor.

8 Grave of the Unknown Warrior

The body of an unknown soldier from the battlefields of World War I was buried here in 1920. He represents Britain's war dead.

9 Chapter House

This octagonal building with a 13th-century tiled floor (above and left) is where the Abbey's monks gathered. The House of Commons met here between 1257 and 1542. It is now run by the Abbey and can also be reached via Dean's Yard.

For more London places of worship **See pp46–7**

33

🔟 Parliament Square

The spiritual and political heart of the city, the Palace of Westminster was built here a thousand years ago as a royal household, seat of government and abbey. The square was planned as part of the rebuilding programme following a fire that destroyed the Palace in 1834. Usually known as the Houses of Parliament, the new Palace of Westminster stands opposite Westminster Abbey. On the north side of the square, Parliament Street leads to Whitehall and No.10 Downing Street, the Prime Minister's residence.

Detail above Central Hall window

☕ The basement café in Central Hall is a good place for a snack.

🕐 To avoid long lines for the Strangers' Galleries go after 6pm Mon–Thu.

• Parliament Square SW1
• Map M6
• www.parliament.uk
• The Strangers' Galleries at the Houses of Parliament have limited seating for visitors during debates. Times are given at St Stephen's gate, or phone 020 7219 4272
• Tours can be arranged through MPs at www.parliament.uk • Tickets for summer opening of parliament are available from 0844 209 0382

Top 10 Sights

1. Westminster Abbey
2. Houses of Parliament
3. Big Ben
4. Westminster Hall
5. St Margaret's Church
6. Winston Churchill Statue
7. Central Hall
8. Dean's Yard
9. Jewel Tower
10. Statue of Oliver Cromwell

1 Westminster Abbey
See pp32–3.

3 Big Ben
The huge Clock Tower of the Palace of Westminster is popularly known as Big Ben. However, the name actually refers to the clock's 14-tonne bell, named after Sir Benjamin Hall, who was Chief Commissioner of Works when it was installed in 1858.

4 Westminster Hall
Westminster Hall *(left)* is about all of the original palace that remained after the 1834 fire. For centuries the high court sat beneath its marvellous hammerbeam roof.

2 Houses of Parliament
A Gothic revival building from 1870 by Sir Charles Barry and Augustus Welby Pugin, the Houses of Parliament cover 8 acres and have 1,100 rooms around 11 courtyards. The Commons Chamber *(right)* is where Members of Parliament sit and debate policy.

7 Central Hall

This large assembly hall, built in a Beaux Arts style, was funded by a collection among the Methodist Church who wanted to celebrate the centenary of their founder John Wesley (1703–91).

8 Dean's Yard

Buildings around this secluded square were used by monks before the Dissolution of the Monasteries in the 1530s, which closed their school here. A new Westminster School was founded by Elizabeth I in 1560 and it remains one of Britain's top public schools.

9 Jewel Tower

Built in 1365 to safeguard the treasure of Edward III, this is an isolated survivor of the 1834 fire. A small museum about the history of parliament is housed inside.

10 Statue of Oliver Cromwell

Oliver Cromwell (1599–1658) presided over England's only republic, which began after the Civil War. He was buried in Westminster Abbey, but when the monarchy was restored in 1660, his corpse was taken to Tyburn and hanged as though he were a criminal.

Parliament

The 659 publicly elected Members of Parliament sit in the House of Commons, where the Prime Minister and his or her government sits on the right-hand side of the Speaker, who ensures the House's rules are obeyed. The opposing "shadow" government sits on his left. The neighbouring House of Lords is for an unelected upper chamber, which has around 700 members and limited powers. The Prime Minister attends a weekly audience with the Queen, who today has only a symbolic role.

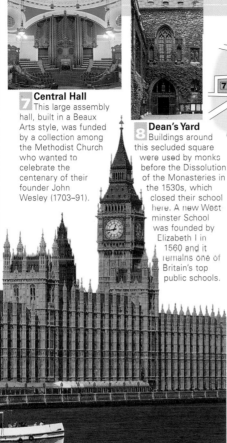

5 St Margaret's Church

Winston Churchill was among many eminent figures to marry in this 15th-century church. William Caxton (1422–91), who set up the first printing press in England, and Sir Walter Raleigh, who established the first British colony in America, are both buried here. Charles I is also remembered *(right)*.

6 Winston Churchill Statue

This powerful statue of Britain's wartime leader (1874–1965), dressed in his famous coat, is one of several statues in the square. These include prime minister Benjamin Disraeli (1804–81), American president Abraham Lincoln (1809–65), and Nelson Mandela (1918–).

🔟 Tower of London

London's great riverside fortress is usually remembered as a place of imprisonment, but it also has a more glorious past. Originally a moated fort, the White Tower was built for William I (the Conqueror) and begun around 1078. Enlarged by later monarchs – including Henry VIII, who famously sent two of his wives to their deaths on Tower Green – it became home to the city arsenal, the Crown Jewels, a menagerie and the Royal Mint.

Yeoman Warders
Some 35 Yeoman Warders now include a female Warder. Former non-commissioned military officers with Long Service and Good Conduct Medals, they wear uniforms dating from Tudor times.

Royal Fusiliers' Museum

🍴 Enjoy a meal at the Tower's café or restaurant.

🕐 Allow at least two hours for your visit.

- Tower Hill EC3
- Map H4
- www.hrp.org.uk
- 0844 482 7777
- Open 9am–5pm Tue–Sat (to 4:30pm winter), 10am–5:30pm Sun & Mon (to 4:30pm winter)
- Admission: adults £18; children 5–15 £9.50 (under 5s free); family tickets (5 people) £50; concessions £15.50

Top 10 Features
1. The White Tower
2. Imperial State Crown
3. Yeoman Warders
4. The Bloody Tower
5. Chapel of St John the Evangelist
6. Ravens
7. Royal Armouries
8. Tower Green
9. Traitors' Gate
10. Beauchamp Tower

The White Tower
The heart of the fortress is a sturdy keep, 30 m (90 ft) tall with walls 5 m (15 ft) thick. It was constructed under William I, and completed in 1097. In 1240 it was whitewashed inside and out, hence its name.

Imperial State Crown
This is the most dazzling of a dozen crowns in the Jewel House. It has 2,800 diamonds, and the sapphire at its top is from the reign of Edward the Confessor (r.1042–66). The crown was made for the coronation of George VI in 1937.

The Bloody Tower
The displays here explore the dark history of the Bloody Tower where murderous deeds, including the killing of the Little Princes, took place.

Chapel of St John the Evangelist
The finest Norman place of worship in London (left), which remains much as it was when it was built, is on the upper floor of the White Tower. In 1399, in preparation for Henry IV's coronation procession, 40 noble knights held vigil here. They then took a purifying bath in an adjoining room and Henry made them the first Knights of the Order of the Bath.

Ravens
When ravens leave the Tower, the saying goes, the building and the monarchy will fall. There are at least six ravens in residence, looked after by the Ravenmaster.

The Royal Armouries
This national collection of arms and armour, shared with the Royal Armouries' other museums in Leeds and Portsmouth, was greatly expanded under Henry VIII.

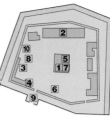

Plan of the Tower

Beauchamp Tower
The displays in this tower explore the different experiences of real prisoners of the Tower, including Lady Jane Grey and the Kray twins. The tower takes its name from Thomas Beauchamp, Earl of Warwick, who was imprisoned here between 1397–99 by Richard II.

Tower Green
The place of execution for nobility, including Lady Jane Grey (1554) and two of Henry VIII's wives – Katherine Howard (1542) and Anne Boleyn (1536).

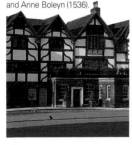

Traitors' Gate
The oak and iron watergate in the outer wall *(above)* was used to bring many prisoners to the Tower, and became known as Traitors' Gate.

Tower History
William I's White Tower, built by Gundolph, Bishop of Rochester, was intended to defend London against attacks – and to be a visible sign to the native Anglo-Saxon population of the conquering Normans' power. Henry III (r.1216–72) built the inner wall with its 13 towers and brought the Crown Jewels here. The city arsenal was kept here, and under Henry VIII (r.1509–47) the Royal Armouries were improved. James I (r.1603–25) was the last monarch to stay in residence. All coinage in Great Britain was minted in the Outer Ward of the Tower until 1810 when the Royal Mint was established nearby, on Tower Hill.

For more on royal London **See pp54–5**

Left **Bell Tower** Centre **Apartment in the Bloody Tower** Right **Beauchamp Tower**

🔟 Tower Prisoners

1 Bishop of Durham
The first political prisoner to be held in the White Tower was Ralph de Flambard, Bishop of Durham. Locked up by Henry I in 1100, he was seen as responsible for the unpopular policies of Henry's predecessor, William II.

2 Henry VI
During the Wars of the Roses, between the rival families of York and Lancaster, Henry VI was kept in Wakefield Tower for five years, until restored to power in 1470.

3 The Little Princes
The alleged murder of Edward, 12, and Richard, 10, in 1483, gave the Bloody Tower its name. It is thought their uncle, Richard III, was responsible.

4 Sir Thomas More
Chancellor Thomas More's refusal to approve Henry VIII's marriage to Anne Boleyn led to his imprisonment in the lower Bell Tower. He was beheaded in 1535.

Chapel of St Peter ad Vincula

5 Henry VIII's Wives
Some of the Tower's most famous victims, such as the beheaded wives of Henry VIII,

Sites of imprisonment

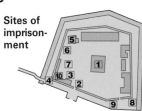

Anne Boleyn and Katherine Howard, are buried in the Chapel Royal of St Peter ad Vincula.

6 The Dudley Family
Lord Dudley and his four brothers were imprisoned (before their execution) in the Beauchamp Tower for supporting Lady Jane Grey's 1554 claim to the throne.

7 Lady Jane Grey
In 1554 Lady Jane Grey was queen for nine days. Aged 16, she was held in the gaoler's house on Tower Green and later executed by order of Queen Mary I.

8 Catholic Martyrs
Under the reign of Elizabeth I (1558–1603), many Catholics were executed. Most, including Jesuits, were held in the Salt Tower.

9 John Gerard
He escaped from the Cradle Tower with a fellow prisoner in 1597, using a rope strung over the moat by an accomplice in a boat.

10 Rudolf Hess
The Tower's last prisoner was Hitler's deputy. He was held in the Queen's House in 1941, after flying to the UK to ask for peace.

For more on royal London See pp54–5

Top 10 Jewels

1. Imperial State Crown
2. St Edward's Crown
3. Imperial Crown of India
4. Queen Victoria's Crown
5. Royal Sceptre
6. Jewelled State Sword
7. George V's Crown
8. The Sovereign's Ring
9. The Sovereign's Orb
10. The Sovereign's Sceptre

The Crown Jewels

The lavish, bejewelled items that make up the sovereign's ceremonial regalia are all in the care of the Tower of London. The collection dates from 1661 when a new set was made to replace those destroyed by Cromwell following the execution of Charles I in 1649. St Edward's Crown was the first subsequent crown to be made, of pure gold, and is the oldest of the 12 crowns here. Other coronation jewels on display include a gold, jewel-studded orb, made in 1661, and a sceptre containing the 530-carat Star of Africa, the biggest cut diamond in the world. The Sovereign's Ring, made for William IV, is sometimes called "the wedding ring of England".

Sovereign's Sceptre

Imperial State Crown
Heavily encrusted with 2,868 diamonds, 17 sapphires, 11 emeralds, 5 rubies and 273 pearls, this crown was designed for the coronation of George VI in 1937.

Queen Elizabeth II wearing the Imperial State Crown, coronation day, 2 June 1953

St Paul's Cathedral

This is the great masterpiece of Sir Christopher Wren, who rebuilt the City's churches after the Great Fire of 1666. Completed in 1708, it was England's first purpose-built Protestant cathedral, and has many similarities with St Peter's in Rome, notably in its enormous ornate dome. It has the largest swinging bell in Europe, Great Paul, which strikes every day at 1pm. The hour bell, Great Tom, strikes the hour and marks the death of royalty and senior churchmen. The cathedral has a reputation for music, and draws its choristers from St Paul's Cathedral School.

St Paul's semi-circular South Porch

🍴 Food and drink in the Crypt Café.

🎵 The most popular service is the choral evensong (usually at 5pm daily) when you can hear the choir.

Guided tours and audio guides are available.

• St Paul's Cathedral, Ludgate Hill EC4
• Map R2
• 020 7236 4128
• www.stpauls.co.uk
• Cathedral: Open 8:30am–4pm Mon–Sat; Galleries: open 9:30am–4pm Mon–Sat
• Admission: adults £12.50; children 6–16 £4 (under-6s free); seniors £11.50; students £9.50; family £29.50; group rates available, call for details • Guided tours at 10:45am, 11:15am, 1:30pm, 2pm (adults £3; concessions £2.50; under 16s £1)

Top 10 Features

1. West Front and Towers
2. Dome
3. Whispering Gallery
4. Quire
5. OBE Chapel
6. High Altar
7. The Light of the World
8. Tijou Gates
9. Mosaics
10. Moore's Mother and Child

Quire

The beautiful stalls and organ case in the Quire are by Grinling Gibbons. Handel and Mendelssohn both played the organ, which dates from 1695.

Dome

One of the largest domes in the world *(above)*, it is 111 m (365 ft) high and weighs 65,000 tonnes. The Golden Gallery at the top, and the larger Stone Gallery, both have great views.

West Front and Towers

The imposing West Front is dominated by two huge towers. The pineapples at their tops are symbols of peace and prosperity. The Great West Door is 9 m (29 ft) high and is used only for ceremonial occasions.

Whispering Gallery

Inside the dome is the famous Whispering Gallery. Words whispered against the wall can be heard on the opposite side of the gallery.

5 OBE Chapel
At the eastern end of the crypt is a chapel devoted to men and women who received the Order of the British Empire, a military and civil honour established in 1917, and the first to include women.

6 High Altar
The magnificent High Altar *(below)* is made from Italian marble, and the canopy is from a sketch by Wren. The large candlesticks are copies of a 16th-century pair made for Cardinal Wolsey.

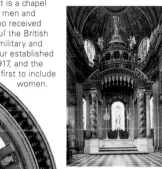

7 The Light of the World
This painting by the Pre-Raphaelite artist Holman Hunt dates from c.1900. It shows Christ knocking on a door that opens from inside, meaning that God can enter our lives only if we invite Him in.

8 Tijou Gates
The French master metal worker Jean Tijou designed these ornate wrought iron gates *(detail above)* in the North Quire Aisle, along with the Whispering Gallery balcony and other cathedral metalwork.

9 Mosaics
Colourful mosaic ceilings were installed in the Quire and Ambulatory *(above)* in the 19th century. They are made with irregular cubes of glass, set at angles so that they sparkle.

Cathedral Floorplan

10 Moore's Mother and Child
The sculptor Henry Moore is commemorated in the crypt. This piece *(right)* is one of a growing number of independent works of art that have been introduced into St Paul's since the 1960s.

St Paul's History
The first known church dedicated to St Paul was built on this site in AD 604. Made of wood, it burned down in 675 and a subsequent church was destroyed by Viking invaders in 962. The third church was built in stone. Following another fire in 1087, it was rebuilt under the Normans as a much larger cathedral, with stone walls and a wooden roof. This was completed in 1300. In 1666 Christopher Wren's plans to restore the building had just been accepted when the Great Fire of London burned the old cathedral to the ground.

Left **View up the Nave** Right **Lord Nelson memorial**

St Paul's Monuments

Tomb of Christopher Wren
St Paul's architect, Sir Christopher Wren (1632–1723), has a plain tomb in the OBE chapel. Its inscription reads, "*Lector, si monumentum requiris, circumspice* – Reader, if you seek a monument, look around you".

Wellington's Tomb
Britain's great military leader and prime minister, Arthur Wellesly, 1st Duke of Wellington (1769–1852), lies in the crypt. He also has a monument in the nave.

Nelson's Tomb
Preserved in brandy and brought home from Trafalgar, sea hero Admiral Lord Nelson (1758–1805) is in the centre of the crypt.

John Donne's Memorial
The metaphysical poet John Donne (1572–1631) was made Dean of St Paul's in 1621. His memorial is in the Dean's Aisle.

American Memorial, detail

Gallipoli Memorial
One of many war memorials in the cathedral, this one is dedicated to those who died in the 1915 Gallipoli campaign.

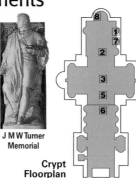

J M W Turner Memorial

Crypt Floorplan

Churchill Memorial Screen
This screen commemorates Sir Winston Churchill (1874–1965) who during the Blitz said "at all costs, St Paul's must be saved".

The Worshipful Company of Masons Memorial
This City guild's plaque near Wren's tomb reads, "Remember the men who made shapely the stones of Saint Paul's Cathedral".

Turner's Tomb
The great landscape painter JMW Turner (1775–1851) is buried in the OBE chapel.

American Memorial
Behind the High Altar, the American Memorial Chapel's roll of honour lists the US servicemen killed while stationed in Britain during World War II.

Fire-Watchers Memorial
In the Nave, this remembers those who saved the church from destruction during the 1940 Blitz.

Top 10 Moments in St Paul's History

1. Elizabeth II's Golden Jubilee (2002).
2. Prince Charles' and Lady Diana's wedding (1981).
3. Winston Churchill's funeral (1965).
4. Martin Luther King Jr preaches (1964).
5. Festival of Britain launched (1951).
6. Cathedral bombed (1940).
7. Queen Victoria's Diamond Jubilee (1897).
8. Duke of Wellington's funeral (1852).
9. Nelson's funeral (1806).
10. First service (1697).

St Paul's Role in History

St Paul's belongs to the nation and to London. It is run by a Dean and Chapter of five priests. Annual services for the City guilds have taken place here for a thousand years. One of the cathedral's main functions is as a place of national mourning and celebration. In the 19th century, 13,000 people filled

Wedding of Prince of Wales, 501, St Paul's

the cathedral for the funeral of the Duke of Wellington. Queen Victoria's Jubilee was a spectacular occasion held on the steps of the cathedral. The Prince of Wales and Lady Diana Spencer chose to be married at St Paul's rather than the royal Westminster Abbey. The decision helped to portray the couple as the people's prince and princess.

Nelson's Funeral
Such was Admiral Nelson's popularity that he was afforded a full state funeral *(left)*. His body was carried up the Thames from Greenwich Hospital to St Paul's by barge.

Wedding of Prince Charles and Lady Diana Spencer, 1981

43

Execution of Charles I outside Banqueting House

10 Moments in London's History

AD 43: Roman Invasion
1 When the Romans arrived in Britain, they built a bridge across the Thames from Southwark and encircled Londinium with a wall, part of which is still visible in the City *(see pp134–9)*. Their forum was in Cornhill and their amphitheatre lies beneath the Guildhall.

Roman invasion of Britain

1066: Norman Conquest
2 The next successful invasion of Britain came from northern France. It was led by William the Conqueror, Duke of Normandy, who was crowned King of England in the newly completed Westminster Abbey *(see pp32–3)* on Christmas Day 1066.

1240: First Parliament
3 The first parliament sat in Westminster and became a seat of government separate from the mercantile City, which continued to expand on the former Roman site.

1534: The Reformation
4 A quarrel between Henry VIII and Pope Clement VII over the king's divorce led to Henry breaking with Rome and declaring himself head of the church in England. Today, the sovereign remains the head of the Church of England.

1649: Charles I Executed
5 Charles I's belief in the divine right of kings led to civil war. The royalist cause was lost and the king was beheaded in 1649. After 11 years of Puritanism, his son Charles II returned to the throne to preside over the Restoration.

1666: Great Fire of London
6 Much of the city, including the medieval St Paul's and 87 parish churches, were destroyed in the fire, which raged for five days. Afterwards Sir Christopher Wren replanned the entire city, including the cathedral *(see p40)*.

1863: First Underground
7 Originally designed to link the main London railway termini, the Metropolitan Line was the world's first underground railway. When it opened, the carriages were little more than trucks.

The Great Fire of London

Bomb damage near St Paul's Cathedral

8 1875: Embankments Built
Built on either side of the river, the Embankments were among the great engineering works of the Victorians. They were designed by Sir Joseph Bazalgette to contain a vast new sewage system to take waste to pumping stations outside London.

9 1940–41: The Blitz
Between September 1940 and May 1941, German air raids left 30,000 Londoners dead. The bombers destroyed much of the Docks, the East End and the City. The House of Commons, Westminster Abbey and the Tower of London were all hit. Many Londoners sought shelter in Underground stations at night.

10 1992 to the Present Day
In 1992, the regeneration of Docklands saw the development of Canary Wharf and creation of City Airport. In July 2005, the London transport system was rocked by four terrorist bombs, with tragic loss of life. In April 2011 the wedding of Prince William to Catherine Middleton took place, and in 2012 London is set to host the Olympic Games.

Top 10 Cultural Highlights

1 Shakespeare Arrives
The first mention of William Shakespeare (1564–1616) as a London dramatist was recorded in 1585.

2 Rubens Knighted
The Dutch painter Peter Paul Rubens was knighted by Charles I in 1629 after painting the Banqueting House ceiling.

3 Purcell's Appointment
The greatest English composer of his age, Henry Purcell was appointed organist at Westminster Abbey in 1679.

4 Handel's Water Music
George Friedrich Handel's *Water Music* was composed for a performance on King George I's royal barge in 1711.

5 Great Exhibition
In 1851, the expanding Empire was celebrated in an exhibition held in a massive glass structure in Hyde Park.

6 J M W Turner Bequest
Turner's paintings were left to the nation on condition that they be seen by the public free of charge *(see pp20–21)*.

7 Royal Opera Highlight
In 1892 Gustav Mahler conducted the first British performance of Wagner's *Ring* at the Royal Opera House.

8 First Radio Broadcast
The BBC made its first broadcast on New Year's Day 1927.

9 Festival of Britain
In 1951, the Festival of Britain was held at the South Bank to mark the centenary of the Great Exhibition.

10 Royal National Theatre
The Royal National Theatre company was founded in 1963 at the Old Vic under Laurence Olivier (later Lord Olivier).

Left **Carving, Westminster Abbey** Centre **Brompton Oratory interior** Right **Cherub, St Bride's**

Churches

St Martin-in-the-Fields

Westminster Abbey
See pp32–3.

St Paul's Cathedral
See pp40–43.

St Martin-in-the-Fields
A parish church of Buckingham Palace, famous for its music events. There has been a church on the site since the 13th century, and the present building was designed by James Gibbs in 1726. Coffee shop in the crypt. ⊗ Trafalgar Square WC2 • Map L4 • Open 8:30am–6pm Mon–Sat; services only Sun • Free • www.smitf.com

Southwark Cathedral
This priory church was elevated to a cathedral in 1905. It has many connections with the area's Elizabethan theatres, and with Shakespeare, who is commemorated in a memorial and a stained-glass window. US college founder John Harvard, who was baptised here, is remembered in The Harvard Chapel. ⊗ London Bridge SE1 • Map G4 • Open 8am–6pm daily • Free • www.cathedral.southwark.anglican.org

Southwark Cathedral stained glass

Temple Church
This circular church was built in the 12th century for the Knights Templar, a crusading order. Effigies of the knights are embedded in the floor. A chancel was added later, and a reredos (screen), designed by Christopher Wren. The church was rebuilt in 1958. ⊗ Inner Temple Lane EC4 • Map P2 • check www.templechurch.com for opening times • Free

Gatehouse, St Bartholomew-the-Great

St Bartholomew-the-Great
A survivor of the Great Fire, this is London's only Norman Church apart from St John's chapel in the Tower of London. It was founded in 1123 by a courtier of Henry I, and its solid pillars and Norman choir have remained unaltered. The 14th-century Lady Chapel, restored by Sir Aston Webb in 1890, once housed a printing press where Benjamin Franklin worked (see p138).

7 Brompton Oratory

This very un-English, Italianate church was established by a Catholic convert, John Henry Newman (1801–90). He introduced England to the Oratory, a religious institute of secular priests founded in 16th-century Rome. The building, designed by Herbert Gribble, opened in 1884, with many of its treasures imported from Italy. ⊗ Brompton Road SW7 • Map C5 • Open 6:30am–8pm daily • Free

Italianate interior of Brompton Oratory

8 Westminster Cathedral

The main Roman Catholic church in England is in Byzantine style, designed by John Francis Bentley and completed in 1903. It has an 83-m (273-ft) campanile, which can be climbed for a great view of the city. Mosaics and over 100 varieties of marble decorate the interior. ⊗ Victoria St SW1 • Map E5 • Open 8am–7pm Mon–Fri, 8am–7pm Sat & Sun • Free • www. westminstercathedral.org.uk

9 St Bride's

There has been a church on this site since Roman times. Sir Christopher Wren's fine church has a wonderful tiered spire that was copied for a wedding cake by a Fleet Street baker, Mr Rich, starting a trend. This is traditionally the journalists' church and memorial services are held here. ⊗ Fleet Street EC4 • Map Q2 • Open 8am–6pm Mon–Fri, 10am–6:30pm Sun • Free • www.stbrides.com

10 All Souls

This distinctive building, with a semi-circular portico and stiletto spire, was designed by John Nash, creator of Regent Street. After the BBC built their headquarters next door, it became the home of religious broadcasts. ⊗ Langham Place W1 • Map J1 • Open 9:30am–5:30pm Mon–Fri, services only Sun • Free

Memorial tablet at All Souls

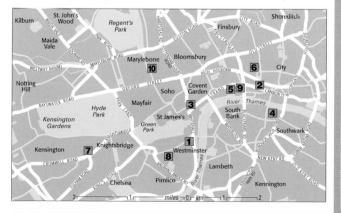

Left **V&A Museum of Childhood** Right **London Transport Museum**

Museums

Victoria and Albert Museum

British Museum
The oldest museum in the world, and one of London's most fascinating, contains treasures and artifacts from all over the world *(see pp8–11)*.

Natural History Museum
Life on Earth and the Earth itself are vividly explained here using hundreds of traditional and interactive exhibits *(see pp22–3)*.

Science Museum
This exciting museum traces centuries of scientific and technological development, with impressive and educational displays *(see pp24–5)*.

Victoria and Albert Museum
This museum of decorative arts is one of London's great pleasures,

Smiling Nun, Museum of London

with 145 astonishingly eclectic galleries. Highlights include the Medieval and Renaissance Galleries with their remarkable collection of treasures. The museum also has displays of jewellery, textiles, metalwork, glass, paintings, prints and sculpture, and boasts rooms full of Indian and Far Eastern treasures *(see p119)*.

Museum of London
This comprehensive museum provides a detailed account of London life from prehistoric times to the present day. It is particularly strong on Roman Londinium, but also has a model recreating the Great Fire of 1666 and a reconstruction of a Victorian street including several original shopfronts *(see p136)*.

National Maritime Museum
The world's largest maritime museum, part of the Maritime Greenwich World Heritage Site, has much to offer. Detailing inspirational stories from Britain's seafaring past, it tells of the continuing effects the oceans still have on the world today. Admiral Nelson's fatally pierced naval coat is on display, the tragic polar expeditions of explorers are recalled and a state-of-the-art simulator gives an idea of what it is like to steer a ship into port *(see p147)*.

7 Imperial War Museum

In this museum, which is housed in part of the former Bethlehem ("Bedlam") Hospital for the Insane, a clock in the basement moves remorselessly on, recording the world's war dead – a figure that has now reached 100 million. Six million of them are commemorated in the Holocaust Exhibition. Other displays include evocative re-creations of World War I trench warfare and the life of Londoners during the World War II Blitz. Now it is "total war" that we have to contemplate, and this, too, is explored *(see p83)*.

Imperial War Museum

8 Design Museum

Based in a clean white 1930s building beside Tower Bridge, this museum is the only one in Britain devoted to 20th- and 21st-century design. Regularly changing exhibitions feature the very best of modern design, including both product and graphic design, fashion, furniture, architecture and engineering. ◎ *Butler's Wharf SE1 • Map H4*
- *Open 10am–5.45pm daily*
- *Admission charge*
- *www.designmuseum.org*

9 London Transport Museum

In this former flower-market building, the history of London's transport system is illustrated with posters, photographs and examples of early buses, tubes and horse-drawn vehicles. There are also interactive "KidZones" for children *(see p100)*.

10 V&A Museum of Childhood

The V&A Museum in Bethnal Green has the largest collection of childhood-related objects in the UK. The museum's array of toys, games, lavish dolls' houses, model trains, furniture and children's clothing dates from the 1600s to the present day *(see p154)*.

Austin Taxi, London Transport Museum

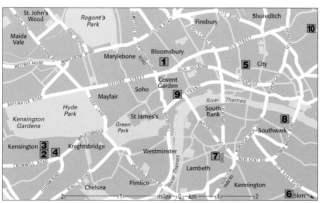

For children's museums **See pp68–9**

Left **The National Gallery** Right *Satan Smiting Job with Sore Boils* by William Blake, Tate Britain

🔟 Art Galleries

1 The National Gallery and National Portrait Gallery

Located adjacent to each other at the top of Trafalgar Square, these comprehensive galleries make up the core of Britain's art collection *(see pp12–15)*.

Renoir's *At The Theatre*, National Gallery

2 Tate Modern

Housed in a huge converted power station on the south bank of the Thames, this exciting gallery covers modern art from 1900 to the present day *(see pp18–19)*.

3 Tate Britain

The other Tate gallery in London, focusing on work from 1500 to the present, has the best collection of British art in London *(see pp20–21)*.

4 Courtauld Gallery

From Fra Angelico to Van Gogh, this is a complete art course in one manageable gallery. The core of the collection is the country's finest Impressionist and Post-Impressionist works, amassed by a textile magnate, Samuel Courtauld (1876–1947). Many of them are instantly recognisable: Manet's *Bar at the Folies- Bergère*, Van Gogh's *Self Portrait With Bandaged Ear*, Gauguin's *Te Rerioa* and Manet's *Déjeuner sur L'Herbe*. Visit the Courtauld café or Somerset House's fountain courtyard and riverside terrace café for a drink afterwards *(see p99)*.

5 Wallace Collection

This wonderful Victorian mansion belonged to Sir Richard Wallace (1818–90). In 1897, his widow bequeathed the house and their amazing art collection to the nation. Covering two floors, the 25 public rooms are beautifully furnished with one of the best collections of French 18th-century pictures, porcelain and furniture in the world. The paintings are rich and voluptuous – notable works include Nicolas Poussin's *A Dance to the Music of Time* and Frans Hals' *The Laughing Cavalier*. There are English portraits by Gainsborough and Reynolds *(see p129)*.

The Laughing Cavalier by Frans Hals, Wallace Collection

Vermeer's *The Guitar Player*, Kenwood House

Dulwich Picture Gallery

If you have time, this suburban gallery is well worth a short train journey. Britain's oldest public art gallery, it was opened in 1817. The important collection includes Murillo's *Flower Girl*, Poussin's *Triumph of David* and Rembrandt's *Girl at the Window* *(see p148)*.

Serpentine Gallery

Major contemporary artists tend to be shown here. Cindy Sherman and Gerhard Richter have both showcased their works. This is one of London's most exciting galleries, often transforming its space to suit the work. Installations have been known to spill out into the park – even to become an outside tearoom. Busy on warm weekends. ✪ *Kensington Gardens W2 • Tube Lancaster Gate*
• *Open 10am–6pm daily*
• *www.serpentinegallery.org*

Royal Academy

The Royal Academy's continual big-name temporary exhibitions draw the crowds, and it is often necessary to reserve a ticket in advance. The traditional Summer Exhibition, which anyone can apply to enter, is also extremely popular *(see p113)*.

Queen's Gallery, Buckingham Palace

Established in 1962 to display works from the Royal Collection, this fascinating gallery shows paintings and other pieces from the royal collection *(see p26)*.

Kenwood House

This majestic mansion with interiors designed by Robert Adam has a small but important collection comprising 17th-century Dutch and Flemish works, 18th-century English portraits, and a small French Rococo section. There are statues by Henry Moore and Barbara Hepworth in the extensive grounds *(see p142)*.

Left **Dickens' house** Right **Carlyle's House interior**

Famous Residents

Sherlock Holmes

The famous but fictitious detective created by Sir Arthur Conan Doyle first appeared in 1891. He still gets regular fan mail sent to 221b Baker Street, which houses the Sherlock Holmes Museum *(see p130)*.

Charles Dickens

The great Victorian novelist and social campaigner (1812–70) lived in Doughty Street for two years from 1837. The house is his only surviving London home, and he thought it "a frightfully first-class family mansion, involving awful responsibilities" *(see p108)*.

Dr Johnson

"When a man is tired of London, he is tired of life," said Dr Samuel Johnson (1709–84). He lived in this house from around 1748 to 1759 and much of his famous dictionary was compiled here. His companion James Boswell reported on the social comings and goings in the house.
◈ *Dr Johnson's House, 17 Gough Square EC4 • Map P2 • Open 11am–5pm Mon–Sat • Admission charge • www.drjohnsonshouse.org*

Freud's famous couch

Sherlock Holmes, London's famous detective

John Keats

The London-born Romantic poet (1795–1821) lived in Hampstead from 1818 to 1820 before leaving for Italy to try to cure his fatal tuberculosis. After falling in love with his neighbour's daughter, Fanny Brawne, he wrote his famous and beautiful *Ode to a Nightingale* in the garden *(see p141)*.

Sigmund Freud

The Viennese founder of psychoanalysis (1856–1939) spent the last year of his life in a north London house. A Jew, he had fled the Nazis, bringing his celebrated couch with him *(see p141)*.

Lord Leighton

Yorkshire-born Frederic Leighton (1830–96) was the most successful painter in Victorian London and president of the Royal Academy. He had this exotic house built for him in 1866 *(see p121)*.

London's Top 10

Thomas Carlyle

The Scottish historian and essayist Thomas Carlyle, famous for his history of the French Revolution, lived in London from 1834. ✪ *Carlyle's House, 24 Cheyne Row SW3 • Map C6 • Open Apr–Oct: 2pm–5pm Wed–Fri, 11am–5pm Sat, Sun & public hols • Admission charge*

The Duke of Wellington

Arthur Wellesley, 1st Duke of Wellington (1769–1852), lived at Apsley House, which has the unique address of No. 1 London, following his victories in the Napoleonic Wars *(see p114)*.

Georg Friedrich Handel

The great German-born composer first visited London in 1710 and settled here permanently in 1712. ✪ *Handel House Museum, 25 Brook Street W1 • Map D3 • Open 10am–6pm Tue–Sat (10am–8pm Thu), noon–6pm Sun • Admission charge*

William Hogarth

The great painter of London life (1697–1764, *see pp20–21*) was used to the gritty life of the city and called his house near Chiswick "a little country box by the Thames". ✪ *Hogarth's House, Hogarth Lane W4 • Check www.hounslow.info for opening times • Closed Jan • Free*

Richly decorated interior of Leighton House

Top 10 Blue Plaques

Circular blue plaques on the walls of some London buildings recall famous residents.

Wolfgang A Mozart

The German composer (1756–91) wrote his first symphony, aged eight, while at No. 180 Ebury Street.

Benjamin Franklin

The US statesman and scientist (1706–90) lived for a time at No. 38 Craven Street.

Charlie Chaplin

The much-loved movie actor (1889–1977) was born at No. 287 Kennington Road.

Charles de Gaulle

The exiled general (1890–1970) organized the Free French Forces from No. 6 Carlton Terrace during World War II.

Dwight Eisenhower

During World War II the Allied Commander (1880–1969) lived at No. 20 Grosvenor Square, near the US embassy.

Mark Twain

The American humorist (1835–1910) lived for a year at No. 23 Tedworth Square.

Mahatma Gandhi

The "father" of India's independence movement (1869–1948) studied law in the Inner Temple in 1889.

Jimi Hendrix

The American guitarist (1942–1970) stayed in central London at No. 23 Brook Street.

Henry James

The American writer (1843–1916) lived in Bolton Street, de Vere Gardens, and in Cheyne Walk, where he died.

Giuseppe Mazzini

From 1837 to 1849 the Italian revolutionary and patriot (1805–72) lived at No. 183 Gower Street.

Left **Buckingham Palace** Right **Kensington Palace**

TOP 10 Royal London

1 Buckingham Palace
See pp26–7

2 Hampton Court
The finest piece of Tudor architecture in Britain, Hampton Court was begun by Henry VIII's ally Cardinal Wolsey in 1514 and later given to the king. It was enlarged first by Henry and then by William and Mary, who employed Christopher Wren as architect. Its many rooms include a huge kitchen, a Renaissance Picture Gallery, the Chapel Royal and fine royal apartments. Set in 60 acres, the gardens, with their famous maze, are as much an attraction as the palace (see p147).

3 Kensington Palace
An intimate royal palace in Kensington Gardens, famous as the home of Princess Diana, the first sovereign residents here were William and Mary in 1689 and Queen Victoria was born here in 1837. Until mid-2012 the State Apartments are the setting for an enchanting, multi-sensory exhibition that reveals intriguing tales of past residents. The Orangery is delightful for coffee (see p119).

4 St James's Palace
Although not open to the public, St James's has a key role in royal London. Its classic Tudor style sets it in the reign of Henry VIII, although it served only briefly as a

Tudor gatehouse, St James's Palace

royal residence. Prince Charles has offices here (see p113).

5 Kew Palace and Queen Charlotte's Cottage
The smallest royal palace, Kew was built in 1631 and used as a residence by George III and Queen Charlotte. Nearby Queen Charlotte's Cottage was used for picnics and housing royal pets. The palace is set in Kew Gardens (see p147). ◈ Kew, Surrey • Palace: open Apr–Oct, call 0844 482 7799 for times; Cottage: open during the summer • www.hrp.org.uk

6 Banqueting House
Built by Inigo Jones, this magnificent building is particularly noted for its Rubens ceiling. It was commissioned by Charles I, who stepped from this room on to the scaffold for his execution in 1649. ◈ Whitehall SW1 • Map L4 • Open 10am–5pm Mon–Sat • Admission charge

Ceiling detail, Banqueting House

Queen's House

7 This delightful home in the midst of Greenwich Park was the first Palladian building by Inigo Jones, and home to the wife of Charles I. Restored to its 17th-century glory, it houses the National Maritime Museum's art collection. ◈ *Romney Road SE10 • Train to Greenwich; DLR Cutty Sark, Greenwich • Open 10am–5pm daily • www.nmm.ac.uk*

Royal Mews

8 See pp26 7.

Queen's Chapel

9 This exquisite royal chapel is open only to its congregation (visitors welcome as worshippers). Built by Inigo Jones in 1627, its furnishings remain virtually intact, including a beautiful altarpiece by Annibale Carracci. ◈ *Marlborough Road SW1 • Map K5*

Clarence House

10 Designed by John Nash and finished in 1827 for William, Duke of Clarence who lived here after he became king in 1830. It was the Queen Mother's home until her death in 2002. ◈ *Stable Yard SW1 • Map K5 • Open Aug & Sep daily, call 020 7766 7303 for times*

Queen's House, Greenwich

Top 10 Royals in Everyday London Life

1 King Charles Spaniel
These were the favourite dogs of King Charles II. Today, the Queen prefers corgis.

2 Queen Anne's Gate
A delightful small Westminster street with a statue of the queen who gave her name to a style of furniture.

3 Regent's Park
The Prince Regent, later George IV, used John Nash for this ambitious urban plan.

4 Duke of York Steps
A statue of the "Grand Old Duke of York", subject of the nursery rhyme, is elevated above these steps off Pall Mall.

5 Victoria Station
All the main London railway termini were built in Victoria's reign. This one serves southern England.

6 Albert Memorial
Prince Albert, beloved consort of Queen Victoria, has a splendid memorial in Kensington Gardens *(see p119)*.

7 George Cross
Instituted in 1940 under George VI, this medal is awarded for acts of heroism by civilians.

8 Princess of Wales Pubs
Several pubs have changed their name to remember Diana, Princess of Wales, "the people's princess".

9 Windsor Knot
The stylish Duke of Windsor, who abdicated the throne in 1938, gave the world a wide tie knot.

10 King Edward Potato
This variety of English potato was named after King Edward VII, who visited Ireland after the 1903 potato famine.

For royal parks and gardens See pp28–9

Left **Colonnade at the ICA** Centre **Royal Court Theatre façade** Right **Performers at Sadler's Wells**

🔟 Performing Arts Venues

1 Royal Opera House
One of the greatest opera houses in the world, this theatre is home to the Royal Ballet Company, and hosts international opera productions. Apart from the sumptuous main auditorium, there are the smaller Linbury and Clore theatres, which have music and dance. There are regular backstage tours and occasional big-screen live simulcasts of opera in the Piazza (see p99).

2 The National Theatre
Seeing a play at the National Theatre takes you to the heart of London's cultural life. Within the grey blocks of this innovative building, designed by Denys Lasdun in 1976, you can see a musical, a classic or a new play in one of its three theatres: the Olivier, the Lyttelton or the Cottesloe. Check for free shows and exhibitions in the foyer. Reduced price tickets are sold from 10am on the day of the performance. ◈ South Bank SE1 • Map N4 • 020 7452 3000

3 Barbican Centre
Home of one of the best music companies in the world – the London Symphony Orchestra – the Barbican is the City's most important arts complex. Theatre, cinema, concerts, dance and exhibitions can all be seen here, and there are plenty of restaurants, cafés

The Nutcracker, Royal Opera House

and bars. The centre also contains a library and convention hall. The Guildhall School of Music and Drama is nearby (see p135).

4 London Coliseum
London's other principal opera house presents productions sung in English by the English National Opera. The largest theatre in London, it is a fine example of Edwardian decoration. ◈ St Martin's Lane WC2 • Map L3 • 0871 911 0200 • www.eno.org

Golden globe atop the London Coliseum

5 Queen Elizabeth Hall
Part of the Southbank Centre, Queen Elizabeth Hall, along with the Purcell Room, Royal Festival Hall and the Hayward Gallery, has a programme of musical, arts and literary activities. ◈ South Bank SE1 • Map N4 • 0871 663 25 01• www.southbankcentre.co.uk

Sadler's Wells

After winning a reputation as the best dance theatre in London in the 1950s, Sadler's Wells now also hosts music and opera. The stunning glass building prides itself on its community events as well as its international dance shows *(see p144)*.

Royal Albert Hall

This distinctive, circular building was designed to resemble a Roman amphitheatre, and has a delicate Classical frieze around the exterior. The excellent acoustic inside makes this a premier venue for every kind of concert, including the "Proms" *(see p120)*.

Royal Court Theatre

The cream of new drama can be seen at this charming small theatre. Both the main and tiny upstairs theatre are important London venues. Play "actor spotting" in the restaurant and bar. ✆ *Sloane Square SW1 • Map C5 • 020 7565 5000 •www.royalcourttheatre.com*

Riverside Studios

With a glorious location by the Thames at Hammersmith Bridge, this is a fascinating arts and media centre. An eclectic programme includes cinema,

theatre, comedy, dance, music and the visual arts. Works of such innovators as Samuel Beckett and Peter Brook have premiered here. Once BBC studios, the venue is still used to make TV shows. The café, bar and river terrace are a draw in themselves. ✆ *Crisp Road W6 • Tube Hammersmith • 020 8237 1111*

ICA

A stately, colonnaded terrace by Nash houses London's hippest gallery, the Institute of Contemporary Arts. The ICA's cutting edge policy on the visual arts includes developing new and challenging digitally-produced works, and Becks Futures, the UK's largest arts prize for students. ✆ *The Mall SW1 • Map K5 • 020 7930 3647*

Performance, Royal Albert Hall

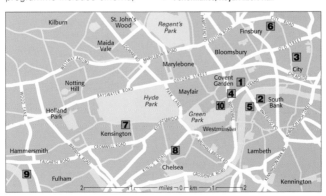

For more theatres **See pp60–61**

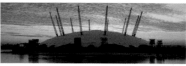

Left **Camden's Jazz Café** Right **The O2 arena**

Live Music Venues

1 Ronnie Scott's
This legendary London jazz club was opened by saxophonist Ronnie Scott (1929–96) in 1959. Intimate lamplit tables surround a tiny stage that has hosted such stars as Ella Fitzgerald and Dizzy Gillespie, and continues to attract top names *(see p93)*.

2 100 Club
Atmospheric jazz and blues dive that stays open up to 2am. This club's heritage is legendary – the Rolling Stones played here, as did the Sex Pistols and other punk bands of the 1970s. Today it also hosts Indie groups. Membership is not required. ✆ *100 Oxford Street W1 • Map K2 • 020 7636 0933*

3 Jazz Café
Top jazz and soul performers, as well as great food make this a popular venue. Best views are to be had from the balcony tables. ✆ *5 Parkway NW1 • Map D1 • 020 7688 8899*

4 HMV Forum
A 2,300-capacity music venue in the heart of Kentish Town that plays host to a

Koko, Camden

Ronnie Scott's jazz club

number of big name acts. ✆ *9–17 Highgate Road NW5 • 020 7485 4080 • Tube Kentish Town*

5 O2 Academy Brixton
This is a great place to see big names from across the music spectrum. Although it holds 4,000, the hall retains an intimate, clubby atmosphere with good views of the performers from across the auditorium. ✆ *211 Stockwell Road SW9 • 0844 477 2000 • Tube Brixton*

6 Koko
Hosting mainly indie gigs as well as big names such as Prince and Madonna, Koko is also home to well known club nights such as the famous "pop" fest, Guilty Pleasures. ✆ *1a Camden High Street NW1 • Map D1 • 0870 432 5527*

7 PizzaExpress Jazz Club
Downstairs from the Pizza Express restaurant is one of London's best jazz venues, where anything from swing,

blues and gospel classics to modern fusion jazz can be heard. ◈ *10 Dean Street W1 • Map 2K • 0845 602 7017*

Borderline
One of London's best small clubs, Borderline has hosted many international bands in its basement. There's at least one different band every weekday evening, playing a wide range of music, from country to metal. ◈ *Orange Yard, off Manette Street W1 • Map L2 • 0844 847 2465*

O2 arena & indigO2
The ill-fated Millennium Dome has been transformed into the huge O2 arena, hosting the biggest names around including the Rolling Stones and Justin Timberlake. The indigO2 offers a more intimate setting, with a capacity of 2,350. Taking the Thames Clipper along the river is all part of the fun. ◈ *Millennium Way, North Greenwich SE10 • Tube North Greenwich • 0844 856 0202*

Live music at the Troubadour

Troubadour Coffee House
An atmospheric and laid-back coffee house club devoted to live music. All the great folk singers of the 1960s played here, and today there is a relaxed feel to the evenings when singers, poets and comedians perform. ◈ *263–7 Old Brompton Road SW5 • Map A6 • 020 7370 1434*

Top 10 Nightclubs

1 Fabric
The best dance venue in town, arranged in three rooms filled with sound: 24-hour music licence. ◈ *77a Charterhouse Street EC1 • Map Q1*

2 333
This three-storey club heaves to drum 'n' bass, hip hop and funky soul. ◈ *333 Old Street, Hoxton EC1 • Map H2*

3 Volupté
Expect top cabaret at this burlesque club. ◈ *9 Norwich Street EC4 • Tube Chancery Lane*

4 Madame Jo-Jo's
Some of the best drag acts in town. ◈ *8–10 Brewer Street W1 • Map K3*

5 Cargo
One of the best places for cutting-edge music. ◈ *83 Rivington Street EC2 • Map H2*

6 Plastic People
Small but perfectly formed basement club with a top sound system. ◈ *147–149 Curtain Road EC2 • Map H2*

7 Brixton Jamm
The South London venue for indie rock, plus electronic, trance and beats. ◈ *261 Brixton Road SW9 • Tube Brixton*

8 Café de Paris
Popular disco with a mix of DJs and a restaurant. ◈ *3 Coventry Street W1 • Map K3*

9 Heaven
London's best-known gay venue has several bars and dance floors beneath Charing Cross station. ◈ *Villiers Street WC2 • Map M4*

10 Storm Nightclub
Nightclub playing R 'n' B and hip hop, and a comedy venue with TV acts. ◈ *28A Leicester Square WC2 • Map L3*

 For more late-night venues See p93

Left **Blood Brothers** Right **Priscilla Queen of the Desert**

West End Shows

1 Les Misérables

Victor Hugo's 1862 French classic novel was adapted for the stage by Trevor Nunn for the Royal Shakespeare Company in 1985. With music by Alain Boublil and Claude-Michel Schönberg, "*Les Mis*" tells the tale of downtrodden poor and the social and political struggles in revolutionary France. Originally at the Palace Theatre on Cambridge Circus, it is now at the Queens Theatre. ⊗ *Queens Theatre, Shaftesbury Avenue W1 • Map K3 • 08444 825 160*

The Lion King, Lyceum Theatre

2 The Mousetrap

Agatha Christie's murder mystery, *The Mousetrap*, has been playing in London since 1952, and has been seen by 100 million people. A few bits of the original set remain. Christie herself predicted a run of only six months, and in 1955, after the 1,000th performance, a critic wrote: "The biggest mystery of the evening is why this play has run so long." ⊗ *St Martin's Theatre, West Street WC2 • Map L3 • 08444 991 515*

3 Chicago

The longest-running Broadway musical to play the West End is this high-kicking tribute to Bob Fosse's 1975 version. ⊗ *Cambridge Theatre, Earlham Street WC2 • Map L2 • 020 7834 6318*

4 Phantom of the Opera

Andrew Lloyd Webber's 1986 hit musical, *The Phantom of the Opera* is based on Gaston Leroux's novel of the same name and is set in the Paris Opera House. Perhaps it is Lloyd Webber's most famous production. ⊗ *Her Majesty's Theatre, Haymarket SW1 • Map L4 • 0844 412 2707*

5 The Lion King

Based on the 1994 animated film of the same name, this story is magically conjured up on stage. The animal costumes and special effects wow children and adults alike. ⊗ *Lyceum Theatre, 21 Wellington Street WC2 • Map N3 • 0844 844 0005*

Cast of *Phantom of the Opera*

Dirty Dancing at the Aldwych Theatre

The Woman in Black
This production, staged in one of London's smallest venues since 1989, has plenty of atmosphere and tells a classic ghost story. This is a story that will keep you on the edge of your seat. ⊗ *Fortune Theatre, Russell Street WC2 • Map M2 • 0844 871 7626*

Wicked
Based on the novel by Gregory Maguire and touted as "the untold story of the witches of Oz", this musical offers a prequel to the story told in *The Wizard of Oz*, leading up to the moment when Dorothy's house falls on the Green Witch's sister. ⊗ *Apollo Victoria, Wilton Road SW1 • Map D5 • 0844 826 8000*

Dirty Dancing
As Baby turns into a woman with the help of a hip-swivelling dance instructor, expect plenty of rock and roll and some sexy moves in this raunchy version of an old favourite. Great fun. ⊗ *Aldwych Theatre WC2 • Map L4 • 0844 847 2330*

Priscilla Queen of the Desert
Based on the Oscar®-winning movie *The Adventures of Priscilla, Queen of the Desert* (1994), it tells a hilarious yet heart-warming tale of three drag queens journeying across the Australian outback in search of love. Outrageously glamorous. ⊗ *Palace Theatre W1 • Map L2 • 0844 755 0016*

Blood Brothers
The story revolves around twins separated at birth because their mother cannot afford to keep them both. One grows up with his poor, natural, mother, the other lives with her wealthy employer. The consequences when they eventually meet are a successful blend of comedy and tragedy. ⊗ *Phoenix Theatre, Charing Cross Road WC2 • Map L2 • 0870 060 6629*

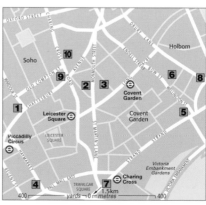

For more entertainment venues **See pp56–7**

Left **Sign, George Inn** Right **Outside the George Inn**

Pubs

The Lamb and Flag

This old-world establishment tucked up an alley looks much as it did in Charles Dickens' day. In the heart of Covent Garden, it can get crowded – during the summer drinkers spill outside into the quiet alley. The 17th-century poet John Dryden was severely beaten up outside the pub which was known as The Bucket of Blood because of the bareknuckle fights held here *(see p104)*.

Dog and Duck

This small, tiled Victorian pub is like a cosy front room in the heart of Soho. The Dog and Duck has a tiny bar, where you might bump into art students and designers, and a blackboard with the latest selection of beers from all corners of England *(see p94)*.

Lamb and Flag, Covent Garden

Dog and Duck, Soho

Ye Olde Cheshire Cheese

In an alley off Fleet Street, this warren of rooms still seems as if it should have sawdust on the floors. Rebuilt in 1667, after the Great Fire of London, it was a favourite of Dr Johnson *(see p52)* and other writers. Never too crowded, its intimate corners make a good meeting place, made cozier with fires in winter. ◈ *Wine Office Court EC4 • Map Q2*

George Inn

Built in 1676, this is the only galleried coaching inn left in London, and was taken over by the National Trust in 1937. You can enjoy excellent beers in its myriad old rooms, with lattice windows and wooden beams, or in the large courtyard *(see p86)*.

Jerusalem Tavern

A delightful little pub with cubicles, a small bar and little more than the 18th-century coffee shop it once was. It serves the full range of a rare but popular brewery, St Peter's in Suffolk. Light meals are served at lunchtime; closed at week-ends. ◈ *55 Britton Street EC1 • Map G2*

Note: Smoking is banned in all pubs, clubs and restaurants

Spaniards Inn
This lovely 16th-century pub north of Hampstead Heath, with a large, attractive beer garden, is steeped in history and romance: the 18th-century highwayman Dick Turpin drank here, along with literary luminaries Keats, Shelley and Byron *(see p145)*.

Princess Louise
The Princess Louise is a beautiful 19th-century pub with stained-glass windows, nooks and alcoves. An unexpected bonus is the beer for under £2 a pint, as well as hearty and delicious pies and puddings. § *208–209 High Holborn WC1* • *Map M1*

The Grapes
Built in the 1720s, with wooden floors and panelling, The Grapes has survived the modern development of Docklands, retaining its traditional charm and informal atmosphere. The back bar has an open fire for the winter months and a terrace by the Thames for the summer. The excellent upstairs restaurant is renowned for its fish dishes. § *76 Narrow Street E14* • *DLR Westferry*

The Eagle
This large Victorian pub is popular, crowded and lively, with many coming here to eat the excellent, mainly Mediterranean, food. Portions are large and inexpensive, and can be washed down with a good selection of beer and wine *(see p76)*. § *159 Farringdon Road EC1* • *Tube Farringdon* • *No bookings*

French House
This was once a meeting place for the French Resistance during World War II, when it was given its name. Gaining a reputation as a bohemian bolthole, it was also frequented by artists and poets such as Francis Bacon, Brendan Behan and Dylan Thomas. It is now well known for its refreshing Breton cider and fine wines. § *49 Dean Street W1* • *Map L3*

Jerusalem Tavern, City

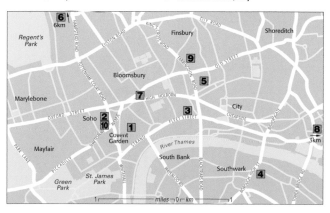

Left **Hamleys** Right **Harrods by night**

🔟 Shops and Markets

Liberty's mock-Tudor façade

Liberty
This handsome, half-timbered building dates from 1925 and its fine wood-floored and panelled interior is part of the shopping experience there. Long associated with the Arts and Crafts movement, it employed artists such as William Morris to design its fabrics. Great for its own Liberty floral fabrics, home furnishings, men's and women's fashions and lovely gifts *(see p110)*.

Fortnum and Mason
London's most elegant store has hardly noticed the arrival of the 21st century. The ground-floor food hall is famous for its traditional English produce, and lavish picnic hampers can be found, along with wines, in the basement. The upper floors are good for designer men's and women's fashion and stylish gifts *(see p116)*.

Harrods
London's most famous and exclusive department store is more of an event than a shop. Covering seven floors, it is full of extraordinary things to buy – from pianos to children's racing cars – all with equally extraordinary prices. The children's toy department is excellent, and the store's food hall is rightly famous, with bars selling upmarket ice-cream, pizzas and countless other treats *(see p123)*.

Harvey Nichols
Almost a parody of itself, "Harvey Nicks" is where the glamorous shop. There's wall-to-wall designer labels, an extravagant perfume and beauty department and stylish homeware. The fifth floor is for consuming, with a food hall, sushi bar and the to-be-seen-in Fifth Floor restaurant *(see p123)*.

Hamleys
The five storeys of London's largest toyshop contain just about anything a child might want, from traditional puppets and games to giant stuffed toys, models, arts and crafts supplies and the latest electronic gadgets. There are also many delights here for adults who haven't let go of their childhood *(see p110)*.

Playing with giant teddies, Hamleys

6 Portobello Road
West London's liveliest street sells a mixture of antiques and bric-à-brac. As it heads north, there are food stalls, crafts, clothes and music. Shops and some stalls open daily but the main antiques market is on Saturday *(see p120)*.

7 Camden Market
A great place to spend a Saturday, this rambling market around Camden Lock takes in several streets and buildings. Street fashion, world crafts… it's as if the 1960s never ended. Sundays are a crush *(see p141)*.

8 Waterstone's Piccadilly
The largest bookshop in Europe, Waterstone's stocks a quarter of a million titles. There's a restaurant, cafés and a champagne bar on the fifth floor *(see p116)*.

Antique shop, Portobello Road

Camden's indoor market

9 John Lewis
This store has a large and loyal clientele, with departments ranging from kitchenware and haberdashery through furniture, fashion and fabrics to electrical goods. Staff are informed, prices are excellent and the quality is guaranteed *(see p132)*.

10 Westfield
Europe's largest inner city shopping centre mixes high fashion with overseas brands and luxury labels (housed in the boutique-style setting, The Village). Also has a 14-screen cinema. ◎ *Ariel Way W12*

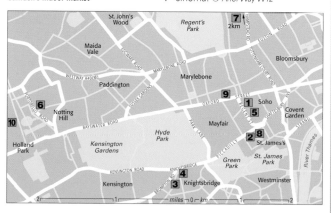

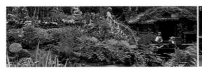

Left **RHS Chelsea Flower Show** Right **Lord Mayor's Show**

🔟 Festivals and Events

1 Notting Hill Carnival
This three-day Caribbean festival is Europe's largest carnival, with steel bands and DJ's playing all imaginable kinds of music, street food, brilliant costumes and lively dancers. Children's parades on Sunday, grown-ups' on Monday. ◈ *Notting Hill W11 • Map A3 • Last Sat–Mon in Aug*

2 RHS Chelsea Flower Show
As much a society outing as a horticultural event, this is the Royal Horticultural Society's prestigious annual show. Beautiful and imaginative gardens are created especially for the event. ◈ *Chelsea Royal Hospital SW1 • Map C6 • Mid-May • Admission charge*

Trooping the Colour, Horse Guards Parade

3 Trooping the Colour
The Queen celebrates her official birthday on Horse Guards Parade where troops of the Household Division, in their famous red tunics and bearskin hats, put on an immaculate display of marching and drilling before escorting her to Buckingham Palace. ◈ *Horse Guards Parade SW1 • Map L5 • Sat closest to 10 Jun*

Extravagant costume, Notting Hill Carnival

4 BBC Promenade Concerts
The most extensive concert series in the world. The famous last concert is relayed live to adjacent Hyde Park, when *Land of Hope and Glory* rocks the Royal Albert Hall *(see p120)* to its foundations. ◈ *Royal Albert Hall SW1 • Map B5 • Mid-Jul–mid-Sep*

5 Royal Academy Summer Exhibition
Around 1,000 works are selected from the public and academicians for the art world's most eclectic summer show. Works sell for as little as £100. ◈ *Piccadilly W1 • Map J4 • Jun–Aug • Admission charge*

6 Lord Mayor's Show
Every year, the City of London elects a Lord Mayor who processes through the Square Mile in a gilded coach. Military bands, floats and city guildsmen in traditional costume go from Guildhall to the Law Courts. Evening fireworks. ◈ *City of London • Map R2 (Guildhall) • 2nd Sat in Nov*

7 Guy Fawkes Night

Effigies of Guy Fawkes, who attempted to blow up Parliament in 1605, are burned on bonfires across the country, with accompanying firework extravaganzas. Children make dummy Guys and ask for pennies to pay for their little arsenals. ◎ *5 Nov*

8 Chinese New Year

Chinatown *(see p89)* is taken over by dancing dragons breathing fire during this vibrant, colourful festival. Food and craft stalls are authentically oriental. ◎ *Soho W1 • Map L3 • Late Jan–early Feb*

9 BFI London Film Festival

Scores of international films are shown in this two-week festival when cinemas, including the National Film Theatre, reduce prices. A booth is set up in Leicester Square to take bookings and distribute programmes. ◎ *West End • Nov*

10 Great British Beer Festival

Organized by the Campaign for Real Ale (CAMRA), this annual festival in a major London exhibition hall is a chance to sample the best beers and ciders produced in Britain. ◎ *Earls Court SW5 • Aug • Admission charge*

Lord Mayor's Show fireworks

Top 10 Sports Events

1 Wimbledon Lawn Tennis Championship
The world's top grass-court championships. ◎ *All England Lawn Tennis and Croquet Club, Wimbledon • Jun/Jul*

2 London Marathon
26.2-mile (42-km) road race from Greenwich Park to The Mall. ◎ *Apr*

3 ECB County Championship Final
The climax of the domestic cricket season. ◎ *Lord's • Sep*

4 Oxford and Cambridge Boat Race
The two universities' annual rowing race covers some 6.5 km (4 miles) on the Thames. ◎ *Putney to Mortlake • Mar*

5 The London International Horse Show
Family fun at this Christmas show. ◎ *Olympia W8 • Dec*

6 Varsity Match
The Oxford-Cambridge rugby union duel. ◎ *Twickenham Rugby Ground • Dec*

7 FA Cup Final
The last match of the Football Association Challenge Cup. ◎ *Wembley Stadium • mid-May*

8 Six Nations Rugby
Annual rugby union contest with England, France, Ireland, Italy, Scotland and Wales. ◎ *Twickenham Rugby Ground • Feb/Mar/Apr*

9 Royal Ascot
All London Society goes to the races in top hats and other glamorous creations. ◎ *Ascot, Berkshire • Jun*

10 Test Matches
These are top-flight international cricket matches, with games lasting up to five days. ◎ *Lord's and The Oval cricket grounds • May–Aug*

Left **London Zoo** Right **London Dungeon**

📖10 Children's London

Science Museum
See pp24–5.

Natural History Museum
See pp22–3.

Madame Tussaud's
One of London's most popular attractions, this is where you can see everyone from Arnold Schwarzenegger to the Queen. A Spirit of London ride takes you on a whistle-stop tour of the city's history. The famous Chamber of Horrors puts you face-to-face with London's most infamous criminals and has the very guillotine that beheaded Queen Marie Antoinette in the French Revolution. Other sections of the exhibition include Premiere Night, which is devoted to the giants of the entertainment world. Get there early to avoid waiting in long lines *(see p129)*.

Waxwork Royalty, Madame Tussaud's

London Zoo
There's a full day out to be had in this 36-acre zoo. Home of the Zoological Society of London, the zoo emphasizes its important international role in conservation and research work. Its enclosures have won awards, such as the aviary designed by Lord Snowdon. The Meet the Monkeys enclosure provides a rainforest habitat for free-roaming monkeys and other wildlife *(see p129)*.

Sea Life London Aquarium
Located on London's South Bank, the aquarium is home to thousands of marine creatures. A journey along the Great Ocean Conveyor Belt shows them in all their glory. Crocodiles, green turtles and zebra sharks are among the sea life. For interactive fun, Eco Pirates can climb aboard the Good Ship SOS *(see p84)*.

London Trocadero
The Trocadero entertainment complex in the heart of the West End is a magnet for children. Aside from its shops, restaurants and cinema, a Ripley's Believe It or Not!, a bowling alley and a bewildering array of hi-tech video games and simulators that will keep them occupied for hours *(see p91)*.

Sharks, Sea Life London Aquarium

7 V&A Museum of Childhood

This East End museum has one of the largest toy collections in the world, including dolls, teddies, puppets, games and children's clothes. Activities are organized on weekends and during school holidays *(see p154).*

Doll's house, V&A Museum of Childhood

8 Coram's Fields

No adults admitted without a child, says the sign on the gate to this 7-acre park for small children. There's a paddling pool, play areas and a city farm with a pets corner and grazing farm animals. ◈ *93 Guilford Street WC1 • Map F2 • Open daily (closed 25–26 Dec) • Free • www.coramsfields.org*

9 Battersea Park

This large south London park is ideal for kids, with an adventure playground, boating lake, deer enclosure and a children's zoo *(see p150).* ◈ *Albert Bridge Road SW11 • Map D6 • Zoo: Open 10am–5:30pm Easter–Oct, weekends in Winter, Admission charge • www. batterseapark.org*

Entrance sign, London Dungeon

10 London Dungeon

The scariest experience in town combines history and horror to celebrate an "orgy of grisly entertainment", with death, torture and violence at every turn. Follow in the bloody footsteps of the Victorian serial killer Jack the Ripper, witness medieval murders, the 17th-century Fire of London, or go to your own execution on Judgment Day. Not for the faint-hearted. ◈ *28/ 34 Tooley Street, SE1 • Map H4 • Opening times vary. For more information on times please check their website www.thedungeons. com • Admission charge*

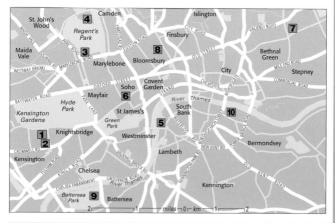

Left **Tower Bridge** Right **St Katharine Docks**

🔟 River Sights

Lambeth Palace
The Archbishop of Canterbury's official London residence is a famous riverside landmark. Part of the palace dates from the 13th century, but it is the red-brick Tudor Gatehouse (1490), that gives the palace a distinctive appearance. 🞄 *Lambeth Palace Road SE1* • *Map F5* • *Closed to the public*

Tudor gatehouse, Lambeth Palace

Houses of Parliament
See pp34–5.

Savoy Hotel
London's first luxury hotel opened in 1889, on the site of the medieval Savoy Palace. Its Chinese lacquered "ascending rooms" were some of the first lifts in Europe. Oscar Wilde objected to the new-fangled built-in plumbing: he wanted

to ring for his hot water like a gentleman. The hotel reopened in 2010 after a multi-million-pound restoration *(see p177)*.

Millennium Bridge
This stunning, blade-like suspension bridge links Tate Modern on Bankside with St Paul's and the City opposite. Unfortunately, this modern footbridge suffered from excessive movement when it first opened in 2000. It has since been fixed and is a delightful and apt approach to Tate Modern. 🞄 *Map R3*

Shakespeare's Globe
This modern reconstruction in oak, thatch and 36,000 handmade bricks is near the site of the original Globe Theatre, which burned down in 1613. The centre of the theatre is uncovered, so performances only happen during part of the year, but an interesting exhibition is open all year round, plus there is a café, restaurant and bar with river views *(see p83)*.

HMS Belfast
The last of the big-gun armoured ships, *HMS Belfast* was built in 1938 and saw active service in World War II and Korea. In 1971 she was saved for the nation and opened as a

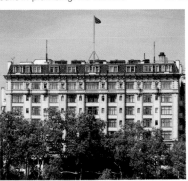

Rear of the Savoy Hotel, overlooking the Thames

museum. Visitors can tour the bridge, the huge engine rooms, the galley and the messdecks, where you get an idea of what life must have been like on board.

🖎 *Morgan's Lane, Tooley Street SE1 • Map H4 • Open Mar–Oct: 10am– 5:15pm daily; Nov–Feb: 10am–4:15pm daily • Admission charge • www. hmsbelfast.iwm.org.uk*

7 Tower Bridge

London's enduring landmark is a neo-gothic wonder. A masterly piece of civil engineering, the bridge was built in 1894 with steam pumps to raise its two halves. Tours of the tower include views from the top *(see p135)*.

8 St Katharine Docks

The first and most successful piece of modern Docklands development was this handsome dock beside Tower Bridge. Designed by civil engineer Thomas Telford in 1824, the site suffered severe bomb damage during

Thames Flood Barrier

World War II and was refurbished in the 1980s. The area is surrounded by luxury apartments, shops and cafés *(see p137)*.

Figurehead of the Cutty Sark

9 The Cutty Sark

Built in 1869, this is the last of the record-breaking tea-clippers that brought the leaves to thirsty London. It has undergone major refurbishment since 2007 when the ship was damaged by fire. There is now a museum space.

🖎 *King William Walk SE10 • Train to Greenwich; DLR Cutty Sark • For opening times, visit www.cuttysark.org.uk*

10 Thames Flood Barrier

This huge barrier across the lower reaches of the Thames, just past Greenwich, was built between 1974 and 1982 to prevent the dangerous combination of wind and tides from flooding the city. The Visitors' Centre explains the problem, detailing a long history of flooding in London *(see p154)*.

Left **Geoffrey Chaucer** Middle **Oscar Wilde** Right **Martin Amis**

Literary London

1 Samuel Pepys

The extraordinary *Diary* of Samuel Pepys (1633–1703) begins on New Year's Day, 1660 and ends on May 31, 1669. He vividly describes contemporary life, the Plague and Great Fire, and an attack on London by the Dutch. The work was written in short-hand and only deciphered in 1825.

2 Dr Johnson

Samuel Johnson (1709–84) was a towering literary figure who presided over gatherings in pubs, coffee houses and literary clubs, as well as in his own home *(see p52)*, and had opinions on everything. His satirical poem, *London* (1738), attacked poverty in the city and his parliamentary sketches and dictionary made him famous.

Engraving of Dr Johnson

3 Geoffrey Chaucer

Chaucer (1343–1400) was a diplomat and son of a London vintner. His *Canterbury Tales* is a classic piece of English literature, and follows a group of pilgrims travelling from Southwark to Canterbury. In 17,000 lines the characters tell their rollicking tales.

Peter Ackroyd

4 Oscar Wilde

Dublin-born Wilde (1854–1900) dazzled London audiences with his plays, and society with his wit. He fell from grace when he was convicted of homosexual activity. His plays, such as *Lady Windermere's Fan* (1892) and *The Importance of Being Earnest* (1895) are frequently revived.

5 Virginia Woolf

Woolf (1882–1941) and her sister Vanessa Bell lived in Gordon Square, where the influential pre-war Bloomsbury Group grew from social gatherings. She developed an impressionistic stream of consciousness in novels such as *Mrs Dalloway* (1925) and *To The Lighthouse* (1927).

6 John Betjeman

A devoted Londoner, with a fine disdain for bureaucracy, mediocrity and hideous architecture, Betjeman (1906–84) was made Poet Laureate in 1972. His poems are full of gentle wit and humour and he remains one of Britain's favourite poets.

7 Colin MacInnes

MacInnes (1914–76) documented the teenage and black immigrant culture in Notting Hill in the 1950s. *City of Spades* (1957) and *Absolute Beginners* (1959) are set among the coffee bars, jazz clubs, drink and drugs scene at a time of great unrest.

8 Martin Amis

Darling of the London literary scene in the 1970s and 1980s, Amis (b.1949) had a famous literary father, Kingsley, and a precocious talent, having his first book, *The Rachael Papers* (1974), published at the age of 24. London has infused novels such as *Money* (1984) and *London Fields* (1989).

9 Zadie Smith

Her first novel, *White Teeth*, about Asian immigrants in north London, made Smith (b.1975) an overnight sensation in 1999. Wickedly funny, it has remarkably well-drawn portraits of London life.

10 Peter Ackroyd

The biographer of Charles Dickens, Ackroyd (b.1949) turned to fiction to examine the lives of other Londoners, such as the architect Nicholas Hawksmoor and Oscar Wilde. Most ambitiously he wrote *London: a Biography* (2000).

Zadie Smith

Top 10 London Songs

1 London's Burning
Commemorating the Great Fire of 1666, this is sung in a round, a device popular since Elizabethan days.

2 London Bridge is Falling Down
A traditional song about old London Bridge, which fell into disrepair.

3 Oranges and Lemons
"...say the bells of St Clement's". This children's song rhymes City churches, and is sung as part of a game.

4 Maybe It's Because I'm a Londoner
The theme song of music-hall duo, Flanagan and Allen, it became a patriotic comfort in post-wartime London.

5 The Lambeth Walk
Made popular by the musical *Me and My Girl* in the 1930s, this has been a Cockney favourite ever since.

6 London Pride
An uncharacteristically sentimental song that celebrates the city.

7 England Swings
This hit US song came out after a 1966 story in *Time* magazine announced the arrival of "Swinging London".

8 Waterloo Sunset
Pop groups don't usually celebrate London, or Britain, but this 1967 record by The Kinks was an exception.

9 A Nightingale Sang in Berkeley Square
A standard sung by Frank Sinatra and others, it is actually very unusual to hear nightingales in central London.

10 Burlington Bertie
A music-hall song about the life of a Mayfair gentleman in Edwardian London.

For famous London residents See pp52–3

73

Left **Battersea Park** Right **Thames path, South Bank**

London on Foot

Thames Path, South Bank
Start by the London Eye and walk along the South Bank downstream to London Bridge and the Design Museum beyond Butler's Wharf. This stretch of the Thames Path has enough to distract you all day. ◈ *South Bank • Map N5*

Regent's Canal
It's possible to walk along the whole 14-km (8.5-mile) canal from Paddington to Limehouse. The most accessible part lies between Camden Lock and Regent's Park, where grand houses back on to the water. Further on, in Little Venice, moored "narrowboats" are owned by the wealthy *(see p130)*.

Houseboat, Regents Canal

Richmond
Richmond has a lovely aspect on the River Thames. Apart from its royal park *(see p29)* there is a lot to see and do, with riverside pubs and cafés, and boats to rent. It's a half-hour walk along the towpath to the 17th-century Ham House, owned by the National Trust. In summer you can take a ferry across to Marble Hill House in Twickenham *(see p148)*.

View over London from Hampstead Heath

Hampstead Heath
This green grandstand overlooking the city covers 8 sq km (3 sq miles) and is a rural mix of meadows, woods, lakes and ponds for both swimming and fishing. Head off in any direction, and make the Spaniards Inn *(see p145)* or Kenwood House a stopping-off point *(see p141)*.

Hyde Park and Kensington Gardens
Central London's largest green area can tire out any walker. It takes about an hour and a half to walk around, but there are plenty of diversions, from the Serpentine Gallery *(see p51)*, to cafés, fountains and flower gardens *(see p28)*. ◈ *Hyde Park W2 • Map C4 • Open 5am–midnight daily*

Battersea Park
This lively park is not just for children *(see p69)*. It has a pleasant riverside promenade beside a Buddhist Peace Pagoda, lakeside walks and the Festival Gardens *(see p150)*.

7 Wimbledon Common

It is easy to get lost in this wild public space. Start by the Windmill and go down to Queens Mere Pond or stride out along the cinder horse track to the pine copse of Caesar's Camp, an old Iron Age hill fort *(see p150)*.

8 Blackheath

This treeless expanse, enjoyed by kite flyers, lies behind Greenwich Park *(see p29)*. Donkey rides are available, and on the far side is Blackheath Village.
◈ *Blackheath SE3 • Train to Blackheath*

9 WWT London Wetland Centre

London's major bird sanctuary covers 105 acres in four disused Victorian reservoirs. It has trails, a visitor centre and an observatory where you can spot some of the 180 species which have been recorded here *(see p150)*.

10 Highgate Cemetery

Filled with grand tombs, many of the rich and famous, this is the best of London's cemeteries. The living have to pay to get in, too, and the cemetery is divided into eastern and western halves, the latter visitable only with a tour *(see p143)*.

Faded grandeur, Highgate Cemetery

Top 10 Outdoor Activities

1 Rowing
Parks with rowing lakes include Hyde Park, Regent's Park and Battersea Park.

2 Ice Skating
Indoors at the Leisure Box in Queensway. Outdoor winter rinks include Broadgate, Somerset House and the Natural History Museum.

3 Kite Flying
Hampstead Heath, Primrose Hill and Blackheath are the best places to get a lift.

4 Swimming
There are a number of public indoor pools. **◈** *The Oasis, Endell Street WC2 • Porchester Centre, Queensway W2 • Chelsea Sports Centre, Chelsea Manor St SW3.*

5 Nature Watching
London's open spaces and woodlands are full of plants and wildlife to discover.

6 Skateboarding
Many parks have skateboard facilities. The South Bank's *(see p83)* concrete spaces have a regular clientele.

7 Cycling
Rent bikes from On Your Bike in London Bridge *(020 7378 6669)* and The London Bicycle Tour Company in Gabriel's Wharf *(020 7928 6838)*.

8 Tennis
For indoors try Islington Tennis Centre, Market Rd N7. Outdoors, Holland Park, Battersea Park or Regent's Park.

9 Skating
Wide paths make Hyde Park the most popular choice.

10 Horse Riding
The best place is the stables at Hyde Park. **◈** *63 Bathurst Mews W2.*

→ *For royal parks and gardens See pp28–9*

Left **Club Gascon** Right **Clarke's**

🔟 Best Places to Eat

1 Pig's Ear
In the heart of Chelsea, just a stone's throw away from the bustle and extremely fashionable shopping in King's Road, this gastropub serves up quality food in a warm and friendly atmosphere. For a calmer experience head upstairs to the Blue Room Restaurant. ☜ *35 Old Church Street SW3 • Map B6 • 0207 352 2908*

2 Clarke's
A steady favourite since it opened in 1984, the food here is wonderfully fresh, and basically Mediterranean, with roast and baked dishes to the fore. The Sally Clarke set menus are the focal point, but there is also a daily changing selection of à la carte dishes. The wine list favours California *(see p125)*.

Rasa Samudra, Fitzrovia

3 Rasa Samudra
Indian curries are almost a national dish in Britain, but this is quite different from the norm. The cooking is stunning, and first-timers will need talking through the unusual menu, which includes delicious fish dishes *(see p111)*.

L'Atelier de Joël Robuchon, Covent Garden

4 Club Gascon
Inspired Gallic cooking means you need to make a reservation weeks in advance. The original idea here is that there are no starter or main courses. Dishes are categorised under half a dozen themed headings, and you put together three of four to make a meal. Each one is a rare combination *(see p139)*.

5 L'Atelier de Joël Robuchon
Michelin-starred Robuchon brings his unbeatable gourmet dining experience to London in this Japanese-inspired restaurant. Lobster ravioli and potato purée are a couple of highlights. The bar on the third floor is a chic place for a drink *(see p105)*.

6 Hakkasan
Alan Yau, the man behind the successful Wagamama chain, created this seriously stylish dining experience. Michelin-starred oriental-inspired food, such as sautéed sweet ginger and pineapple roasted duck, with dim sum specialities, is served in luxurious surroundings designed by Christian Liaigre. The cocktails are sublime *(see p111)*.

7 Orrery

Sir Terence Conran is London's most prominent restaurateur. This intimate restaurant is at the peak of perfection and prices. The menu changes regularly, and has a distinctly French bias – including the best fish, beef and game *(see p133)*.

8 Rules

London's oldest restaurant (1798), Rules has a wonderful, genuine Belle Epoque atmosphere, and remains a great British institution, not resting on its laurels. It specializes mainly in game but is also known for its oysters, pies and traditional puddings *(see p105)*.

9 Barrafina

One of the coolest tapas bars around, Barrafina uses top-quality ingredients to excellent effect. Sit at the bar with a glass of *fino* or a small *Cruzcampo* and watch the experts at work. Expect to queue *(see p95)*.

10 St John

A great restaurant near Smithfield meat market, this is in a converted smokehouse. It serves a delicious range of high-quality British cooking, and has its own bakery. Try the amazing Eccles cakes with Lancashire cheese. Bar-menu snacks are not expensive *(see pp139, 155, 157)*.

Orrery, Marylebone

Top 10 Places to Eat with a View

1 Oxo Tower
Terrific river views from this South Bank landmark *(see p87)*.

2 Vertigo 42
On the 42nd floor of the City's tallest skyscraper. ⊗ *Tower 42, Old Broad Street EC2 • Map H3 • 020 7877 7842*

3 Le Pont de la Tour
Modern French cuisine overlooking Tower Bridge. ⊗ *36d Shad Thames SE1 • Map H4 • 020 7403 8403*

4 Tate Modern Restaurant: Level 7
Panoramic river views and great food. ⊗ *Bankside SE1 • Map R4 • 020 7887 8888*

5 Portrait Restaurant
Views over Trafalgar Square and Whitehall. ⊗ *National Portrait Gallery, St Martin's Place WC2 • Map L4 • 020 7312 2490*

6 Blue Print Café
A restaurant with a spectacular view of London Bridge. ⊗ *Design Museum, Shad Thames SE1 • Map H4 • 020 7378 7031*

7 Skylon
One of the finest river views in town. ⊗ *Royal Festival Hall SE1 • Map N4 • 020 7654 7800*

8 Swan At The Globe
Look over to the City through mullioned windows. ⊗ *New Globe Walk SE1 • Map G4 • 020 7928 9444*

9 Top Floor at Smiths of Smithfield
Above a vast warehouse, the dining room has lofty rooftop views of St Paul's *(see p139)*.

10 Coq d'Argent
Fine City sights from this rooftop garden bar and French restaurant. ⊗ *1 Poultry EC2 • Map G3 • 020 7395 5000*

→ For more restaurants See pp87, 95, 105, 111, 117, 125, 133, 139, 145, 151, 157

AROUND
TOWN

LONDON'S TOP 10

Left **Houses of Parliament** Right **Shakespeare's Globe**

Westminster, the South Bank and Southwark

HERE THERE IS A RICH MIX *of things to do. Sights range from Westminster Abbey and the Houses of Parliament to the Tate's stunning art institutions, the Southbank Centre and Shakespeare's Globe. In between there's the spectacular London Eye and other entertainments around County Hall, former headquarters of the Greater London Council. Two footbridges – one at Hungerford Bridge, the other at Tate Modern – help to bring the two sides of the river together.*

Sights

1. Westminster Abbey
2. Tate Modern
3. London Eye
4. Houses of Parliament
5. Tate Britain
6. Downing Street
7. Churchill War Rooms
8. Southbank Centre
9. Shakespeare's Globe
10. Imperial War Museum

Statue of Queen Boadicea, near Westminster station

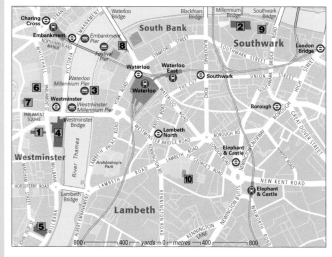

Preceding pages: View from London Eye towards Big Ben and Westminster Abbey

View down Whitehall towards Big Ben

Westminster Abbey
London's most venerable and most beautiful church, the scene of coronations and royal weddings and the resting place of monarchs *(see pp32–3)*.

Tate Modern
One of the world's great contemporary art galleries. A boat service connects Tate Britain and Tate Modern. It leaves from Bankside Pier outside Tate Modern every 20 minutes *(see pp18–19)*.

London Eye
The world's tallest cantilevered observational wheel offers amazing views of the city. While waiting for a flight, visit the attractions in County Hall – the Sea Life London Aquarium, Namco Station and the London Film Museum *(see pp16–17 and p84)*.

Houses of Parliament
The ancient Palace of Westminster is the seat of the two Houses of Parliament – the Lords and the Commons. A Union flag flies on the Victoria Tower when the Commons is in session. Night sittings are indicated by a light on the Clock Tower – the tower that houses Big Ben, the 14-ton bell whose hourly chimes are recognized around the world *(see pp34–5)*.

Tate Britain
The best of British art is held at the Tate and works range from 1500 to the present. Look downstream to see the home of British Intelligence (MI5). This large building, known as Thames House, is built inside a bug-proof "Faraday cage" *(see pp20–21)*.

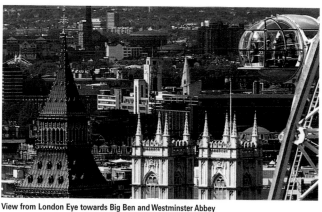

View from London Eye towards Big Ben and Westminster Abbey

Downing Street

6 The official home and office of Britain's Prime Minister is one of four surviving houses built in 1680 for Sir George Downing (1623–84) who went to America as a boy and returned to fight for the Parliamentarians in the English Civil War. The building contains a State Dining Room and the Cabinet Room, where a group of 20 senior government ministers meets regularly to formulate policy. Next door, No. 11, is the traditional residence of the Chancellor of the Exchequer. Downing Street has been closed to the public for security reasons since 1989. ◈ *Downing Street SW1 • Map L5 • Closed to public*

No. 10 Downing Street

Churchill War Rooms

7 During the dark days of World War II, Winston Churchill and his War Cabinet met in these War Rooms beneath the Government Treasury Chambers. They remain just as they were left in 1945, with spartan rooms and colour-coded phones. Take a guided

Whitehall and Horse Guards

The wide street connecting Parliament Square and Trafalgar Square takes its name from the Palace of Whitehall built for Henry VIII in 1532. The palace was guarded on the north side at what is now Horse Guards, where the guard is still mounted every morning at 11am (10am on Sundays), with a dismounting inspection at 4pm.

audio tour through the rooms where ministers plotted the course of the war, or visit the Churchill Museum which records Churchill's life and career. ◈ *Clive Steps, King Charles Street SW1 • Map L6 • Open 9:30am–6pm daily • Admission charge • www.cwr.iwm.org.uk*

Southbank Centre

8 The most accessible arts centre in London still has the air of friendly, egalitarian optimism that brought it into life in the 1950s and 60s. The Royal Festival Hall and the Queen Elizabeth Hall have diverse programmes, while the Hayward Gallery is a major venue for art exhibitions. The BFI Southbank, run by the British Film Institute, has a varied programme of movies. The National Theatre's three theatres (Olivier, Cottesloe and Lyttelton) are to the east along the river *(see p56)*. ◈ *Southbank Centre SE1 • Map N4*

Left **Churchill War Rooms** Right **Hayward Gallery**

Exhibits in the Imperial War Museum

Shakespeare's Globe

To see a Shakespeare play at the reconstructed Globe is a magical experience. The theatre is open to the skies, with seating in three tiers around the sides and standing in the central courtyard. Except when a matinee is playing, visitors to the exhibition next door are given guided tours of the theatre by staff (see p70).
⊗ New Globe Walk, Bankside SE1 • Map R4 • Bookings (plays from Apr–Oct only). 020 7401 9919 • Exhibition/theatre tour: Apr–Oct: 9am–5pm daily; Oct–Apr: 10am–5pm daily • Admission charge

Imperial War Museum

It is well worth the effort to visit this museum, which documents the social effects of war as much as the technology involved in fighting it, with displays on food rationing, censorship, air-raid precautions and morale-boosting strategies. Concerned mainly with conflicts in the 20th century to the present, it has changing exhibitions and an excellent shop that will appeal to those with a nostalgia for wartime London (see p45). ⊗ Lambeth Road SE1 • Map F5 • Open 10am–6pm daily • www.iwm.org.uk

A Day By the River

Morning

Start at Waterloo with breakfast and a self-guided tour of the Marriott Hotel, based in the splendid former headquarters of the Greater London Council. Cross Westminster Bridge to visit **Westminster Abbey** (see pp32–3) and nearby St Margaret's Church.

Continue along Abingdon Street to Lambeth Bridge and re-cross the river. Have a coffee at the delightful little café at Lambeth Pier, passing **Lambeth Palace** (see p70) on your way. Walk along the Albert Embankment for a stunning view of the **Houses of Parliament** (see p81) across the river.

For lunch, try **Skylon** (see p87) within the Royal Festival Hall at the **Southbank Centre**. The restaurant boasts fantastic river views.

Afternoon

Walk along the embankment and browse the second-hand bookstalls outside the BFI Southbank. Continue past the craft shops of **Gabriel's Wharf** (see p85) to the **Oxo Tower's** (see p84) designer galleries just beyond and take the lift to the tower's viewing platform for a great view of the city.

Afterwards, head along the embankment to **Tate Modern** (see pp18–19) – a wonderful place to spend the rest of the afternoon. Have a drink with more views in the **Espresso Bar: Level 4**. Further downriver, the **Anchor** pub (see p86) is a good place to relax and have dinner.

Left **Oxo Tower** Right **County Hall building**

The Best of the Rest

Clink Exhibition
London's first prison now houses a small exhibition devoted to crime and punishment. ❧ *1 Clink Street SE1 • Map G4 • Open 10am–6pm daily (to 9pm Jul–Sep) • Admission charge*

Sea Life London Aquarium
See thousands of marine creatures in exciting themed settings at one of Europe's largest aquariums *(see p68)*. ❧ *County Hall SE1 • Map N6 • Open 10am–6pm daily • Admission charge*

Duck Tours
This unique guided tour takes in several sights by road before plunging into the Thames for a river tour in an amphibious vehicle. ❧ *55 York Road SE1 • Map N5 • Open 10am–dusk daily • Admission charge*

BFI London IMAX
Giant-screen cinema that shows exciting movies set in the natural world. ❧ *South Bank SE1 • Map N4 • Open daily (screening times vary) • Admission charge*

Namco Station
Popular with children, this centre has arcade games, bumper cars and a bowling alley. ❧ *County Hall SE1 • Map N6 • Open 10am–midnight*

Florence Nightingale Museum
Fascinating museum devoted to the life and work of 19th-century nurse Florence Nightingale. ❧ *2 Lambeth Palace Road SE1 • Map N6 • Open 10am–5pm daily • Admission charge*

Golden Hinde
A full-size replica of the ship in which Sir Francis Drake circumnavigated the world from 1577 to 1580. ❧ *St Mary Overie Dock SE1 • Map G4 • Open 10am–5:30pm daily • Admission charge*

Fashion and Textile Museum
Zandra Rhodes' museum showcases the best of contemporary fashion, textiles and jewellery. ❧ *83 Bermondsey Street SE1 • Map H4 • Open 11am–6pm Tue–Sat • Admission charge*

Young Vic Theatre
This famous independent theatre company nurtures the talent of young actors and attracts diverse audiences with its critically acclaimed productions. ❧ *The Cut SE1 • Map Q6*

Oxo Tower Wharf
For great city views, take a lift to the public viewing gallery next to the restaurant *(see p77)*. Check out the boutiques and galleries below. ❧ *Bargehouse Street SE1 • Map P4 • Open daily*

Left **Gabriel's Wharf**, Centre **Signs, Southbank Centre** Right **Llewellyn Alexander art gallery**

🔟 Shopping

Parliamentary Bookshop
Buy the day's political reading, plus parliamentary-related prints and other souvenirs. ✪ *12 Bridge Street SW1 • Map L6*

Lower Marsh
Once London's longest street market, stalls sell inexpensive music, clothes, hardware and food. Open mornings Mon–Fri. ✪ *Lower Marsh SE1 • Map P6*

Llewellyn Alexander
This art gallery has changing, quality exhibitions, notably in the summer. ✪ *124–126 The Cut SE1 • Map Q5 • Open 10am–7:30pm Mon–Sat • Free*

Southbank Centre
Free concerts are held at the Royal Festival Hall and the National Theatre. Both have shops selling books and music. Second-hand books are sold under Waterloo Bridge. ✪ *South Bank SE1 • Map N4*

Gabriel's Wharf
Shops in riverside Gabriel's Wharf display hand-painted glassware, fashion, interiors, jewellery and ceramics. ✪ *56 Upper Ground SE1 • Map P4*

Bankside Gallery
The gallery for the Royal Watercolour Society and Royal Society of Painter-Printmakers has work for sale, and a shop. ✪ *48 Hopton Street SE1 • Map R4 • Open 11am–6pm daily during exhibitions • Free*

Oxo Tower Wharf
Two floors are given over to designers of fashion, jewellery and interiors and "the.gallery@ oxo" showcases cutting-edge photography, art, design and architecture. ✪ *Bargehouse Street SE1 • Map P4 • Open daily*

Konditor & Cook
This urban village bakery has a cult following amongst the cake connoisseurs. Its funky iced Magic cakes are legendary. ✪ *22 Cornwall Road SE1 • Map P5 • Open 7:30am–6:30pm Mon–Fri, 8:30am–3pm Sat*

Vinopolis
Wines can be tried out on a tour of this exhibition of viticulture, and the shop stocks over a thousand varieties. ✪ *1 Bank End SE1 • Map G4 • Open noon–10pm Thu, Fri & Sat, noon–9pm Sun • Admission charge*

Borough Market
Good food from all over the country comes to this traditional covered market near Southwark Cathedral. ✪ *8 Southwark Street SE1 • Map R4 • Open 11am–5pm Thu, noon–6pm Fri, 8am–5pm Sat*

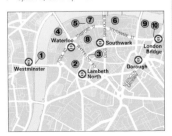

Left **Pub, The Anchor** Right **Swan at the Globe**

Pubs and Cafés

1 The Southwark Tavern
A popular pub with a wide range of drink and food. The debtors bar, down below, has individual booths that come with televisions. ✪ *22 Southwark Street SE1 • Map G4*

2 Footstool
In the basement of St John's, Smith Square, this is a good spot for a lunchtime snack. ✪ *St John's, Smith Square SW1 • Map E5*

3 Anchor and Hope
Don't be put off by the queues. The food is some of the best around. Great English ingredients make this a wonderful gastropub experience. ✪ *36 The Cut SE1 • Map Q5*

4 Monmouth Coffee Company
Serving arguably the best coffee in London, this atmospheric café in the heart of Borough Market also has delicious pastries and snacks. ✪ *2 Park Street SE1 • Map G4*

5 The Anchor at Bankside
Snug, old English pub with tables outside in summer. The dining room upstairs serves traditional English food.
✪ *34 Park Street SE1 • Map Q4*

6 Vinopolis Wine Wharf
The bar of this modern temple to viticulture has a vast wine list plus 20 varieties of champagne served by the glass. ✪ *Stoney Street SE1 • Map G4*

7 Swan at the Globe
Wonderfully located café on the first floor of this handsomely restored Shakespearean theatre building, with a fine view of St Paul's *(see p83)*.
✪ *New Globe Walk SE1 • Map R4*

8 Market Porter
A popular, historic market pub. Open for traders and all-night ravers from 6–8:30am.
✪ *9 Stoney Street SE1 • Map G4*

9 Rake
A fine selection of beers is on offer at this pub near Borough Market. The outdoor decking area is great for summer drinks. ✪ *14 Winchester Walk SE1 • Map G4*

10 George Inn
London's only surviving galleried coaching inn is a maze of plain, wood-panelled rooms and upstairs bars. Food is served from noon to 9pm Monday to Saturday and from noon to 5pm on Sundays. Courtyard tables are pleasant for dining in the summer months. ✪ *77 Borough High Street SE1 • Map G4*

For more pubs See pp62–3

Price Categories

For a three-course meal for one with half a bottle of wine (or equivalent meal), taxes and extra charges.

£	under £15
££	£15–£25
£££	£25–£35
££££	£35–£50
£££££	over £50

Turkish restaurant, Tas

🔟 Restaurants

1 The Cinnamon Club
Innovative Indian cuisine served in comfortable, club-like premises. ✆ *The Old Westminster Library, Great Smith Street SW1 • Map E5 • 020 7222 2555 • ££££*

2 Skylon
Named after the symbol of the 1950s Festival of Britain, the Southbank Centre's restaurant is a classy affair. Guests have a fine river view, along with classic British dining. ✆ *Southbank Centre, Belvedere Road SE1 • Map N4 • 020 7654 7800 • £££££ • Grill: ££££*

3 Baltic
London's most spectacular eastern European restaurant offers excellent dishes such as sorrel soup, smoked fish, and caviar in glamorous surroundings. ✆ *74 Blackfriars Road SE1 • Map Q5 • 020 7928 1111 • ££££*

4 Roast
Bang in the middle of popular Borough Market *(see p85)* is this handsome restaurant with views of St Paul's. Serves excellent and well-sourced British cooking. ✆ *The Floral Hall, Stoney Street SE1 • Map G4 • 0845 034 7300 • ££££*

5 The Archduke
Set in beautifully converted railway arches, this restaurant serves modern British food in a smart but relaxing atmosphere. Open daily with live jazz Mon–Sat. ✆ *Concert Hall Approach SE1 • Map N5 • 020 7928 9370 • £££*

6 Tas
Two branches of an exciting, modern, yet inexpensive Turkish restaurant. ✆ *33 The Cut SE1. Map P5. 020 7928 2111 • 72 Borough High Street SE1. Map G4. 020 7403 7200 • ££*

7 Gourmet Pizza Company
A range of pizza toppings is offered at this wonderful riverside shack. ✆ *Gabriel's Wharf SE1 • Map P4 • 020 7928 3188 • ££*

8 Oxo Tower Restaurant Bar and Brasserie
Delicious modern dishes are served in the restaurant. The bar has live jazz *(see p77)*. ✆ *Oxo Tower Wharf SE1 • Map G4 • 020 7803 3888 • ££££ • Brasserie: £££*

9 Cantina Vinopolis
Huge, vaulted dining room serving excellent Mediterranean food. ✆ *1 Bank End SE1 • Map P4 • 020 7940 8333 • £££–££££*

10 fish!
Innovative fish dishes are served in this modern, stylish restaurant. ✆ *Cathedral Street SE1 • Map G4 • 0871 963 3075 • £££–££££*

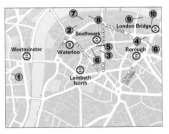

Left **Fountain, Trafalgar Square** Middle **Old Compton Street** Right **Leicester Square statue**

Soho and the West End

LONDON'S WEST END *is where everyone heads for a night out. Clubbers from outside London catch the last trains into the capital and head for its bars and music venues, knowing they won't leave till dawn. Here are the great theatres of Shaftesbury Avenue and Charing Cross Road, the star-struck cinemas of Leicester Square and, at its heart, Soho, abuzz with activity as the night wears on. But it's not all for the night owl – Trafalgar Square has the National Gallery, the National Portrait Gallery and free lunchtime concerts at St Martin-in-the-Fields.*

🔟 Sights

1. **National Gallery**
2. **National Portrait Gallery**
3. **Trafalgar Square**
4. **Piccadilly Circus**
5. **Chinatown**
6. **Soho Square**
7. **Old Compton Street**
8. **Berwick Street Market**
9. **London Trocadero**
10. **Leicester Square**

Share your travel recommendations on **traveldk.com**

Statue of Eros, Piccadilly Circus

National Gallery
See pp12–13.

National Portrait Gallery
See pp14–15.

Trafalgar Square
Trafalgar Square – once the royal mews – is a hub of the West End and a venue for public rallies and events. From the top of a 50-m (165-ft) column, Admiral Lord Nelson, who famously defeated Napoleon's fleet at the Battle of Trafalgar in 1805, looks down Whitehall towards the Houses of Parliament. The column is guarded at its base by four huge lions – the work of Edwin Landseer. At the northwest corner of the square, the Fourth Plinth features temporary artworks by leading national and international artists. On the north side of the square is the National Gallery *(see pp12–13)* and St-Martin-in-the-Fields church *(see p46)*; to the southwest, Admiralty Arch leads to Buckingham Palace. ✎ WC2 • Map L4

Piccadilly Circus
Designed by John Nash as a junction in Regent Street, the Circus is the endpoint of the street called Piccadilly. Its Eros statue – erected as a memorial to the Earl of Shaftesbury – is a familiar London landmark and a popular meeting place. The Circus is renowned for its neon advertising displays, which mark the entrance to the city's entertainment district. To the south is the Criterion Theatre, next to Lillywhite's – a leading sporting-goods store. ✎ W1 • Map K3

Chinatown
Ornate oriental archways in Gerrard Street mark the entrance to Chinatown, an area of London that has, since the 1950s, been the focus of the capital's Chinese residents. Here you can shop at Chinese supermarkets, street stalls and gift shops. The Chinese New Year, celebrated in late January or early February, is a particular highlight. Chinatown abounds with excellent-value restaurants. ✎ Streets around Gerrard Street, W1 • Map L3

Left **Admiralty Arch** Right **Chinese dragon, Chinatown**

Around Town – Soho & the West End

6 Soho Square

This pleasant square, spiked with palms, is popular at lunchtime, after work and at weekends, when there's always a friendly atmosphere, especially in summer. With the most fashionable address in London, many of the square's buildings are now occupied by film companies. On the north side is a church built for French Protestants under a charter granted by Edward VI in 1550. The redbrick St Patrick's, on the east side, sometimes has music recitals. On the corner of Greek Street is the House of St Barnabas in Soho, a charitable foundation in an 18th-century building which is occasionally open to visitors.
✣ Map K2

7 Old Compton Street

The main street in Soho is a lively thoroughfare both day and night. It is also the centre of London's sex scene, and now the site of popular gay pubs, Compton's of Soho and the Admiral Duncan. Soho's vibrant streetlife spills into Frith, Greek and Wardour streets, where pubs, clubs, restaurants and cafés have pavement tables, often warmed by gas heaters in winter. Some, like Bar Italia in Frith Street and

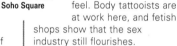

Mock-Tudor shed, Soho Square

Balans Café at 34 Old Compton Street, are open until the early hours. Everywhere fills up when the evening's performance at the Prince Edward Theatre ends. A delicious breakfast is to be had at Patisserie Valerie at No. 44, and such long-standing shops as the Italian delicatessen I Camisa, and the Vintage House (over 1400 malts in stock), give the area its village feel. Body tattooists are at work here, and fetish shops show that the sex industry still flourishes.
✣ Map L2

8 Berwick Street Market

There has been a market here since the 18th century, and the daily fruit and vegetable stalls remain cheap, cheerful and thoroughly Cockney. Half the time, traders talk in old money

Left **Old Compton Street** Right **Berwick Street Market**

Bar Italia, Frith Street

("ten bob" is 50p) and round things up to a "nicker" or a "quid" (£1). It opens around 9am six days a week. ◈ *Map K2*

London Trocadero

Take the escalator to the top of Funland and make your way down through this electronic jungle of video games and virtual-reality rides. There are dodgem cars, a race-track simulator and a bowling alley. Themed restaurants, bars, shops and cinemas fill up the space, as well as an HMV record store. ◈ *Piccadilly Circus W1 • Map K3 • 10am–midnight Sun–Thu, 10am–1am Fri & Sat*

Leicester Square

When this square was originally laid out in 1670 it was a grand and fashionable place to live. Celebrities of the 17th and 18th centuries to live here include Sir Isaac Newton and the painters Joshua Reynolds and William Hogarth. Today the square forms the heart of London's West End entertainment district and houses the Empire and Art Deco Odeon cinemas. There is also a cut-price theatre ticket booth called "Tkts" on the southside of the square. ◈ *Leicester Square W1 • Map L3*

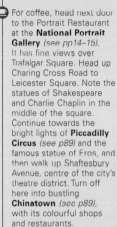

A Walk Around the West End

Morning

Start the day in **Trafalgar Square** *(see p89)* at 8:30am when the fountains are switched on and view the latest art on the Fourth Plinth. You could spend a day at the **National Gallery** *(see pp12–13)*, but limit yourself to an hour or two, perhaps just visiting the Sainsbury Wing.

For coffee, head next door to the Portrait Restaurant at the **National Portrait Gallery** *(see pp14–15)*. It has fine views over Trafalgar Square. Head up Charing Cross Road to Leicester Square. Note the statues of Shakespeare and Charlie Chaplin in the middle of the square. Continue towards the bright lights of **Piccadilly Circus** *(see p89)* and the famous statue of Eros, and then walk up Shaftesbury Avenue, centre of the city's theatre district. Turn off here into bustling **Chinatown** *(see p89)*, with its colourful shops and restaurants.

Lunch in Chinatown is obligatory. Enjoy the bustle of the Golden Dragon on Gerrard Street, or the calm of the excellent Joy King Lau in Leicester Street, just off Lisle Street.

Afternoon

Give the afternoon over to colourful and lively **Soho**. Eat a peach fresh from the stall in **Berwick Street Market**, then stroll up Wardour Street, home of the movie industry. Reward yourself with tea and a slice of cake at the delightful **Maison Bertaux** *(see p94)* in **Greek Street**.

Left **Façade, Algerian Coffee Stores** Right **Coffee makers, Algerian Coffee Stores**

🔟 Shopping

1 Ann Summers
When in Soho, you have to do something naughty. Ann Summers sex shops have been around so long they seem quite tame – but their products really are rather risqué. ✆ *79 Wardour Street W1 • Map K3*

2 Merc
A Carnaby Street classic, fans may still buy clothes cut from original 1960s patterns here. ✆ *10 Carnaby Street W1 • Map J3*

3 Foyles
In a street of bookshops, this grandmother of all bookshops is something of an institution. A vast range of subject matter is covered. ✆ *113–19 Charing Cross Road WC2 • Map L2*

4 Lillywhites
Infamous for its vast array of sporting goods that are spread over six enormous floors, there are plenty of bargains to be found at Lillywhites. ✆ *24–36 Lower Regent Street SW1Y • Map K3*

5 Milroy's of Soho
A West End whisky specialist, Milroy's has a small bar where malts can be sampled. ✆ *3 Greek Street W1 • Map L2*

6 Scribbler
A unique gift card shopping experience in Soho, Scribbler sells funny, well-designed cards and wrapping paper. ✆ *104 Wardour Street W1F • Map K3*

7 Agent Provocateur
Seriously sexy high-quality lingerie, from Joseph Corré, Vivienne Westwood's son, and his wife Serena Rees. Give in to temptation! ✆ *6 Broadwick Street W1 • Map E3*

8 I. Camisa
One of London's best-known delicatessens, famous for its fresh pasta, this is like stepping into a 1950s Italian grocery store. ✆ *61 Old Compton Street W1 • Map K3*

9 Algerian Coffee Stores
Opened in 1887, this is one of the oldest shops in Soho. It exudes a wonderful aroma of the many kinds of coffee it sells. Speciality teas and herbal infusions can also be bought here. ✆ *52 Old Compton Street W1 • Map K3*

10 The Witch Ball
Original French lithographs, antique travel posters and prints are sold here. The street is lined with antiquarian print and book shops. ✆ *2 Cecil Court WC2 • Map L3*

For more on shopping See p170

Left **Bar 101's colourful interior** Centre **Neon sign, Ronnie Scott's** Right **Café Boheme**

🔟 Late Night Venues

1 Ronnie Scott's
London's premier jazz venue (see p58). ✆ 47 Frith Street W1 • Map L2 • 020 7439 0747

2 Floridita
A long cuban cocktail bar serving Havana's original recipes. Interpretations of Cuban and Latin American cuisine make up the menu. ✆ 100 Wardour Street W1 • Map K3

3 Café Boheme
French-style bistro: sandwiches, salads and light meat and fish dishes are served until 3am Monday to Saturday. ✆ 13 Old Compton Street W1 • Map L2

4 Cork and Bottle
A range of champagnes and wines are available at this base-ment bar near Leicester Square. Open until midnight, Monday to Saturday and to 10:30pm on Sunday evenings. ✆ 46 Cranbourn Street WC2 • Map L3

5 Balans Café
This lively bar is open 24-hours a day. Hot dishes and sandwiches are on hand to keep people on their feet. Their eggs benedict is to die for! ✆ 34 Old Compton Street W1 • Map L2

6 Punk
A venue that is taking the West End by storm as it veers away from traditional door policy and ushers in a more hip, casual crowd. Boasts a huge bar. ✆ 14 Soho Street W1 • Map K2

7 Bar 101
Open till the early hours, this funky venue, on two floors, attracts cocktail drinkers and has live DJs at weekends. ✆ 101 New Oxford Street, St Giles WC1 • Map L2

8 Jazz After Dark
Things don't get going here much before 9pm, and the jazz and blues go on until 2am Mon–Thu, 3am Fri–Sat. BBQ mixed grill, tex mex and tapas are on the menu. ✆ 9 Greek Street, W1 • Map L2

9 Jewel Piccadilly
A chic bar and club attracting the young, the beautiful and occasionally the famous. Serves great cocktails and gourmet snacks including sharing platters. Funk and house on Friday nights. ✆ 4–6 Glasshouse Street, W1 • Map K3

10 PizzaExpress Jazz Club
One of a chain of 80 outlets in London, this one is open until midnight, with regular jazz nights a big draw. ✆ 10 Dean Street W1 • Map K2

For more live music venues See pp58–9 93

Around Town – Soho & the West End

Left **Fernandez and Wells** Right **Patisserie Valerie**

Pubs and Cafés

1 Patisserie Valerie
A classic Soho café with a wide range of delicious cakes and pastries: the fresh croissants make it a good place for breakfast. Its Frenchness extends to the Toulouse-Lautrec style cartoons by Terroni. ◈ 44 Old Compton Street W1 • Map L3

2 Maison Bertaux
This little corner of Paris in the heart of Soho attracts a faithful clientele, who love its delicious coffee and heavenly cakes. ◈ 28 Greek Street W1 • Map L3

3 French House
A small, one-bar establishment where conversation flows freely among strangers, this Soho pub was once the haunt of the artist Francis Bacon (1909–92). ◈ 49 Dean Street W1 • Map L3

4 Bar Italia
Sit at the bar or out on the heated pavement and enjoy the best Italian coffee in London. A huge screen at the back of the bar shows Italian football matches. Open 24 hours. ◈ 22 Frith Street W1 • Map L2

5 Fernandez and Wells
This lovely coffee shop serves quality coffee along with delicious croissants, pastries and cakes. It is also open for breakfast when you can order grilled pancetta or black pudding with egg mayonnaise in a roll. ◈ 73 Beak Street W1 • Map K3

6 The Admiral Duncan
A small, lively bar in Old Compton Street – one of dozens in the area with a gay clientele. ◈ 54 Old Compton Street W1 • Map L3

7 Endurance
This is what gastropubs are all about – great food, plenty of atmosphere (especially on market day) and a selection of wines by the glass. ◈ 90 Berwick Street W1 • Map L2

8 Beatroot
A small, bright vegetarian restaurant serving delicious salads and hot dishes, packed in boxes. ◈ 92 Berwick Street W1 • Map K2

9 The Cork and Bottle
A 1970s basement wine bar with vintage music, bistro food and a fine selection of wines (see p93). ◈ 44–6 Cranbourn Street WC2 • Map L3

10 The Dog and Duck
Small, friendly pub with Victorian tiled walls, classic pub food and British cask ales (see p62). ◈ 18 Bateman Street W1 • Map L2

For more pubs See pp 62–3

For a three-course meal for one with half a bottle of wine (or equivalent meal), taxes and extra charges.

£	under £15
££	£15–£25
£££	£25–£35
££££	£35–£50
£££££	over £50

Left **Arbutus dining room** Right **J Sheekey**

Around Town – Soho & the West End

🔟 Restaurants

1 Italian Grafitti
This bustling trattoria sells quality pizzas as well as pasta, and swordfish simply grilled with oil and garlic. ✆ *163–165 Wardour Street W1 • Map K2 • 020 7439 4668 • No disabled access • £££*

2 Arbutus
Black leather banquette seating and wood flooring, with typical dishes including squid and mackerel "burgers" and bavette of beef. ✆ *63 Frith Street W1 • Map L2 • 020 7734 4545 • ££££*

3 Incognico
Solid French food, such as fried goose liver, is served here. The restaurant was set up by Nico Ladenis, one of London's best chefs, who is now retired. ✆ *117 Shaftesbury Avenue WC2 • Map L3 • 020 7836 8866 • Disabled access • £££*

4 New World
Choose from the trolleys that trundle past at this popular dim sum venue, or from the menu of stir fries. ✆ *1 Gerrard Place W1 • Map L3 • 020 7734 0396 • ££*

5 Criterion
With its prime location in the heart of Piccadilly Circus, the Criterion is a fabulous place to dine. The gold, wood and marble furnishings provide a captivating retreat from the hustle and bustle outside, particularly at lunchtime. Modern European menu. ✆ *224 Piccadilly W1 • Map K3 • 020 7930 0488 • Lunch and pre-theatre menus • ££££*

6 Yauatcha
Be prepared to book ahead and dress up to enjoy steamed scallop *shu mai* or venison in puff pastry. ✆ *15 Broadwick Street W1 • Map K2 • 020 7494 8888 • ££££*

7 J Sheekey
The best fish restaurant in London in a charming setting, with dishes including shellfish and fishcakes. ✆ *28–34 St Martin's Court WC2 • Map L3 • 020 7240 2565 • ££££*

8 Itsu
An oriental conveyor-belt restaurant serving imaginative dishes. ✆ *103 Wardour Street • Map K3 • 020 7479 4790 • ££*

9 Busaba Eathai
Trendy Thai restaurant with a minimal interior. ✆ *110 Wardour Street W1 • Map K2 • 020 7255 8686 • ££*

10 Barrafina
Enjoy quality tapas at the counter in this stylish restaurant. Expect to queue. ✆ *54 Frith Street W1 • Map L2 • 020 7813 8016 • ££££*

Unless otherwise stated, all restaurants accept credit cards and serve vegetarian options

Left **Covent Garden piazza and central market** Right **Somerset House**

Covent Garden

ONE OF LONDON'S LIVELIEST AREAS, *Covent Garden is a popular destination for Londoners and tourists alike. At its heart is the capital's first planned square, laid out in the 17th century by Inigo Jones and completed by the addition of the Royal Opera House. In spite of such grandeur, there is still a local feel to the surrounding streets and lanes, especially around Neal's Yard and Endell Street. To the south of Covent Garden is Somerset House, which contains the Courtauld Gallery and is the setting for outdoor concerts in summer and a superb ice skating rink in winter. To get the full impact of the imposing riverside setting, enter from the Embankment side.*

TOP 10 Sights

1. The Piazza and Central Market
2. Royal Opera House
3. Courtauld Gallery
4. Somerset House
5. Seven Dials
6. Benjamin Pollock's Toyshop
7. London Transport Museum
8. Neal's Yard
9. St Paul's Church
10. Theatre Royal, Drury Lane

Clowns in Covent Garden

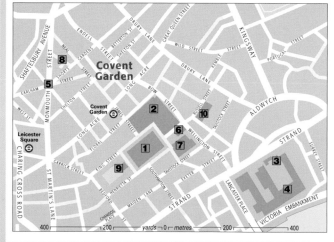

Preceding pages **Phantom of the Opera**, Her Majesty's Theatre

Shops and cafés in the former market area

The Piazza and Central Market
For 300 years, Covent Garden was a fruit, vegetable and flower market – immortalized by Lerner and Loewe's hit musical *My Fair Lady*. In 1980 the Victorian halls, with their lovely iron and glass roofs, were transformed into a vibrant, modern day market place, surrounded by cafés and bars and enlivened by regular street entertainment. ◈ *WC2 • Map M3*

Royal Opera House
London's impressive premier music venue is home to both the Royal Opera and Royal Ballet Companies. The present Neo-Classical theatre was designed in 1858 by E M Barry and incorporated a portico frieze recovered from the previous building, which had been destroyed by fire. The

Opera House has spread its wings into the lovely Floral Hall, once part of Covent Garden market and now housing a champagne bar *(see p56)*. ◈ *Bow Street WC2 • Map M2 • Open to visitors 10am–3:30pm • 020 7304 4000 • www.roh.org.uk*

Courtauld Gallery
Founded in 1932 for the study of the history of European art, the Courtauld is part of Britain's oldest institute for teaching the history of art. Located in the North Block of Somerset House *(below)* the gallery rooms are particularly strong on Impressionist paintings. A range of events is held here including monthly curator and weekday lunchtime talks. ◈ *Strand WC2 • Map N3 • Open 10am–6pm daily • Admission charge • www.courtauld.ac.uk*

Somerset House
Once a grand riverside palace, and later home to the Navy Board, Somerset House is now partly occupied by the Civil Service. A large amount of the building, though, is open to the public. Aside from housing the Courtauld Gallery *(above)*, there are the Embankment Galleries, which put on a varied programme of exhibitions spanning design, fashion, architecture and photography. ◈ *Strand WC2 • Map N3 • Open 10am–6pm daily • Admission charge*

Left **Street entertainment in Covent Garden** Right **Royal Opera production of** *Platee*

5 Seven Dials

Also known as "Covent Garden's hidden village", this characteristic street layout was created by Thomas Neale (1641–99), MP. The sundial at the central monument has only six faces, as Neale's original scheme included only six streets. Nowadays, it is known for its unusual mix of shops and leisure and entertainment venues, including restaurants, spas and four theatres. ◈ WC2 • Map E3

Benjamin Pollock's Toyshop, Covent Garden

6 Benjamin Pollock's Toyshop

Established in the 1880s, this independent, family-run shop specializes in toy theatres, theatrical gifts and traditional toys for both children and adult collectors. The colourful range on offer includes marionettes and puppets, musical boxes and paper dolls. ◈ 44 The Market, Covent Garden WC2 • Map M3 • Open 10:30am–6pm Mon–Sat (to 8:30pm Thu), 11am–4pm Sun • www.pollocks-coventgarden.co.uk

Covent Garden Architect

Inigo Jones (1573–1652) designed Covent Garden as London's first planned square. The low roofs and classical portico of St Paul's Church were influenced by the Italian architect Andrea Palladio (1518–80). As set designer for royal masques, Jones was responsible for introducing the proscenium arch and moveable scenery to the London stage.

7 London Transport Museum

Some of the most innovative British designers have worked for London Transport, and their posters and furnishings are on display here. See vehicles that have served the city for two centuries. The bookshop sells souvenir model buses, taxis and goods displaying the distinctive London Underground symbol (see p49). ◈ The Piazza WC2 • Map M3 • Open 10am–6pm Mon–Thu, Sat & Sun; 11am–6pm Fri • Admission charge • www.ltmuseum.co.uk

8 Neal's Yard

This delightful enclave is full of colour, with painted shop fronts, flower-filled window-boxes and oil-drums, and cascades of plants tumbling down the walls. This is alternative London, with wholefoods and such alternative therapies as Chinese medicines, walk-in back rubs and acupuncture.

Left **London Transport Museum** Right **Theatre Royal, Haymarket**

Neal's Yard, Covent Garden

Visit Neal's Yard Remedies for natural cures and beauty products. Try British cheese at Neal's Yard Dairy round the corner in Short's Gardens. ◈ *Neal Street WC2 • Map M2*

St Paul's Church

Inigo Jones built this church (known as the actors' church) with the main portico facing east, on to the Piazza, and the altar at the west end. Clerics objected to this unorthodox arrangement, so the altar was moved. The entrance is through the burial ground while the grand east door is essentially a fake. ◈ *Bedford Street WC2 • Map M3*

Theatre Royal, Drury Lane

Drury Lane is synonymous with the London stage and this glorious theatre explains why. It has a splendid entrance, with magnificent stairways leading to the circle seats. The auditorium is large enough to put on the biggest musical extravaganzas, including *South Pacific, My Fair Lady, Hello Dolly* and *Miss Saigon*. The first theatre on this site was built in 1663 for Charles II whose mistress Nell Gwynne trod the boards. ◈ *Catherine Street WC2 • Map M2 • Guided tours*

A Walk around Covent Garden

Morning

Take the tube to Leicester Square and head up Monmouth Street, where the delicious smell of coffee roasting will lead you to the Monmouth Coffee Company *(see p104)* for coffee and a pastry. Continue up Monmouth Street to the small entrance to **Neal's Yard** and buy soap at Neal's Yard Remedies. Check out Neal's Yard Dairy round the corner in Short's Gardens, and explore the shops in Earlham Street. Visit **Covent Garden Piazza** *(see p99)* for the street entertainers outside Inigo Jones' elegant **St Paul's Church**. Take a look inside before lunch in the **Royal Opera House's** *(see p99)* Amphitheatre Restaurant, with its wonderful views.

Afternoon

Before leaving the Piazza, pop into **Benjamin Pollock's Toyshop**, then turn down Russell Street and Wellington Street to the Strand. Cross the road and turn left to **Somerset House**, home of the **Courtauld Gallery** *(see p99)*. Start with their collection of Impressionist and Post-Impressionist paintings. Pause to relax by the Courtyard fountains or at the River Terrace Café before checking out the Embankment Galleries at riverside level, with exhibitions dedicated to a programme of contemporary arts, including design, fashion, architecture and photography. For more photography, exit Somerset House and walk along the Strand to Proud's Strand Gallery at 32 John Adam Street.

Left **Street entertainment, Covent Garden** Right **Globe atop London Coliseum**

The Best of the Rest

Free Entertainment
Every day from 10am–10pm there are street entertainers in the Piazza, while opera singers and classical musicians perform in the South Hall of the Central Market building. ❧ *WC1 • Map M3*

The Sanctuary
Spend a totally hedonistic day in this women-only spa with pools, jacuzzis, saunas, treatment rooms, a restaurant and a tranquil koi carp relaxation lounge. ❧ *12 Floral Street WC2 • Map M3 • Open 9:30am–6pm Mon–Fri, 9:30am–8pm Sat & Sun; evening spa: Mon (Oct–May), Wed–Thu 5–10pm • Admission charge*

The Tintin Shop
Everything from keyrings and Snowy toys to limited edition models – Tintin fans will love this shop. ❧ *34 Floral Street WC2 • Map M3*

Victoria Embankment Gardens
In summer, outdoor concerts are held in these attractive gardens by the river. ❧ *WC2 • Map M4*

Savoy Hotel
Enjoy a traditional afternoon tea in the Thames Foyer of this grand old London hotel *(see p70)*. ❧ *Strand WC2 • Map M3*

London Coliseum
Built in 1904, the home of the English National Opera has retained its Edwardian flavour, with gilded cherubs and scarlet curtains in the foyer *(see p56)*.

River Cruises
Embankment Pier is the boarding point for a range of trips, from sightseeing and dining cruises to the striking Tate Boat that links both branches of the Tate Gallery *(see also pp20 & 168)*. ❧ *Embankment WC2 • Map M4*

Oasis Sports Centre
Famous for its heated outdoor pool, there is also an indoor pool, studios, squash courts, gym, sauna and sun terrace. ❧ *32 Endell Street WC2 • Map M2 • Admission charge*

Players Theatre
The company at this tiny Victorian theatre recreates traditional music hall shows at various London venues. Check their website for details of upcoming events. ❧ *www. playerstheatre.co.uk*

Bush House
Home of the BBC World Service, Bush House has an imposing portico on its north side. In the arcade on the south side, the BBC World Service Shop sells DVDs, tapes, videos and books. ❧ *Strand WC2 • Map N3*

Left **Benjamin Pollock's Toyshop** Right **Specialist travel book shop, Stanford's**

🔟 Shopping

1 Floral Street
This stylish street is home to Paul Smith, which sells trendy clothes, Camper shoes and cool French designer Agnes B.
◈ *Floral Street WC2 • Map M3*

2 Shorts Gardens
One of the best places for streetwear, this street is home to G-Star Raw, Boxfresh and Miss Sixty, along with beauty shops and Neal's Yard Dairy.
◈ *Covent Garden WC2 • Map M2*

3 Neal's Yard Remedies
Remedies and toiletries, all made with purely natural ingredients, have been sold at this shop for over twenty years.
◈ *15 Neal's Yard WC2H • Map M3*

4 Stanford's
With an extensive range of travel guides, literature, maps and gifts, this shop is a traveller's paradise. ◈ *12–14 Long Acre WC2 • Map M3*

5 St Martin's Courtyard
London's latest shopping and dining destination is a stylish yet charming urban village enclave, with alfresco tables and top-name stores. ◈ *Long Acre WC2 • Map L3*

6 Octopus
Home to a kooky collection of colourful bags, eye-catching jewellery, luggage and household goods. Ideal for unusual gifts for children and adults alike. ◈ *54 Neal Street • Map M2*

7 Penhaligon's
In business since 1870, this eccentric British perfumery has a glorious range of fragrances and accessories for men and women. Perfect for elegant gifts.
◈ *41 Wellington Street WC2E • Map M3*

8 Benjamin Pollock's Toyshop
The place to go for toy theatres, theatrical gifts and traditional toys such as puppets and musical boxes.
◈ *44 The Market WC2E • Map M3*

9 The Tea House
Over a hundred teas – from Moroccan Minty to Mango & Maracuja – are on sale at this speciality shop in Neal Street. There are also novelty teapots and books on how to master the very English art of tea-making.
◈ *15a Neal Street WC2 • Map M2*

10 Thomas Neal Centre
This upmarket designer shopping mall has a range of fashionable boutiques over two floors. On the lower floor there is a pleasant café and restaurant.
◈ *Earlham Street WC2 • Map L2*

Left **World food café sign** Centre **Enjoying a snack at Paul** Right **Outside the Lamb and Flag**

Pubs & Cafés

1 Amphitheatre Bar at the Royal Opera House
Head upstairs to the Amphitheatre Bar for coffees, cakes and drinks. © Covent Garden WC2 • Map M2

2 World Food Café, Neal's Yard Dining Room
Have a pot of tea or a coffee, an Indian mango ice cream or a vegetarian snack in this pretty corner of Covent Garden. © 14 Neal's Yard WC2 • Map M2

3 Freud
This small basement attracts a designer crowd in the evenings. Huge choice of coffees (some with liqueurs), cocktails and bottled beers. © 198 Shaftesbury Avenue W1 • Map L2

4 Canela
Portuguese and Brazilian treats await the hungry here. Try the black bean stew with pork, chunky sandwiches filled with *chorizo*, and filling desserts. © 33 Earlham Street WC2 • Map L2

5 The Lamb and Flag
This traditional pub, serving cask bitter, is one of the oldest in the West End *(see p62)* and is deservedly popular. Delicious roasts are served upstairs at weekday lunchtimes. © 33 Rose Street WC2 • Map M3

6 Paul
The best patisserie in Covent Garden has authentic French fruit tarts, croissants, breads and cakes, as well as filled baguettes and real French coffee. © 29 Bedford Street WC2 • Map M3

7 Gordon's Wine Bar
An ancient cellar where wine, port and Madeira are served from the barrel in schooners or beakers. © 47 Villiers Street WC2 • Map M4

8 Lowlander
Belgian beer and European cuisine served in a relaxed setting attract drinkers and diners alike at this popular spot. © 36 Drury Lane WC2 • Map M2

9 Porterhouse
Excellent beers and a great atmosphere in this pub, which boasts snugs and bars over 11 levels. © 21–22 Maiden Lane WC2 • Map M3

10 Monmouth Coffee Company
The best place in London to buy and sample really good coffee, as well as a wonderful small café of great character that serves delicious French pastries *(see also p86)*. © 27 Monmouth Street WC2 • Map L2

Left **The Ivy** Right **View of Covent Garden from Chez Gerard**

Price Categories

For a three-course meal for one with half a bottle of wine (or equivalent meal), taxes and extra charges.

£	under £15
££	£15–£25
£££	£25–£35
££££	£35–£50
£££££	over £50

🔟 Restaurants

1 The Ivy
Mere mortals need to reserve several months ahead for London's most star-struck restaurant, but it's worth waiting for the delicious brasserie-style food and lively atmosphere. ◈ *1–5 West Street WC2 • Map L2 • 020 7836 4751 • £££££*

2 Abeno Too
Okonomiyaki – Japanese comfort food, rather like a cross between omelette and a savoury pancake – is cooked on a hot grill right in front of you. ◈ *17–18 Great Newport Street WC2 • Map L3 • 020 7379 1160 • ££*

3 Mon Plaisir
One of the oldest French restaurants in London. Daily specials keep the menu fresh. ◈ *19–21 Monmouth Street WC2 • Map L2 • 020 7836 7243 • Set lunch and pre-theatre set menus • £££*

4 Rock and Sole Plaice
This is simply the best place in central London for traditional British fish and chips. ◈ *47 Endell Street WC2 • Map M2 • 020 7836 3785 • £*

5 Chez Gerard
This airy branch of a popular chain of French restaurants has a glass roof and spectacular setting overlooking Covent Garden market. Robust, unfussy French food at its best. The café is open 11am–5pm. ◈ *The Market, Covent Garden Piazza WC2 • Map M2 • 020 7379 0666 • No disabled access • Prix Fixe menus • £££*

6 Souk Medina
A taste of Marrakech, from the exotic ambience to the mint tea and tagines. ◈ *1A Short's Gardens, WC2 • Map L2 • 020 7240 1796 • £££*

7 Orso
A popular, atmospheric, mid-priced Italian restaurant. ◈ *27 Wellington Street WC2 • Map N3 • 020 7240 5269 • ££££*

8 L'Atelier de Joël Robuchon
Experience fine dining from the man who mentored such luminaries as Gordon Ramsay. ◈ *13–15 West Street WC2 • Map L2 • 020 7010 8600 • £££££*

9 Rules
London's oldest restaurant has been famed since 1798 for its "porter, pies and oysters" *(see p77)*. ◈ *35 Maiden Lane WC2 • Map M3 • 020 7836 5314 • No disabled access • £££££*

10 Tom's Kitchen
Tom Aiken reinvents classic brasserie cuisine. In summer, Tom's Terrace offers lovely river views. ◈ *Somerset House, The Strand WC2 • Map N3 • 020 7845 4646 • ££££*

Note: Unless otherwise stated, all restaurants accept credit cards and serve vegetarian meals

Left **Museum Street** Right **Fitzroy Square**

Bloomsbury and Fitzrovia

LITERARY, LEGAL AND SCHOLARLY, *this is the brainy quarter of London.* Dominated by two towering institutions, the British Museum and University College London, and bolstered by the Inns of Court, it could hardly be otherwise. It is an area of elegant squares and Georgian façades, of libraries, bookshops and publishing houses. Most famously, the Bloomsbury Group, known for novelist Virginia Woolf (see p72) lived here during the early decades of the 20th century. Fitzrovia's reputation as a raffish place was enhanced by the characters who drank at the Fitzroy Tavern, such as Welsh poet Dylan Thomas (1914–53) and the painter Augustus John (1878–1961).

🔟 Sights

1. British Museum
2. British Library
3. Sir John Soane's Museum
4. Charles Dickens Museum
5. University College London
6. Wellcome Collection
7. BT Tower
8. Pollock's Toy Museum and Shop
9. St George's Church
10. St Pancras International Station

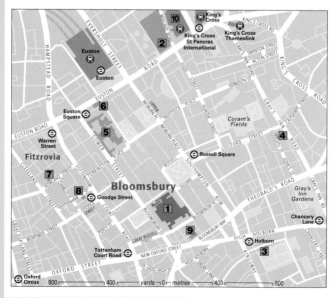

Sign up for DK's email newsletter on **traveldk.com**

Sir John Soane's Museum

British Museum
See pp8–11.

British Library
Located in the heart of St Pancras, the British Library holds copies of everything published in Britain, as well as many historical publications from around the world. Members have free access to these, while non-members can enjoy the magnificent space and the regular exhibitions put on here. A dazzling, permanent display in the Sir John Ritblatt Gallery includes the earliest map of Britain (1250), a Gutenberg Bible (1455), Shakespeare's first folio (1623), Handel's *Messiah* (1741) and many breathtaking illuminated manuscripts. The glass walls in the core of the building reveal the huge leather volumes from the King's Library, donated by George III. There are regular talks and events, a café, restaurant and, of course, a well-stocked bookshop. ✪ *96 Euston Road NW1 • Map L1 • Open 9:30am–6pm Mon, Wed, Thu, Fri, 9:30am–8pm Tue, 9:30am–5pm Sat, 11am–5pm Sun & public hols • Permanent exhibitions are free • www.bl.uk*

Sir John Soane's Museum
A particular pleasure of this unique museum is watching visitors' faces as they turn a corner and encounter yet another unexpected gem. Sir John Soane, one of Britain's leading 19th-century architects, crammed three adjoining houses with antiques and treasures, displayed in the most ingenious ways. The basement crypt, designed to resemble a Roman catacomb, is particularly original. *The Rake's Progress* (1753), a series of eight paintings by Hogarth, is another highlight.

The houses are on the northern side of Lincoln's Inn Fields, the heart of legal London, where gowned and bewigged lawyers roam. Lincoln's Inn, on the east side of the square, is one of the best preserved Inns of Court in London, part of it dating from the 15th century. ✪ *13 Lincoln's Inn Fields WC2 • Map N1 • Open 10am–5pm Tue–Sat, 6–9pm first Tue of month • Free • www.soane.org*

Left **Illuminated manuscript, British Library** Right **Sir John Soane's Museum**

For more on London's literary figures See pp72–3

Charles Dickens Museum

Home to Charles Dickens from 1837–39, during which time he completed some of his best work (including *The Pickwick Papers, Oliver Twist* and *Nicholas Nickleby*), this four-storey terraced house offers a fascinating glimpse into the life and times of the great Victorian author and social reformer. Some rooms have been laid out exactly as they were in Dickens' time. Nearby Doughty Mews provides another step back to Victorian times. ◊ *48 Doughty Street WC1 • Map F2 • Open 10am–5pm Mon–Sun, 11am–5pm Sun • Admission charge*

University College London

Founded in 1836, UCL is one of the world's leading multi-disciplinary universities and has many fascinating collections of international importance, including the Petrie Museum of Egyptian Archaeology, the Grant Museum of Zoology and the UCL Art Collections. The university hosts public lectures, workshops and exhibitions as well as performances at its Bloomsbury Theatre in Gordon Street. ◊ *Gower Street WC1 • Map K1 • Bloomsbury Theatre • Map E2 • 020 7388 8822 • www.ucl.ac.uk/ museums*

Bloomsbury Connections

Many Bloomsbury streets and squares are named after members of the Russell family – the Dukes of Bedford. The first duke features in Shakespeare's *Henry V*. In 1800, the 5th Duke sold the mansion in Bedford Place and retired to the country. The current Duke has turned the family seat, Woburn Abbey, into a huge tourist attraction *(see p167)*.

Wellcome Collection

The medical collection of American businessman and philanthropist Sir Henry Wellcome (1853–1936), who founded one of the world's leading pharmaceutical companies, explores the connections between medicine, life and art. ◊ *183 Euston Road NW1 • Map E2 • Open 10am–6pm Tue, Wed, Fri & Sat, 10am–10pm Thu, 11am–6pm Sun • Free • www. wellcomecollection.org*

BT Tower

At 190 m (620 ft), this was the tallest building in London when it opened in 1965. It is now used as a media and telecommunications hub and is closed to the public. The Tower Tavern in Cleveland Street has a good large-scale diagram explaining the tower's constituent parts (as well as hand-pulled beer). ◊ *Map D2*

BT Tower

Left **Façade, St Pancras International Station** Right **Carved figures, St Pancras Parish Church**

For more London museums See pp48–9

Pearly dolls, Pollock's Toy Museum

8 Pollock's Toy Museum and Shop

This delightful child-sized museum is a treasure-trove of historic toys. The shop below is crammed with old-fashioned playthings including Victorian toy theatre sheets, originally published by Benjamin Pollock. ⊗ *1 Scala Street W1 • Map E2 • Open 10am–5pm Mon–Sat • Admission charge • www.pollockstoymuseum.com*

9 St George's Church

This church was described in a 19th-century guide book as "the most pretentious, ugliest edifice in the metropolis". The steeple is topped with a statue of King George I posing as St George. There are music events, and an exhibition in the crypt. ⊗ *Bloomsbury Way WC1 • Map M1 • Open 1–4pm daily and for services on Wed & Fri (1pm), Sun (10:30am) • www.stgeorgesbloomsbury.org.uk*

10 St Pancras International Station

One of the glories of Victorian Gothic architecture, this railway terminus was designed in 1874 by Sir George Gilbert Scott. Most of the frontage is in fact the Midland Grand Hotel. The Eurostar International Terminal opened here in 2007. ⊗ *Euston Road NW1 • Map E1*

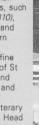
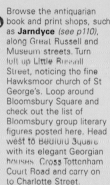

Bloomsbury & Fitzrovia on Foot

Morning

Arrive at the **British Museum** *(see pp8–11)* at 10am (opening time) so that you can enjoy the Great Court in peace. View Norman Foster's glass dome while having coffee at the café here. Stroll past the great Assyrian bas-reliefs on your way out.

Browse the antiquarian book and print shops, such as **Jarndyce** *(see p110)*, along Great Russell and Museum streets. Turn left up Little Russell Street, noticing the fine Hawksmoor church of St George's. Loop around Bloomsbury Square and check out the list of Bloomsbury group literary figures posted here. Head west to Bedford Square with its elegant Georgian houses. Cross Tottenham Court Road and carry on to Charlotte Street.

Afternoon

See the photos of literary figures such as Dylan Thomas in the basement bar of **Fitzroy Tavern** *(see p111)* at No.16 Charlotte Street, while enjoing a pre-lunch drink. If you fancy something more substantial than bar food, try a curry from **Rasa Samudra** *(see p111)* at No. 5.

After lunch, amble up to the **Brunswick Centre** for some shopping, from food to fashion. This awesome concrete-and-glass megastructure is one of London's iconic buildings. Catch a cult flick at arthouse cinema **The Renoir**, or have a coffee at **Carluccio's** (One, The Brunswick).

Left **Stylish glasses at Heals** Centre **Choosing a teddy at Hamley's** Right **Liberty**

🔟 Shopping

Around Town – Bloomsbury & Fitzrovia

Liberty
One of London's most appealing department stores, Liberty sells cutting-edge contemporary design in clothing, jewellery and household items. Opened in 1875, to specialise in goods and silks from the Empire, the shop remains famous for its "Liberty Print" fabric *(see p64)*. ✆ *210–220 Regent Street W1 • Map J2*

Hamleys
London's largest toy shop sells everything from dolls to computer games. Worth a visit just to see their fabulous window displays *(see p64)*. ✆ *188–196 Regent Street W1 • Map J2*

Heals
London's leading furniture store is a showcase for the best of British design. There is a café on the first floor. ✆ *196 Tottenham Court Road W1 • Map E2*

French's Dairy
This jewel of a shop in the heart of Bloomsbury sells chic, contemporary jewellery and accessories for both men and women. ✆ *13 Rugby Street WC1 • Map F2*

British Museum Shop
Find exquisite crafts and jewellery in this museum shop. Everything from a pair of ear-rings modelled on those of ancient Egypt or a replica Roman bust to contemporary crafts. ✆ *22 Great Russell Street WC1 • Map L1*

Contemporary Applied Arts
CAA promotes British art and crafts, and you can find glass, ceramics, textiles and jewellery within. ✆ *2 Percy Street W1 • Map K1*

James Smith and Son
Established in 1830, James Smith is a beautiful shop that will meet all your umbrella, cane and walking stick needs. ✆ *53 New Oxford Street WC1 • Map L1*

Cornelissen & Son
The most appealing art shop in town has wood panelling and rows of glass jars full of pigments. ✆ *105 Great Russell Street WC1 • Map M1*

Jarndyce
The handsome antiquarian bookshop is best for 18th- and 19th-century British literature. ✆ *46 Great Russell Street WC1 • Map L1*

Shepherd's
Write a letter home on these fine hand-made papers. The shop is also a specialist on bookbinding. ✆ *76 Southampton Row • Map M1*

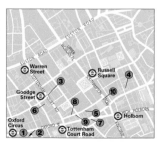

110 *For more on shopping See p170*

Price Categories

For a three-course meal for one with half a bottle of wine (or equivalent meal), taxes and extra charges.

£	under £15
££	£15–£25
£££	£25–£35
££££	£35–£50
£££££	over £50

Left **Carluccio's Caffè** Right **Smithy's**

Eating and Drinking

1 Rasa Samudra
Exquisite dishes from the Kerala region of southern India, including fish and vegetarian curries. A cookbook on display helps explain dishes you have never heard of. ◈ 5 Charlotte Street W1 • Map K1 • 020 7637 0222 • Disabled access, ground floor only • £££

2 Truckles of Pied Bull Yard
This wine bar comes to life in summer when the terrace is filled with drinkers enjoying chilled rosé and Pimm's.
◈ Off Bury Place WC1 • Map M1 • 020 7404 5338 • No disabled access • £££

3 Bam-Bou
Set in a lovely four-storey Georgian townhouse, this is a traditional South Asian restaurant.
◈ 1 Percy Street W1 • Map K1 • 020 7323 9130 • No disabled access • £££

4 Hakkasan
Its location may not be salubrious but this Chinese restaurant and cocktail bar is certainly classy. ◈ 8 Hanway Place W1 • Map K1 • 020 7927 7000 • £££££

5 Fitzroy Tavern
The pub that gave its name to the area (Fitzrovia) has a large central bar that attracts a lively after-work crowd. Good Samuel Smith beer is reasonably priced.
◈ 16 Charlotte Street W1 • Map K1

6 Salt Yard
Spanish grazing dishes here include Old Spot pork belly with cannellini beans and fried courgette flowers. ◈ 54 Goodge Street W1 • Map K1 • 020 7637 0657 • ££££

7 Villandry Foodstore
Attached to an excellent food shop, the restaurant has a simple modern French-brasserie style menu. There is also a café and bar. ◈ 170 Great Portland Street W1 • Map J1 • 020 7631 3131 • ££££

8 Smithy's
A hidden gem in King's Cross serving European cuisine with fine wine and real ales.
◈ 15–17 Leeke Street WC1 • Map F2 • 020 7278 5949 • ££££

9 Carluccio's Caffè
A touch of authentic Italy in this quiet square behind Oxford Street. Eat handmade pasta at pavement tables. ◈ 8 Market Place W1 • Map J2 • 020 7636 2228 • ££

10 Tas
This branch is well placed, offering Turkish food made for sharing. ◈ 22 Bloomsbury Street WC1 • Map L2 • 020 7637 4555 • ££

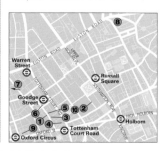

Note: Unless otherwise stated, all restaurants accept credit cards and serve vegetarian meals

Left **Buckingham Palace** Right **Burlington Arcade**

Mayfair and St James's

THIS IS WHERE *royalty shop and the rest of us go to gaze.* Many of the wonderful small shops around here were established to serve the royal court at St James's Palace. Piccadilly – named after the fancy collars called "picadils" sold at a shop in the street in the 18th century – divides St James's to the south from Mayfair to the north, where top shops continue up Bond Street, Cork Street and Savile Row to Oxford Street. Home to the Royal Academy of Arts since 1868, Mayfair has long been one of the best addresses in town. Today most of London's top-flight art galleries are here.

🔟 Sights

1. Buckingham Palace
2. St James's Park
3. Royal Academy of Arts
4. St James's Palace
5. Bond Street
6. Shepherd Market
7. Apsley House
8. Berkeley Square
9. Burlington Arcade
10. Royal Institution

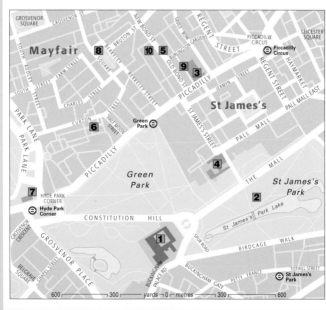

Victoria Memorial, Buckingham Palace

Buckingham Palace
See pp26–7.

St James's Park
This is undoubtedly London's most elegant park, with dazzling flower beds, exotic wildfowl on the lake, an excellent restaurant/café next to the lake (*Inn the Park, 020 7451 9999 to book*) and music on the bandstand in summer. The bridge over the lake has a good view to the west of Buckingham Palace and, to the east, of the former Colonial Office where just 125 civil servants once governed the British Empire that covered one fifth of the world (*see p28*). ✆ SW1 • Map K5–L5 • Open 5am–midnight daily

Royal Academy of Arts
Major visiting art exhibitions are staged at Burlington House, home of Britain's most prestigious fine arts institution. The building is one of Piccadilly's few surviving 17th-century mansions – you can see the former garden front on the way up to the Sackler Galleries. Near the entrance is Michelangelo's *Madonna and Child* (1505) – part of the Royal Academy's permanent collection and one of only four Michelangelo sculptures outside Italy. In the Academy's popular annual summer exhibition, new works by both established and unknown artists are displayed (*see p51*).
✆ Burlington House, Piccadilly W1 • Map J4 • Open 10am–6pm daily (10pm Fri) • Free (admission charge for temporary exhibitions) • www.royalacademy.org.uk

St James's Palace
Built by Henry VIII, on the site of the former hospital of St James, the palace's red brick Tudor gatehouse is a familiar landmark (*see p54*). ✆ The Mall SW1 • Map K5 • Closed to public

Left **St James's Park** Right **Gatehouse, St James's Palace**

5 Bond Street

London's most exclusive shopping street, Bond Street (known as New Bond Street to the north and Old Bond Street to the south) has long been the place for high society to promenade: many of its establishments have been here for over 100 years. The street is home to top fashion houses, elegant galleries such as Halcyon and the Fine Art Society, Sotheby's auction rooms and jewellers such as Tiffany and Asprey. Where Old and New Bond Street meet, there is a delightful sculpture of wartime leaders Franklin D Roosevelt and Winston Churchill – well worth a photograph. ◈ Map J3–J4

6 Shepherd Market

The market was named after Edward Shepherd who built a two-storey house here in around 1735. Today, this pedestrianized area in the heart of Mayfair is a good place to visit on a summer evening for a drink or meal. Ye Grapes, dating from 1882, is the principal pub, while local restaurants include L'Artiste Musclé, Le Boudin Blanc and The Village Bistro. During the 17th century, an annual May Fair was held here, giving the area its name. ◈ Map D4

Americans in Mayfair

America's connection with Mayfair dates from World War II when General Eisenhower stayed in a house on Grosvenor Square. In 1960 the Embassy building opened on land leased from the Grosvenor Estate, who refused to sell the freehold unless 12,000 acres of their estate in Florida, confiscated after the War of Independence, was returned.

7 Apsley House

The home of the Duke of Wellington (see p53), Apsley House is still partly occupied by the family. Designed by Robert Adam in the 1770s, the mansion is given over to paintings, and memorabilia of the great military leader. Paintings include several fine works by Diego Velázquez, including The Waterseller of Seville. Antonio Canova's nude statue of Napoleon has special poignancy. ◈ Hyde Park Corner W1 • Map D5 • Open Apr–Oct: 11am–5pm Wed–Sun (to 4pm Nov–Mar) • Admission charge

Sumptuous interior, Apsley House

8 Berkeley Square

This pocket of green in the middle of Mayfair was planted in 1789 and its 30 huge plane trees may be the oldest in London.

Left **Shepherd Market** Right **Berkeley Square**

Beadle, Burlington Arcade

In 1774 Clive of India, hero of the British Empire in India, committed suicide at No. 45. Memorial benches in the square bear moving inscriptions, many from Americans who were billeted here during World War II. A Bentley and Rolls-Royce dealer's showroom is on the east side of the square. ⊗ *Map D4*

Burlington Arcade

This arcade of bijou shops was built in 1819 for Lord George Cavendish of Burlington House *(see Royal Academy of Arts p113)* to prevent people from throwing rubbish into his garden. The arcade is patrolled by uniformed beadles who control unseemly behaviour. ⊗ *Piccadilly W1 • Map J4*

Royal Institution

Michael Faraday (1791–1867), a pioneer of electro-technology, experimented in the laboratories of the Royal Institution, where he was Professor of Chemistry from 1833–67. These Neo-classical buildings house high-spec laboratories, the famous Faraday theatre and a fascinating science museum. ⊗ *The Royal Institution, 21 Albemarle Street W1 • Map J3 • Museum open 9am–9pm Mon–Fri • Free • www.rigb.org*

Exploring St James's

Morning

🕐 Starting from St James's Park Underground, walk up through Queen Anne's Gate, noting the lovely 18th-century houses. Pass through the alley in the corner into Birdcage Walk then into **St James's Park** *(see p113)*. Get a coffee from the café, Inn the Park, and watch the pelicans before heading up to **Buckingham Palace** *(see p26)* for the Changing of the Guard at 11:30am. After the ceremony, head up The Mall, past **St James's Palace** *(see p113)* and into St James's Street. Turn right into Jermyn Street, and check out such traditional shops as cheese seller, Paxton and Whitfield, and perfumery, Floris. Walk through Wren's St James's Church near the end of the street, leaving by the north exit where a craft market is held. Head west down Piccadilly to Fortnum's.

Afternoon

Fortnum & Mason *(see p64)* is the perfect place to buy tea, as a souvenir, and to have lunch, in the Fountain restaurant, where the dieter's choice is caviar and half a bottle of champagne.

Cross Piccadilly to the **Royal Academy of Arts** *(see p113)* and spend an hour on their permanent collection, including Michelangelo's sculpture, *Madonna and Child*. Window shop along Burlington Arcade and then the **Cork Street** galleries *(see p116)*. Turn left into Bond Street, heading for **Brown's** *(see p177)* stylish hotel in Albemarle Street, and relax over a lavish (and expensive) English tea.

Left **Sotheby's auction house** Right **Designer dresses, Browns**

Shopping

Fortnum and Mason
Famous for its food hall and restaurants, this elegant department store still has male staff who wear coat tails. Try the extravagant ice creams in the Parlour restaurant *(see p64)*. ◈ *181 Piccadilly W1 • Map J4*

Asprey
The British royal family have bought their jewels here for more than a century. Other gift items to be found here include pens and silver picture frames. ◈ *167 New Bond Street W1 • Map J3*

Charbonnel et Walker
One of the best chocolate shops in town selling a tempting array of handmade chocolates. Fill one of the pretty boxes, which come in a range of sizes, with your own choice of chocolates. ◈ *1 The Royal Arcade, 28 Old Bond Street W1 • Map J4*

Gieves and Hawkes
Purveyors of fine, handmade suits and shirts to the gentry since 1785, this shop is one of the best-known in a street of expert tailors. Off-the-rack clothes are also available. ◈ *1 Savile Row W1 • Map J3*

Browns
London's most famous designer clothing store stocks pieces by Lanvin, Balenciaga and Alexander McQueen among many others. ◈ *23–7 South Molton Street W1 • Map D3*

Mulberry
Come here for the complete country-house look, including clothing, household items and gorgeous leather goods. ◈ *41–2 New Bond Street W1 • Map J3*

Cork Street Galleries
Cork Street is famous for its art galleries. You can buy works by the best artists here, from Picasso and Rothko to Damien Hirst and Tracey Emin. ◈ *Map J3*

Sotheby's
View everything from pop star memorabilia to Old Master paintings at this fine arts auction house founded in 1744. ◈ *34–5 New Bond Street W1 • Map J3*

Fenwick
An up-market, small department store with designer labels, accessories and lingerie. ◈ *63 New Bond Street W1 • Map J3*

Waterstone's
This is possibly Europe's largest bookshop *(see p65)*. ◈ *203–206 Piccadilly • Map K4*

For more on shopping **See p170**

Price Categories

For a three-course	**£** under £15
meal for one with half	**££** £15–£25
a bottle of wine (or	**£££** £25–£35
equivalent meal), taxes	**££££** £35–£50
and extra charges	**£££££** over £50

The dining room at Tamarind

🔟 Eating and Drinking

1 Sketch
The cooking here is some of the finest London has to offer. The Gallery is buzzy and informal, while the pricier Lecture Room attracts the fashionable and famous. ✆ *9 Conduit Street W1 • Map J3 • 020 7659 4500 • £££££*

2 Momo
Brilliantly-decorated in a kasbah style, this modern, North African restaurant serves *tajines* and couscous. The Mo Café and Bazaar next door serves tea and snacks. ✆ *25 Heddon Street W1 • Map J3 • 020 7434 4040 • ££££*

3 The Avenue
Join the smart set in this vast, lively restaurant. Food is European and caters to the British preference for large portions. ✆ *7–9 St James's Street SW1 • 020 7321 2111 • ££££*

4 Tamarind
This Indian restaurant doesn't disappoint. The food is modern, original and seasonal while staff are helpful and efficient. The set menus are great value. ✆ *20 Queen Street W1 • Map J4 • 020 7629 3561 • ££££*

5 The Square
Wonderful French food is on offer at this sophisticated modern restaurant. Only set-course meals are served; at lunchtime 2- and 3-course meals are £30 and £35. ✆ *6–10 Bruton Street W1 • Map J3 • 020 7495 7100 • Disabled access • £££££*

6 The Wolseley
The art-deco interior gives this famous brasserie an air of glamour. Opens 7am (8am Sat & Sun). Book well ahead for the formal restaurant. ✆ *160 Piccadilly W1 • Map J4 • 020 7499 6996 • ££££*

7 Nicole's Restaurant
Located in the Nicole Farhi fashion shop, Nicole's is a popular lunch stop. ✆ *158 New Bond Street W1 • Map J3 • 020 7499 8408 • ££££*

8 Alloro
This Mayfair restaurant has an airy first-floor dining room, and good Italian food. ✆ *19–20 Dover Street W1 • Map J4 • 020 7930 0493 • £££££*

9 ICA Café
Good food at reasonable prices is on offer at this arts centre restaurant. ✆ *The Mall SW1 • Map L4 • 020 7930 0493 • £££*

10 The Greenhouse
Michelin-star modern European cuisine in a serene Mayfair location. ✆ *27a Hay's Mews W1 • Map D4 • 020 7499 3331 • £££££*

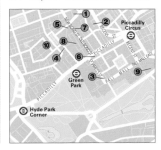

Left **Tiles, Holland House** Centre **Kensington Palace Gardens** Right **Natural History Museum**

Kensington and Knightsbridge

THIS IS WHERE *London's gentry live. Nannies push prams around Kensington Gardens, uniformed school children line up in Hans Crescent and the social "in-crowd" gossip in the Fifth-Floor Café at Harvey Nichols. Whatever time of year, nobody is without a tan. Harrods is the light beacon of the area; the solid rocks are the great museums established in South Kensington by Prince Albert, whose name is never far away. Kensington is the Royal Borough where Lady Diana roamed. She lived in Kensington Palace, the choicest of royal residences, and shopped in Beauchamp Place. Foreign royalty have homes here, too. Such mansions need the finest furnishings and some of London's best antique shops are in Kensington Church Street and Portobello Road, the most fun place to be on Saturday mornings.*

🔟 Sights

1. Natural History Museum
2. Science Museum
3. Victoria and Albert Museum
4. Kensington Palace
5. Albert Memorial
6. Harrods
7. Albert Hall
8. Portobello Road
9. Holland Park
10. Leighton House

Decorative relief, Natural History Museum

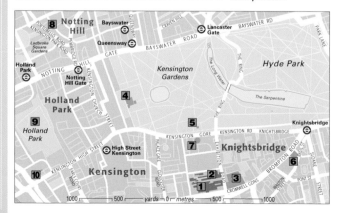

1 Natural History Museum
The whole world of animals and minerals is vividly explained *(see pp22–3)*.

2 Science Museum
Traces the history of scientific and technical innovation *(see pp24–5)*.

3 Victoria and Albert Museum
A cornucopia of treasures is housed in this enchanting museum named after the devoted royal couple. There are fine and applied arts from all over the world, from ancient China to contemporary Britain.

Turkish table from 1560 at the V&A Museum

Highlights include extraordinary plaster copies of statues, and monuments and artifacts from the Italian Renaissance. Displays are arranged over six floors of galleries. The stunning British Galleries display more than 3,000 objects illustrating the best of British art and design since 1500 *(see p48)*. 🟦 *Cromwell Road SW7 • Map B5–C5 • Open 10am–5:45pm daily (to 10pm every Fri) • Free • www.vam.ac.uk*

4 Kensington Palace
This is a delightful royal residence on a domestic scale, which is still in use by members of the royal family: Diana, Princess of Wales lived here as did Princess Margaret, the Queen's sister. The Enchanted Palace, a unique multi-sensory exhibition, combines fashion, performance and dazzling spectacle to reveal the palace's magnificent State Apartments in a magical light. The Wildworks theatre company cast a spell over the palace, creating a mysterious and atmospheric world in which the hidden stories of this historic royal residence are brought dramatically to life *(see p54)*. 🟦 *Kensington Palace Gardens W8 • Map A4 • Open 10am–5pm Mon–Sun • Admission charge • www.hrp.org.uk*

5 Albert Memorial
This edifice to Queen Victoria's beloved consort, Prince Albert, is a fitting tribute to the man who played a large part in establishing the South Kensington museums. Located opposite the Royal Albert Hall, the memorial was designed by Sir George Gilbert Scott and completed in 1876. At its four corners are tableaux representing the Empire, which was at its height during Victoria's reign. 🟦 *Kensington Gardens SW7 • Map B4*

Left **Earth Galleries, Natural History Museum** Right **Albert Memorial**

For more London museums **See pp48–9**

Harrods

6 No backpacks, no torn jeans... Harrods' doormen ensure even the people in the store are in the best possible taste. This world-famous emporium began life in 1849 as a small, impeccable grocer's, and the present terracotta building was built in 1905. It is most striking at night, when it is illuminated by 11,500 lights. It has more than 300 departments and on no account should you miss the wonderfully tiled and decorated food halls. Pick up a floor plan as you go in. In May 2010, Mohamed Al-Fayed sold the store to Qatar Holdings for £1.5 billion *(see pp64 and 123)*. ◈ *Knightsbridge SW1*
• *Map C4*

Royal Albert Hall

7 When Queen Victoria laid the foundation stone for The Hall of Arts and Sciences, to everyone's astonishment she put the words *Royal Albert* before its name, and today it is usually just referred to as the Albert Hall. It is a huge, nearly circular building, modelled on Roman amphitheatres, and seats 5,000. Circuses, film premieres and all manner of musical entertainments are held here, notably the Sir Henry Wood Promenade Concerts *(see p57)*.
◈ *Kensington Gore SW7* • *Map B5*
• *Open for performances and tours*

Prince Albert

Queen Victoria and her first cousin Prince Albert of Saxe-Coburg-Gotha were both 20 when they married in 1840. A Victorian in every sense, his interest in the arts and sciences led to the founding of the great institutions of South Kensington. He died at the age of 41, and the Queen mourned him for the rest of her life. They had nine children.

Portobello Road

8 Running through the centre of the decidedly fashionable Notting Hill, Portobello Road, with its extensive selection of antique shops, is a great place to spend some time. The famous market starts just beyond Westbourne Grove, with antiques, fruit and vegetables, bread, sausages, cheeses, then music, clothes and bric-à-brac. Under the railway bridge there is a young designers' clothes market on Fridays and Saturdays. Beyond that it becomes a flea market. Sit upstairs in the Café Grove (No. 253a) and watch it all go by, or grab a juice in Fluid (13 Elgin Crescent). Ethnic food is otherwise what goes down best, and the West Indian flavour spills over into the colourful clothes stalls *(see p65)*. ◈ *Map A3–A4*

Statue of Prince Albert, outside Albert Hall

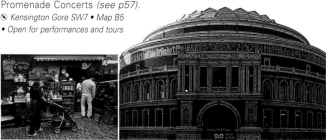

Left **Portobello Road Market** Right **Royal Albert Hall**

Café, Holland Park

9 Holland Park
There is a great deal of charm about Holland Park, where enclosed gardens are laid out like rooms in an open-air house. At its centre is Holland House, a beautiful Jacobean mansion, which was destroyed in a bombing raid in 1941. What remains is used as a youth hostel and the backdrop for summer concerts. Peacocks roam in the woods and in the gardens, including the Dutch Garden, where dahlias were first planted in England.
⊗ *Abbotsbury Road W14 • Map A4–A5*

10 Leighton House
All the themes of the Victorian Aesthetic movement can be found in Leighton House. It was designed by Lord Leighton *(see p52)* and his friend George Aitchison in the 1860s. Its high point is the fabulous Arab Hall, with a fountain and stained-glass cupola. Other friends contributed friezes and mosaics, but many features are original, notably the Islamic tiles, collected by Leighton and his friends on their travels. ⊗ *12 Holland Park Road W14 • Map A5 • Open 10am–5:30pm Wed–Mon • Admission charge*

Kensington on Foot

Morning

🕐 Start at South Kensington Underground station, and follow the signs to the **Victoria & Albert Museum,** *(see p119)*. Spend a delightful hour in the Medieval and Renaissance Galleries. Follow Old Brompton Road to the **Brompton Oratory** *(see p47)*, where you should take a look at its sumptuous Italianate interior, with 12 marble Apostles. Cross the road for a coffee and a pastry at Patisserie Valerie.

Turn right into Beauchamp Place, where window shopping takes in creations by such English designers as Bruce Oldfield and Caroline Charles. Continue down into Pont Street, and turn left up Sloane Street. Check out Hermès, Chanel and Dolce e Gabbana before turning left along Knightsbridge to Harrods.

Harrods has a choice of 29 bars and restaurants, including the food hall's Deli and Oyster Bar and legendary Caffè Florian on the third floor.

Afternoon

Just five minutes north of Harrods, **Hyde Park** *(see p28)*, offers a peaceful walk along the south bank of the Serpentine. Heading for **Kensington Palace** *(see p119)* you pass the famous statue of JM Barrie's *Peter Pan* and the Round Pond, where model-makers sail their boats. West of here, the palace's costume exhibit includes many of Princess Diana's dresses. Next door, **The Orangery** *(see p124)* provides a restorative cup of tea.

Around Town – Kensington & Knightsbridge

Left **Riding, Hyde Park** Centre **Serpentine Gallery** Right **Holland Park Orangery**

TOP 10 The Best of the Rest

1 Royal College of Music
The UK's leading music college stages musical events throughout the year. It also houses a Museum of Musical Instruments. ✪ *Prince Consort Road SW7 • Map B5 • Museum open four days per week during term time, phone 020 7589 3643 for details • Free*

2 Holland Park Concerts
The open-air theatre in Holland Park hosts an annual summer season of opera, while art exhibitions are held regularly in the Ice House and Orangery (see p121). ✪ *Abbotsbury Road W14 • Map A4–A5 • Admission charge*

3 Serpentine Gallery
In the southeast corner of Kensington Gardens, this gallery houses temporary exhibitions of contemporary art (see p51). ✪ *Kensington Gardens W2 • Map B4 • Open 10am–6pm daily • Free*

4 Christie's
Visiting the salerooms here is like going to a small museum. Their experts will value items brought in by the public. ✪ *85 Old Brompton Road SW7 • Map B5 • Open 9am–5pm Mon–Fri (7:30pm Mon), 11am–5pm Sat & Sun*

5 Electric Cinema
London's oldest purpose-built movie theatre, it remains one of the prettiest and offers luxury seats and 3-D technology; it also has a bar and restaurant. ✪ *191 Portobello Road W11 • Map A3*

6 Queens Ice and Bowl
Enjoy ice-skating, karaoke and ten-pin bowling here – but try to avoid the after-school crowd. ✪ *17 Queensway W2 • Map A3 • Bowling 10am–11pm daily, Skating 10am–10:45pm daily (10pm Sun) • Admission charge*

7 V&A Friday Late
On the last Friday of the month the ground-floor galleries at the V&A Museum are open until 10pm, with a themed evening of events (see p119). ✪ *Cromwell Road SW7 • Map B5 • Free*

8 Lido Café
Alongside the Serpentine Lido, the Lido Café has lakeside tables. Jazz and poetry sessions take place on summer evenings. ✪ *Hyde Park W2 • Map C4*

9 Speakers' Corner
This corner of Hyde Park attracts assorted public speakers, especially on Sundays. ✪ *Hyde Park W2 • Map C3*

10 Hyde Park Stables
Ride around Hyde Park or take lessons – this is the best place for horse riding in London. ✪ *63 Bathurst Mews W2 • Map B3*

Share your travel recommendations on **traveldk.com**

Left **Harvey Nichols** Right **Harvey Nichols mannequin**

🔟 Shopping

1 Harrods
London's most famous store has over 300 departments full of the finest goods that money can buy. Specialities include food, fashion, china, glass and kitchenware *(see p64 and p120)*. ⊗ *87–135 Brompton Road SW1 • Map C5*

2 Harvey Nichols
Another top London store. There are eight glorious floors of fashion, beauty and home collections alongside one floor dedicated to high-quality food *(see p64)*. ⊗ *109–125 Knightsbridge SW1 • Map C4*

3 Burberry
Burberry sells its famous trenchcoats as well as checked clothing and distinctive luggage. ⊗ *2 Brompton Road SW1 • Map C5*

4 Charity Shops
Browse the many charity shops around Kensington and Knightsbridge for the chance to pick up a designer bargain. ⊗ *Map B5–C5*

5 Artisan du Chocolat
Combining artistry and craftsmanship, Gerard Coleman creates some of London's most innovative chocolates. ⊗ *89 Lower Sloane Street SW1 • Map C6*

6 Rigby & Peller
Famous for their high quality lingerie, swimwear, corsetry and superb fitting service, this company has held the Royal Warrant since 1960. Expect service fit for a Queen. ⊗ *2 Hans Road SW3 • Tube Knightsbridge*

7 Antiquarius
Up to 60 dealers housed under one roof sell vintage jewellery and silverware as well as more unusual antiques. ⊗ *131–141 King's Road SW3 • Map C6*

8 Cutler and Gross
Treat yourself to the latest eyewear and browse the superb collection of retro classics. ⊗ *16 Knightsbridge Green SW1 • Map C5*

9 The Shop at Bluebird
As to be expected on King's Road, the stock here is always chic and fashionable. Women's and men's clothing, books, furniture and even a spa for decadent treatments. ⊗ *350 King's Road SW3 • Map B6*

10 The Travel Bookshop
Excellent specialist bookshop selling both new and old books. The shop achieved fame when it appeared in the film *Notting Hill*. ⊗ *13–15 Blenheim Crescent W11 • Tube Ladbroke Grove*

Left **Fifth Floor Café, Harvey Nichols** Right **Churchill Arms**

🔟 Pubs and Cafés

Around Town – Kensington & Knightsbridge

1 Beach Blanket Babylon
Famous for its wildly gothic interior, this bar serves lunch during the day, and becomes a swanky cocktail lounge in the evenings. A good place to mingle with the fashionable Notting Hill crowd. ✪ 45 Ledbury Road W11 • Map A3

2 Churchill Arms
Filled with intriguing bric-à-brac and Churchill memorabilia, this is a large, friendly Victorian pub. Inexpensive Thai food is served in the conservatory at lunchtime and for dinner until 9:30pm. ✪ 119 Kensington Church Street W8 • Map A4

3 The Orangery
Open for tea, coffee and lunch, this delightful café is located in a pretty conservatory overlooking Kensington Gardens (see p121). ✪ Kensington Palace W8 • Map A4

4 Portobello Gold
This trendy bar, used by local antique dealers, has a suitably alternative atmosphere and an upstairs Internet bar. There is also a conservatory restaurant. ✪ 95–97 Portobello Road W11 • Map A3

5 Nag's Head
A short walk from Hyde Park is this little gem serving Adnams beer and quality pub food. The low ceilings and wood panelling add to the cosy, village-like atmosphere here. ✪ 53 Kinnerton Street SW1 • Map C4

6 Paxton's Head
A popular watering hole for both locals and visitors, this old pub caters for all tastes, with cocktails and flavoured vodkas as well as real ales. ✪ 153 Knightsbridge SW1 • Map C4

7 Caffè Florian
Expect an authentic Venetian experience with divine food, impeccable service and charming atmosphere. This quintessential Italian café is on the third floor of Harrods department store. ✪ Knightsbridge SW1 • Map C5

8 Fifth Floor Café
Open all day for breakfast, lunch, tea and dinner. ✪ Harvey Nichols, 67 Brompton Road SW3 • Map C4

9 Market Bar
This atmospheric pub is popular with locals. ✪ 240A Portobello Road W11 • Map A3

10 Portobello Stalls
Along the market there are stalls offering ethnic food of every kind. The area also has a good choice of cafes around Portobello Green. ✪ Portobello Road W11 • Tube Westbourne Park

Price Categories

For a three course meal for one with half a bottle of wine (or equivalent meal), taxes and extra charges.

£	under £15
££	£15–£25
£££	£25–£35
££££	£35–£50
£££££	over £50

Opulent dining room at Belvedere

🔟 Restaurants

1 Clarke's
The menu consists of whatever chef Sally Clarke decides to cook for the evening meal. Whatever it is will be excellent. ✆ *124 Kensington Church Street W8 • Map A5 • 020 7221 9225 • ££££*

2 Belvedere
The restaurant's romantic setting in Holland Park is enhanced by its good European food. From the patio in summer, you may hear distant opera from the park's open-air theatre. ✆ *Holland Park W8 • Map A4 • 020 7602 1238 • ££££*

3 Kitchen W8
Fillet of bream with mussel and bacon chowder is typical of this chic but comfortable restaurant, perfect for a romantic dinner. ✆ *11–13 Abingdon Road W8 • Map A5 • 020 7937 0120 • ££££*

4 Amaya
Amaya's dishes take modern Indian cuisine to a new level. Flash-grilled scallops, charcoal-grilled aubergine and tandoori duck are served up in a rosewood-panelled dining room. ✆ *Halkin Arcade, Motcomb Street SW1 • Map C5 • 020 7823 1166 • Disabled access • £££££*

5 O Fado
Friendly staff serve authentic Portuguese delights, including *bacalau* (salt cod). There's also *fado* – Portuguese folk music – at the oldest Portuguese restaurant in London. ✆ *49–50 Beauchamp Place SW3 • Map C5• 020 7589 3002 • ££££*

6 Royal China
A tempting variety of dim sum, including delicious *char siu* buns, are the main attraction here. ✆ *13 Queensway W2 • Map A3 • 020 7221 2535 • £££*

7 Magic Wok
The menu offers an exciting range of Cantonese dishes. ✆ *100 Queensway W2 • Map A3 • 020 7792 9767 • No disabled access • £££*

8 Wódka
Vodka comes in carafes at this leading East European restaurant. Try the smoked salmon and caviar blinis. ✆ *12 St Albans Grove W8 • Map B5 • 020 7937 6513 • Disabled access (except toilets) • ££££*

9 Racine
Authentic French cooking, including plenty of garlic, in a wonderfully "Parisian" atmosphere. ✆ *239 Brompton Road SW3 • Map C5 • 020 7584 4477 • £££££*

10 Mr Chow
You'll find authentic Chinese dishes such as drunken fish in this long-established and fashionable restaurant. ✆ *151 Knightsbridge SW1 • Map C4 • 020 7589 7347 • ££££*

Note: Unless otherwise stated, all restaurants accept credit cards and serve vegetarian meals

Left **Madame Tussaud's** Right **Regent's Park**

Regent's Park and Marylebone

ORTH OF OXFORD STREET *and south of the park are the grand mansion blocks of Marylebone. Once a medieval village surrounded by fields and a pleasure garden, now it is a fashionable and elegant inner city area. In the 19th century, doctors started using these spacious houses to see wealthy clients. The medical connection continues today in the discreet Harley Street consulting rooms of private medical specialists. Madame Tussaud's in Marylebone Road may be less fashionable, but the queues outside testify to their popularity. Behind Marylebone Road, encircled by John Nash's magnificent terraces, is Regent's Park where the residents' tranquillity is ruffled only by the muezzin calling from the London Central Mosque and the bellowing of elephants in London Zoo.*

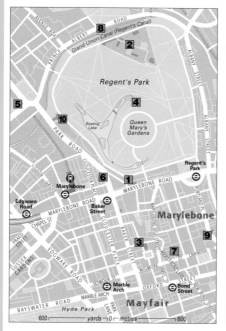

John Nash's Cumberland Terrace dating from 1828

Sights

1. Madame Tussaud's
2. London Zoo
3. Wallace Collection
4. Regent's Park
5. Marylebone Cricket Club Museum
6. Sherlock Holmes Museum
7. Wigmore Hall
8. Regent's Canal
9. BBC Broadcasting House
10. London Central Mosque

Around Town – Regent's Park & Marylebone

Preceding pages **Notting Hill Carnival**

Lord Snowdon's aviary, London Zoo

Madame Tussaud's

Madame Tussaud's museum of waxwork models of the famous has long been one of London's major attractions. The famous Chamber of Horrors puts visitors face-to-face with London's most infamous criminals. Arrive early to avoid the queues or book ahead to get a timed ticket *(see p68)*. ❧ Marylebone Road NW1 • Map C2 • Open 9am–7:30pm daily; Summer: 9am–8:30pm daily • Admission charge • www.madametussauds.com

London Zoo

Lying on the northern side of Regent's Park, London Zoo is home to 600 different animal species. The zoo is heavily into conservation and you can see the breeding programmes of endangered animals, such as the western lowland gorillas and Sumatran tigers. A map is provided and their booklet is full of fascinating animal lore *(see p68)*. ❧ Regent's Park NW1 • Map C1 • Open 10am–4pm (5:30pm in summer) daily • Admission charge • www.zsl.org

Wallace Collection

"The finest private collection of art ever assembled by one family," is the claim of the Wallace Collection, and it is hard to disagree. Sir Richard Wallace, who left this collection to the nation in 1897, was not only outrageously rich but a man of great taste. As well as 25 galleries of fine Sèvres porcelain and an unrivalled collection of armour, there are old masters by English, French and Dutch artists, including Frans Hals's *The Laughing Cavalier* *(see p50)*. ❧ Manchester Square W1 • Map D3 • Open 10am–5pm daily • Free • www.wallacecollection.org

Regent's Park

The best part of Regent's Park is the Inner Circle. Here are Queen Mary's Gardens, with beds of wonderfully fragrant roses, the Open Air Theatre with its summer Shakespeare plays, and the Garden Café, which, along with the Honest Sausage near London Zoo, is the best park café. Rowing boats, tennis courts and deck chairs can be rented and in summer musical performances take place on the bandstand *(see p29)*. ❧ NW1 • Map C1–D2 • Open 5am–dusk daily

Left **Barack Obama, Madame Tussaud's** Right **Boating lake, Regent's Park**

5 Marylebone Cricket Club Museum

Founded in 1787, the MCC is the governing body of the game, and its home ground, Lord's, is a venue for Test matches. The world's oldest sporting museum is included in a guided tour of the ground. Its star exhibit is the tiny trophy known as The Ashes. Ⓢ St John's Wood NW8 • Map B2 • Open Mon–Fri (call 020 7616 8595 as hours vary on match days) • Admission charge

Lord's Cricket Ground

6 Sherlock Holmes Museum

Take a camera when you visit here so you can have your picture taken sitting by the fire in the great detective's front room, wearing a deerstalker hat and smoking a pipe. This museum is great fun, with some entertaining touches. A Victorian policeman stands guard outside, uniformed maids welcome you and, upstairs, wax dummies re-enact moments from Holmes's most famous cases (see p52). Ⓢ 221b Baker Street NW1 • Map C2 • Open 9:30am–6pm daily • Admission charge • www. sherlock-holmes.co.uk

Regency London

Regent's Park was named after the Prince Regent (the future George IV) who employed John Nash in 1812 to lay out the park on the royal estate of Marylebone Farm. Nash was given a free hand and the result is a harmonious delight. Encircling the park are sumptuous Neo-classical terraces, including Cumberland Terrace, intended to be the Prince Regent's residence.

7 Wigmore Hall

One of the world's most important recital venues presents 400 events a year, including song, early music, chamber music and jazz strands as well as a diverse education programme. This beautiful Arts and Crafts style hall, built in 1901, is reputed to have one of the best concert acoustics in the world. Ⓢ 36 Wigmore Street W1 • Map D3 • www.wigmore-hall.org.uk

8 Regent's Canal

John Nash wanted the canal to go through the centre of his new Regent's Park, but objections from neighbours, who were concerned about smelly canal boats and foul-mouthed crews, resulted in it being sited on the northern side of the park. In 1874, a cargo of explosives demolished the North Gate bridge beside London Zoo (see p168). Ⓢ Map C1

Left **Residential narrow boats, Regent's Canal** Right **BBC Broadcasting House**

London Central Mosque

9 BBC Broadcasting House

Synonymous with the BBC, Broadcasting House has sailed majestically down Portland Place like a great liner since it was built in 1932. The expansion in radio and, later, television, meant that additional, larger premises were soon required, and now most broadcasting is done from other studios. Redevelopment is under way to turn Broadcasting House into a state-of-the-art digital centre for BBC Radio, the BBC World Service and BBC News. ✇ *Broadcasting House, Portland Place W1 • Map J1 • Closed to public*

10 London Central Mosque

Five times a day the muezzin calls the faithful to prayer from the minaret of the London Central Mosque. Built in 1978, with a distinctive copper dome, it acts as a community and cultural centre for followers of Islam. It is a hospitable place: step inside and see the sky blue domed ceiling and its shimmering chandelier. Prayer mats cover the floor for the faithful who turn towards Mecca to pray. ✇ *146 Park Road NW8 • Map C2*

Exploring Marylebone

Morning

🕐 Before setting out for the day, reserve a ticket for Madame Tussaud's *(see p68)* for the afternoon. Start at Bond Street Underground, exiting on Oxford Street. Opposite is St Christopher Place, a narrow lane with charming shops, which opens into an attractive pedestrian square. Stop for a coffee break at one of Sofra's pavement tables.

Continue into Marylebone Lane, a pleasant side street of small shops, which leads to Marylebone High Street and its wide choice of designer shops, including The Conran Shop *(see p132)*. Stop awhile in the peaceful memorial garden of St Marylebone Parish Church, planted with various exotic trees. Methodist minister and hymn-writer Charles Wesley (1707–88) has a memorial here.

Afternoon

For lunch, the Orrery *(see p133)*, beside The Conran Shop, is recommended. For a lighter snack, try Patisserie Valerie at 105 Marylebone High Street.

After lunch, bypass the legendary lines of people outside **Madame Tussaud's** and spend an hour and a half checking out the celebrity wax figures.

Cross Marylebone Road to Baker Street, for tea and a sandwich at Reubens *(see p133)*, before heading for the charming **Sherlock Holmes Museum** at No. 221b, a faithful reconstruction of the fictional detective's home.

Left **Selfridges columned façade** Centre **John Lewis department store** Right **Selfridges window**

TOP 10 Shopping

1 Daunt's Books
All kinds of travel books, including fiction, are arranged along oak galleries in this atmospheric Edwardian travel bookshop. 🛇 *83–84 Marylebone High Street W1 • Map D3*

2 Marylebone Farmers' Market
With over 40 producers, this is London's biggest farmers' market. Held every Sunday. 🛇 *Cramer Street Car Park W1 • Map D3*

3 The Conran Shop
Conran sells homeware and furniture in the best of both modern British and historic European design, such as a classic Mies Van der Rohe reclining chair. 🛇 *55 Marylebone High Street W1 • Map D3*

4 Divertimenti
This innovative London kitchen store has a huge variety of cooking implements, utensils and tableware. Open Sunday afternoons. 🛇 *33/34 Marylebone High Street W1 • Map D3*

5 Alfie's Antiques Market
Vintage jewellery, fashion, art and furniture are all under one roof, plus there is a café for when you're all shopped out. 🛇 *13–25 Church Street NW8 • Map C2*

6 Marylebone Lane
This charming lane off Marylebone High Street still has plenty of quirky gems to tempt the shopper. 🛇 *Off Marylebone High Street W1 • Map D3*

7 John Lewis
This sophisticated department store prides itself on being "never knowingly undersold". If you can prove another shop sells the same item for less, you pay the lower price. It has a thoughtful gifts department on the ground floor, and the staff are both helpful and knowledgeable. 🛇 *278–306 Oxford Street W1 • Map D3*

8 Selfridges
Opened in 1909, this store has a handsome neoclassical façade. A London institution, Selfridges is great for women's designer fashion. Its award-winning food hall is wonderful. 🛇 *400 Oxford Street W1 • Map D3*

9 Marks & Spencer
This flagship British brand is known for its underwear and food. 🛇 *458 Oxford Street W1 • Map D3*

10 Debenhams
A middle-of-the-road department store that sells everything from tools to toys. 🛇 *334–348 Oxford Street W1 • Map D3*

For more on shopping See p170

Price Categories

For a three-course meal for one with half a bottle of wine (or equivalent meal), taxes and extra charges.	£ under £15
	££ £15–£25
	£££ £25–£35
	££££ £35–£50
	£££££ over £50

Left **Orrery** Right **Patogh logo**

🔟 Eating and Drinking

1 The Wallace Restaurant
Located in the courtyard of the Wallace Collection, this smart café serves delicious lunches, including big salads. There is a café and à la carte menu, both change regularly *(see p50)*. ❧ *Hertford House, Manchester Square W1 • Map D3 • 020 7563 9505 • Disabled access • £££££*

2 Original Tajines
A distinctive Moroccan wine list complements the hearty tagines and couscous, including vegetarian versions, offered here. ❧ *7A Dorset Street W1 • Map C3 • 020 7935 1545 • ££*

3 Caffè Caldesi
This light and airy Italian eaterie offers classic dishes and a good wine list. The upstairs restaurant is slightly more formal. ❧ *118 Marylebone Lane W1 • Map D3 • 020 7935 1144 • ££££*

4 Reubens
One of London's best kosher restaurants offering such comfort food as chopped liver and salt beef. ❧ *79 Baker Street W1 • Map C3 • 020 7486 0035 • ££££*

5 Mandalay
A Burmese café where the food is a pleasing mix of Thai, Chinese, and Indian. Friendly, inexpensive and unpretentious. ❧ *444 Edgware Road W2 • 020 7258 3696 • Map B2 • ££*

6 Patogh
Kebabs are a speciality at this Iranian restaurant. It is unlicensed, but you can take your own beer or wine. ❧ *8 Crawford Place W1 • Map C3 • 020 7262 4015 • £ • No credit cards*

7 La Fromagerie
Sample the fine cheese and charcuterie plates here, along with delicious seasonal dishes. ❧ *2–6 Moxon Street W1 • Map D3 • 020 7935 0341 • ££*

8 Orrery
This is a lovely restaurant, serving French-inspired food. ❧ *55 Marylebone High Street W1 • Map D3 • 020 7616 8000 • Disabled access • ££££*

9 The Providores and Tapa Room
On the ground floor, the Tapa Room serves exciting fusion cuisine; upstairs is a more sophisticated foodie experience. ❧ *109 Marylebone High Street W1 • Map D3 • 020 7935 6175 • ££££–£££££*

10 Golden Hind
Indulge yourself here with traditional fish and chips, or fish cakes with Greek salad. ❧ *73 Marylebone Lane W1 • Map D3 • 020 7486 3644 • £*

Left **Fish weathervane at Old Billingsgate Market** Right **Old Billingsgate Market**

The City

THE ANCIENT SQUARE MILE OF LONDON, *defined roughly by the walls of the Roman city, is a curious mixture of streets and lanes with medieval names, state-of-the-art finance houses and no fewer than 38 churches, many of them, including St Paul's Cathedral, designed by Sir Christopher Wren. Don't miss the City's old markets: Smithfield still operates as a meat market, Leadenhall is in many ways more attractive than Covent Garden, while the former fish market of Billingsgate offers a great view of the once busy Pool of London.*

🔟 Sights

1 Tower of London
2 St Paul's Cathedral
3 Tower Bridge
4 Barbican Centre
5 Museum of London
6 Guildhall
7 Guildhall Art Gallery
8 Bank of England Museum
9 Monument
10 St Katharine Docks

Stone dragon in Smithfield market

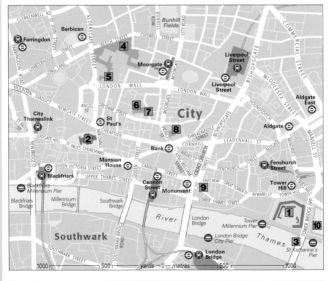

Tower Bridge and the Pool of London

Tower of London
See pp36–9.

St Paul's Cathedral
See pp40–43.

Tower Bridge
When the Pool of London was the gateway to the city's larder, this flamboyant bridge *(see p71)* was constantly being raised and lowered for sail and steam ships bringing their cargoes from all corners of the Empire. Pedestrians who needed to cross the river when the bridge was open had to climb up the 200 steps of the towers to the walkway overhead. Today, visitors on the 60-minute Tower Bridge Exhibition tour still have views from the 42-m (140-ft) high walkways. The entrance is at the northwest tower. It ends with a hands-on experience in the massive engine room, and exits via a shop on the south bank of the river. ◈ *SE1 • Map H4 • Open Apr–Sep: 10am–6:30pm; Oct–Mar: 9:30am–6pm • Admission charge*

Barbican Centre
The cultural jewel of the City, the Barbican Centre is an important arts complex. Music, dance, theatre, film and art all take place here, with top visiting performers and artists. There is also an excellent library, restaurants and cafés. Opened in 1982, the arts complex is part of the Barbican, a major development covering 20 acres and flanked by large blocks of flats. Access from the Barbican tube station is along a marked route. Moorgate, Liverpool Street, St Paul's and Bank stations are all within walking distance. The Centre looks across a lake to the church of St Giles Cripplegate, dating from 1550 *(see p56).* ◈ *Silk Street EC2 • Map R1 • Box office: 020 7638 8891 • www.barbican.org.uk*

Left **Barbican Centre** Right **Tower of London**

Museum of London

The world's largest urban history museum reveals insights into prehistoric, Roman, medieval and early Stuart London, along with "London's Burning", a display showing how the Great Fire of 1666 transformed the city. Visitors can also experience a re-creation of a Victorian Street. ◈ *London Wall EC2* • *Map R1* • *Open 10am–6pm daily* • *Free* • *www.museumoflondon.org*

Medieval shoes, Museum of London

Guildhall

For around 900 years the Guildhall has been the administrative centre of the City of London. City ceremonials are held in its magnificent 15th-century Great Hall, which is hung with banners of the main livery companies. In the Guildhall Library are rotating displays of historic manuscripts and an intriguing collection of watches and clocks, from the Worshipful Company of Clockmakers – some from 1600. ◈ *Guildhall Yard, Gresham Street EC2* • *Map G3* • *Call to check opening times on 020 7332 3700* • *Free*

Dick Whittington

A stained-glass window in St Michael, Paternoster Royal, depicts Dick Whittington (and his cat) – hero of a well-known London rags-to-riches fairy-tale. In fact, Richard Whittington, who was Lord Mayor of London four times between 1397 and 1420, was a wealthy merchant and the City's first major benefactor. He pioneered public lavatories, building them to overhang the Thames.

Guildhall Art Gallery

On the east side of Guildhall Yard is the Guildhall Art Gallery, two floors of paintings of varying quality and enormous interest. Many are associated with the City, and there are a number of highly romantic 19th-century paintings, including pre-Raphaelite works. With the aid of a computerized cataloguing system, it is possible to view all the Guildhall's 31,000 prints and paintings. ◈ *Gresham Street EC2* • *Map G3* • *Call to check opening times on 020 7332 3700* • *Admission charge*

Bank of England Museum

This fascinating museum, located within the impressive walls of the Bank of England, tells the history of the bank from its foundation in 1694 to the present day. Its unique collections of coins, banknotes and artefacts are supplemented by audio-visual

Yacht haven, St Katharine Docks

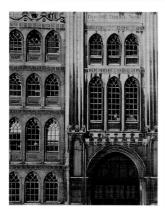
Façade, Guildhall

and interactive displays. Visitors can even handle a real gold bar!
⊛ Bartholomew Lane EC2 • Map G3 • 020 7601 5545 • Open 10am–5pm Mon–Fri • Free

Monument

Standing at 61-m (202-ft), this monument by Sir Christopher Wren offers panoramic views of the City of London. The height of this free-standing stone column is equal to its distance from the baker's shop in Pudding Lane where the Great Fire of London began in 1666 – the event that it marks. Inside, 311 stairs spiral up to a viewing platform; when you return to the entrance, you will receive a certificate to say that you have made the climb.
⊛ Monument Street EC3 • Map H4 • Open 9:30am–5:30pm daily • Admission charge

St Katharine Docks

Near Tower Bridge and the Tower of London, this is the place to come and relax, to watch the rich on their yachts and the working sailors on the Thames barges. There are several cafés, the Marble Quay and a number of popular bars and restaurants (see p71). ⊛ E1 • Map H4

The City on Foot

Morning

Start the day with a brisk trot up the 311 steps of the Monument and see how the surrounding narrow streets all slope down towards the Thames. Descend and carry on down Fish Street Hill across Lower Thames Street to the historic church of **St Magnus the Martyr** (see p138), where a model of the former London Bridge shows the city's great landmark as it was until the 18th century

Return up Fish Street Hill and Philpot Lane to Lime Street to see the glass elevators of the Lloyd's of London building and the affectionately named "Gherkin", 30 St Mary Axe. Enter the ornate, 1881 Leadenhall Market building for trendy shops, restaurants and bars. Have a delicious lunch at Luc's Brasserie in the market.

Afternoon

After lunch, see the City's historic financial buildings along Cornhill. Notice the Royal Exchange building's grand Corinthian portico and hear its carillon of bells at 3pm. Opposite is the Mansion House, the official residence of the Lord Mayor of London. To the north, across Thread-needle Street, is the Bank of England. Continue into Lothbury and along Gresham Street to Guild-hall, where you should look at the medieval Great Hall.

Head up Wood Street to the **Barbican Centre** (see p135) for tea by the lake at the Waterside Café. Check the programme for the day's events and maybe take in a performance.

Around Town – the City

Left **Organ at St Katharine Cree** Right **Carved capital in St Paul's Cathedral**

🔟 City Churches to Visit

St Paul's Cathedral
See pp40–43.

St Bartholomew-the-Great
This is one of London's oldest churches, built in the 12th century. Some Norman architectural details may be seen *(see p46)*. ◊ *West Smithfield EC1 • Map R1 • Open 8:30am–5pm (4pm in winter) Mon–Fri, 10:30am–4pm Sat, 8:30am–8pm Sun • Adm*

St Mary-le-Bow
St Mary-le-Bow was rebuilt by Wren after its destruction in the Great Fire of London in 1666. ◊ *Cheapside EC2 • Map G3 • Open 7am–6pm Mon–Wed, 7am–6:30pm Thu, 7am–4pm Fri, 9am–4pm Sat & Sun • Free*

St Sepulchre-without-Newgate
The largest church in the City after St Paul's, St Sepulchre is famous for its peal of 12 bells. Recitals are held on Wednesdays. ◊ *Holborn Viaduct EC1 • Map Q1 • Open 11:30am–2:30pm Mon & Tue, Thu–Fri, 11am–3pm Wed • Free*

St Katharine Cree
One of eight churches to survive the Great Fire, it dates from about 1630. Purcell and Handel both played on its organ. ◊ *Leadenhall Street EC3 • Map H3 • Open 10:30am–4:30pm Mon–Fri, Holy Communion on Thu (closed Aug) • Free*

St Magnus the Martyr
Designed by Wren in the 1670s, the church retains his elegant pulpit. Regular recitals take place throughout the year. ◊ *Lower Thames Street EC3 • Map H4 • Open 10am–4pm Tue–Fri, 10am–1pm Sun • Free*

All Hallows by the Tower
Take a guided tour of the church, which dates from Saxon times. ◊ *Byward Street EC3 • Map H3 • Open 8am–6pm Mon–Fri, 10am–5pm Sat & Sun • Free*

St Stephen Walbrook
The Lord Mayor's parish church is considered to be Wren's finest. ◊ *Walbrook EC4 • Map G3 • Open 10am–4pm Mon–Fri • Free*

St Anne and St Agnes
This Lutheran church has a long tradition in music (especially Baroque). Lunchtime concerts are held on Mon and Fri. ◊ *Gresham Street EC2 • Map R2 • Open 10am–3pm Mon, Tue, Thu & Fri • Free*

St Lawrence Jewry
Beautiful stained-glass windows of historic figures are the highlight here. ◊ *Guildhall EC2 • Map R2 • Open 8am–4pm Mon–Fri • Free*

For more London churches See pp46–7

Top Floor at Smiths of Smithfield

Eating and Drinking

1 St John
A delightful restaurant serving excellent British food. Delicious light bar meals available (see also St John Bread & Wine, p157). ® 26 St John Street EC1 • Map F2 • 020 7251 0848 • Disabled access to bar but not to restaurant or toilets • ££££

2 Top Floor at Smiths of Smithfield
This warehouse restaurant serves meat market specials (see also p77). A café on the ground floor turns into a bar in the evening and there is an informal restaurant on the second floor. ® 66–77 Charterhouse Street EC1 • Map Q1 • 020 7251 7950 • £££ £££££

3 Club Gascon
Top-notch cuisine from southwest France. Pick three or four "taster" dishes, such as venison scallops, or there is a five-course gourmet "tasting" menu, including wines. ® 57 West Smithfield EC1 • Map R1 • 020 7796 0600 • ££££

4 Sweetings
This is a weekday lunchtime haven for fish lovers. Starters such as potted shrimp are followed by plaice and Dover sole. Desserts include bread-and-butter pudding. ® 39 Queen Victoria Street EC4 • Map R2 • 020 7248 3062 • No credit cards • £££

5 Sauterelle
Stylish French dining in the gallery of the City's Royal Exchange. ® Royal Exchange EC3 • Map H3 • 020 7618 2483 • £££££

6 Eastway @ Andaz
New York style brasserie serving hearty dishes including grilled meats. ® 40 Liverpool Street EC2 • Map H3 • 020 7618 7400 • ££

7 1 Lombard Street
Modern European fare served in a former banking hall. This is one of the city's most striking dining locations. ® 1 Lombard Street EC3 • Map G3 • 020 7929 6611 • £££££

8 Café Below
Canteen in the crypt of St Mary-le-Bow church. Serves breakfast, lunch and dinner. ® Cheapside EC2 • Map G3 • 020 7329 0789 • ££

9 Shaw's Booksellers
Quirky pub and bar with a splendid array of beers and wines. ® 31–34 St Andrew's Hill EC4 • Map Q2 • 020 7489 7999 • £££

10 Vertigo 42
Take in the incredible views at this ostentatious, sky-scraping champagne bar on the 42nd floor. ® Tower 42, 25 Old Broad Street EC2 • Map H3 • 020 7877 7842 • £££££

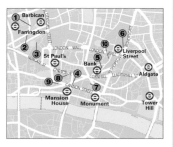

Note: Unless otherwise stated, all restaurants accept credit cards and serve vegetarian meals. Many City restaurants close at weekends.

Left **View over London from Hampstead Heath** Right **Camden Lock Market**

Heading North

BEYOND REGENT'S PARK AND THE RAILWAY TERMINI *of Euston, King's Cross and St Pancras, North London drifts up into areas that were once distant villages where the rich built their country mansions to escape the city. Many of these houses remain and several are open for the public to wander around and imagine a bygone age. Parts of their extensive grounds now make up the wild and lofty expanse of Hampstead Heath. Some of the "villages", such as Hampstead and Highgate, are still distinct from the urban sprawl that surrounds them. Home to the wealthy, cultured and famous, their attractive streets are full of well-preserved architecture as well as dozens of inviting pubs and restaurants. Other parts of North London have different flavours, however – from bustling Camden, with its canal-side market, lively pubs and clubs, to fashionable Islington, with its clothes and antique shops, good restaurants, smart cafés and bars.*

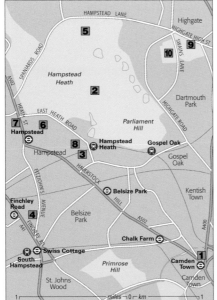

Site of the well on Well Walk, Hampstead

🔟 Sights

1. Camden Markets
2. Hampstead Heath and Parliament Hill
3. Keats House
4. Freud Museum
5. Kenwood House
6. Burgh House
7. Fenton House
8. 2 Willow Road
9. Lauderdale House
10. Highgate Cemetery

Hampstead Heath

Camden Markets
The most exciting North London markets are open every weekend, and linked by the busy and colourful Camden High Street. Camden Market, near the tube station, is packed with stalls selling clothes, shoes and jewellery. Further up the road, by the canal, Camden Lock Market focuses on crafts and ethnic goods. Stalls in the warehouses of Stables Market have great food on sale. Open weekends only between 8am and 6pm *(see p65)*. ✆ *Camden High Street & Chalk Farm Road NW1 • Tube Camden Town*

Hampstead Heath and Parliament Hill
A welcome retreat from the city, this large, open area is one of the best places in London for walking. Covering 800 acres of countryside, it contains ancient woodlands and ponds for swimming and fishing. The high point of Parliament Hill has great city views and is a popular place for kite-flying *(see p74)*. ✆ *Heath Information Centre, Staff Yard, Highgate Road NW5 • Tube Hampstead • 020 7482 7073*

Keats House
Keats Grove, off Downshire Hill, is one of the loveliest areas of Hampstead. The house where the poet John Keats wrote much of his work is a pretty white villa, containing facsimiles of his fragile manuscripts and letters, as well as some personal possessions. Poetry readings and talks take place regularly *(see p52)*. ✆ *Keats Grove NW3 • Train Hampstead Heath, tube Hampstead or Belsize Park • 020 7332 3868 • Open 1–5pm Tue–Sun (Fri–Sun in winter) • Admission charge*

Freud Museum
Sigmund Freud, the founder of psychoanalysis, came to live here when he fled Nazi-occupied Vienna. The house contains Freud's collection of antiques, his library, including first editions of his own works, and the famous couch on which his patients related their dreams. *(see p52)*. ✆ *20 Maresfield Gardens NW3 • Tube Finchley Road • Open noon–5pm Wed–Sun • Admission charge • www.freud.org.uk*

Regent's Canal, Camden Lock

Kenwood House

5 This magnificent mansion, filled with Old Masters, is set in an idyllic lakeside estate on the edge of Hampstead Heath. Vermeer's *The Guitar Player* and a self-portrait by Rembrandt are among the star attractions. Concerts are held by the lake in summer – audiences sit in the grassy bowl, with picnics to sustain them *(see p51)*. ✍ *Hampstead Lane NW3 • Tube Highgate • 020 7973 3893 • Open 11:30am–4pm daily • Pre-booked tours available • Free*

Burgh House

6 Built in 1703, Burgh House houses Hampstead Museum, which has a good selection of local books and a map of the famous people who have lived in the area. The panelled music room is used for art exhibitions, concerts and meetings, and there is a pleasant café with garden tables. ✍ *New End Square NW3 • Tube Hampstead • 020 7431 0144 • Open noon–5pm Wed–Fri, Sun • Free*

Fenton House

7 This splendid 1686 mansion is the oldest in Hampstead. Its exceptionally fine collection of Oriental and European porcelain, furniture and needlework was bequeathed to the National Trust

Hampstead Wells

Hampstead's heyday began in the early 18th century, when a spring in Well Walk was recognized as having medicinal properties. This brought Londoners flocking to take the waters in the Pump Room within the Great Room in Well Walk, which also housed an Assembly Room for dances and concerts. The spa gradually fell into disrepute, but Hampstead retained its fashionable status.

with the house in 1952. A formal walled garden contains an orchard. ✍ *Hampstead Grove NW3 • Tube Hampstead • 020 7435 3471 • Open Mar–Nov: 11am–5pm Wed–Sun • Admission charge*

2 Willow Road

8 Designed in 1939 by the architect Ernö Goldfinger for himself and his wife, the artist Ursula Blackwell, this is one of the most important examples of modern architecture in the UK. Goldfinger designed all the furniture and collected some fine works by Henry Moore, Max Ernst and Marcel Duchamp. Admission is strictly limited to hourly tours, which are non-bookable. ✍ *2 Willow Road NW3 • Train to Hampstead Heath • 020 7435 6166 • Open Mar–Oct: 11am–5pm Wed–Sun • Admission charge*

Left **Staircase, Burgh House** Right **Fenton House**

Memorial, Highgate Cemetery

Lauderdale House

9 Dating from the late 16th century, Lauderdale House was once associated with Charles II and his mistress Nell Gwynne. It now houses a popular arts and cultural centre, with regular concerts, exhibitions and Sunday craft and antique fairs. ◎ *Highgate Hill N6 • Tube Highgate • Open 11am–4pm Tue–Fri, varies Sat (call 020 834 88716 to check), noon–5pm Sun*

Highgate Cemetery

10 On the opposite side of the Heath to Hampstead, Highgate grew up as a healthy, countrified place for nobility who built large mansions here. Many famous people who lived in the area are buried in Highgate Cemetery. Consecrated in 1839, its Victorian architecture and fine views soon made it a popular outing for Londoners. Karl Marx and novelist George Eliot are buried in the less glamorous East Cemetery *(see p75)* ◎ *Swain's Lane N6 • Tube Archway • 020 8340 1834 • East Cemetery: open Mar–Oct: 10am–5pm Mon–Fri, 11am–5pm Sat–Sun; Nov–Feb: 10am–4pm Mon–Fri, 11am– 4pm Sat–Sun. Closed for funerals (phone to check) • West Cemetery: tours only • Admission charge for both • www.highgate-cemetery.org*

Exploring the North

Morning

🕑 Starting at Hampstead tube station, head left down pretty Flask Walk (The Flask pub once sold spa water) to the local museum in **Burgh House** for some background on the area. Then spend some time exploring the many attractive back streets, which are lined with expensive Georgian houses and mansions. Visit Well Walk, fashionable in the days of the Hampstead spa (a fountain in Well Passage on the left still remains), and Elm Row, where D H Lawrence lived at No. 1.

☕ Stop for a coffee at one of the many cafés along Hampstead High Street and then make your way to **Keats House** *(see p141)*, spending half an hour looking around. Afterwards, a stroll across Hampstead Heath to **Kenwood House** will prepare you for lunch.

Afternoon

🍴 The Brew House at Kenwood serves excellent light meals and has a fine position beside the house, overlooking the lake. After lunch, a visit to the house will take an hour or so.

Leave the Heath by the nearby East Lodge and catch a No. 210 bus back towards Hampstead. The bus passes the **Spaniards Inn** *(see p63)* and Whitestone Pond – the highest point on the Heath. Alight at the pond and walk to the tube station, taking a train to Camden Town. Get lost for the rest of the afternoon in lively **Camden Lock Market** *(see p141)*, ending the day with a drink and some food on the **Lock Tavern** roof terrace.

Left **Almeida Theatre** Right **Crafts Council Research Library façade**

Best of the Rest

1 Sadler's Wells
London's premier venue for dance attracts internationally renowned artists and companies from around the world *(see p57)*.
Ⓢ *Rosebery Avenue EC1 • Map F2*
• 0844 412 4300 • www.sadlerswells.com

2 Freightliners Farm
A little bit of the countryside in the city with animals, produce, gardens and a vegetarian café.
Ⓢ *Sheringham Road N7 • Tube Highbury & Islington, Caledonian Road • 020 7609 0467*
• www.freightlinersfarm.org.uk

3 Almeida Theatre
This famous local theatre attracts the best actors and directors from the UK and the US.
Ⓢ *Almeida Street N1 • Tube Angel or Highbury & Islington • 020 7359 4404*
• www.almeida.co.uk

4 Alexandra Palace
Located in a beautiful park, this reconstructed 1873 exhibition centre offers a range of amusements, including regular antique fairs. Tours of the 1920s BBC studios may be booked.
Ⓢ *Tube Wood Green • BBC tours: 020 8365 2121*

5 King's Head Theatre Pub
A busy but delightful Victorian pub with a 110-seat theatre showing musicals and fringe performances at the back. A wide selection of wines and real ale. Bands and DJs also feature. Ⓢ *115 Upper Street N1 • Map F1 • 020 7226 4443 • www.kingsheadtheatre.com*

6 Camden Arts Centre
Known for its fascinating contemporary art exhibitions and excellent art book shop.
Ⓢ *Arkwright Road NW3 • Train or Tube to Finchley Road & Frognal • 020 7472 5500*
• www.camdenartscentre.org

7 Crafts Council Research Library
Books, videos and an image database on British contemporary craftwork. By appointment only.
Ⓢ *44a Pentonville Road N1 • Map F1*
• 020 7806 2501 • Free

8 Hampstead Theatre
This important fringe theatre is a venue for ambitious new writing, and has produced plays by such innovative British artists as Harold Pinter, Michael Frayn and Mike Leigh. Ⓢ *Eton Avenue NW3 • Tube Swiss Cottage (exit 2) • 020 7722 9301 • www.hampsteadtheatre.com*

9 Regent's Park Golf and Tennis School
This floodlit facility is open for golf and tennis from 8am–9pm daily. Ⓢ *Outer Circle, Regent's Park NW1 • Tube Camden Town*

10 Emirates Stadium Tours
Home to Arsenal Football Club, the tour offers a look behind the scenes of the stadium: the directors' box, home changing room, players' tunnel and press conference room as well as the Arsenal Museum. Ⓢ *Highbury N5 • Tube Arsenal • 020 7619 5000*

For more London theatres **See pp56–7**

Price Categories

For a three-course meal for one with half a bottle of wine (or equivalent meal), taxes and extra charges.

£	under £15
££	£15–£25
£££	£25–£35
££££	£35–£50
£££££	over £50

Left **Metrogusto** Right **Camino, King's Cross**

🔟 Eating and Drinking

1 Afghan Kitchen

This great little restaurant is popular among Islington locals and serves a tempting selection of home-cooked Afghan food. ◈ *35 Islington Green N1 • Map F1 • 020 7359 8019 • £*

2 Manna

Global vegan cuisine is served with style in this modern restaurant with a welcoming ambience. Seasonal menus. ◈ *4 Erskine Road, Primrose Hill NW3 • Tube Chalk Farm • 020 7722 8028 • ££££*

3 S&M Café

A great alternative to the British greasy spoon, this café serves sausages and mash as well as other comfort food made from quality ingredients. Choose from over half a dozen varieties, from traditional pork to steak and guiness sausages. ◈ *4–6 Essex Road N1 • Map G1 • 020 7359 5361 • ££*

4 Metrogusto

This restaurant offers simple, classic Italian food, from the grill, as well as home-made bread, pasta and ice cream. Excellent house wines. ◈ *14 Theberton Street N1 • Map F1 • 020 7226 9400 • ££££*

5 Camino

Offering tapas and great cocktails as well as Spanish wines, sherries and traditional cider, Camino is a welcome addition to King's Cross. ◈ *3 Varnisher's Yard N1 • Map E1 • 020 7841 7331 • £££*

6 Lemonia

Traditional and modern Greek dishes are served in a brasserie-style setting. There is an attractive conservatory. ◈ *89 Regent's Park Road NW1 • Tube Chalk Farm • 020 7586 7454 • £££*

7 Rotunda

A classy restaurant with fine views of the Battlebridge Basin. The menu changes regularly and uses seasonal ingredients; the meat is sourced from their own farm. ◈ *90 York Way N1 • Map E1 • 020 7014 2840 • £££*

8 Louis Patisserie

This wonderful old tea room is part of Hampstead folklore. Sink into a comfortable sofa and sample some of the tempting cakes on display in the window. ◈ *32 Heath Street NW3 • Tube Hampstead • 020 7435 9908 • £*

9 The Flask

Dating from 1700, this pub has a country atmosphere and good cask beer. Home-made pub food, lunchtime and evenings. ◈ *14 Flask Walk NW3 • Tube Hampstead • 020 7435 4580 • £££*

10 Spaniards Inn

Opposite the toll house on Hampstead Heath, this is one of London's most famous old pubs. Traditional English pub food is mingled with more exotic choices such as *calamari* (squid). ◈ *Spaniards Road NW3 • 020 8731 8406 • Tube Hampstead, Golders Green • ££*

Left **Old Royal Naval College, Greenwich** Right **Deer in Richmond Park**

South and West

THE PALACES THAT ONCE GRACED LONDON'S *river to the south and west of the city centre* were built in places that remain popular today, from Hampton Court and Richmond in the west, downriver to Greenwich. There, on a deep meander in the Thames, a vast Tudor palace was the dramatic first sight of the city for anyone arriving by ship. That palace has been replaced by Wren's handsome Royal Naval College, a stunning riverside building that is the high point of this World Heritage Site and the start of the many delights of Greenwich Park. These include the Royal Observatory Greenwich, home of world time. Richmond's palace has also disappeared, but opposite the Park lies Kew Palace in the grounds of the incomparable Royal Botanic Gardens. Chiswick House, Ham House and Syon House are the best of a number of palatial mansions near Richmond, while culture is catered for in the Dulwich Picture Gallery and the Horniman Museum.

 Sights

1. Hampton Court
2. Greenwich
3. Royal Botanic Gardens, Kew
4. Richmond
5. Dulwich Picture Gallery
6. Chiswick House
7. Horniman Museum and Gardens
8. Syon House and Park
9. Ham House
10. Wimbledon Lawn Tennis Museum

Carving over entrance to remains of Richmond Palace

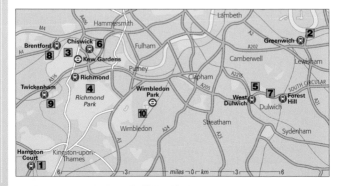

Palm House, Kew Gardens

Hampton Court

Visiting this historic, royal Tudor palace and its extensive grounds is a popular day out from London. As well as family trails and special exhibitions, tours of six separate areas with costumed or audio guides are available. Events held here throughout the year include a week-long music festival in June, which regularly attracts big-name performers. In July, the grounds are filled by the world's largest flower show, organized by the Royal Horticultural Society. Trains from Waterloo take about half an hour but for a delightfully leisurely trip, catch a boat from Westminster Pier, which takes about four hours (see pp54–5).

East Molesey, Surrey • Train Hampton Court • 0844 482 7777 • Open Apr–Oct: 10am–6pm daily; Nov–Mar: 10am–4:30pm daily (last adm 1 hour before closing) • Admission charge • www.hrp.org.uk

Greenwich

The World Heritage Site of Greenwich includes Sir Christopher Wren's Old Royal Naval College, Greenwich Park (see p29), the Planetarium and the Royal Observatory Greenwich where the Prime Meridian, Longitude 0°, was established. In the fine park are the Queen's House (see p55) and National Maritime Museum (see p48). Greenwich has several excellent restaurants and marine-related shops as well as a market selling arts, crafts and antiques. The old tea clipper, the *Cutty Sark* (see p71), is being restored nearby. *Greenwich SE10 • Train to Greenwich; DLR Cutty Sark, Greenwich • Royal Observatory Greenwich: Open 10am–5pm daily • Admission charge*

Royal Botanic Gardens, Kew

This former royal garden holds the world's largest plant collection of around 30,000 specimens. Kew Palace and Queen Charlotte's Cottage (see p54) were used as residences by George III, whose mother, Princess Augusta, laid the first garden here. Take a Kew Explorer Land train tour of the gardens – you can get on and off it any time. *Kew TW9 • Train & tube Kew Gardens • 020 8332 5655 • Open 9:30am daily; closing times vary between 4:15–5:30pm in winter and from 6–7:30pm in summer. Call for information • Admission charge • www.kew.org*

Left **Hampton Court** Centre **Clock at Royal Observatory** Right **Queen Charlotte's Cottage**

For more on royal London See pp54–5

Richmond

4 This attractive, wealthy riverside suburb, with its quaint shops and pubs and pretty lanes, is particularly worth a visit for its attractive riverside walks *(see p74)* and its vast royal park *(see p29)*. There is also a spacious Green, where cricket is played in summer, which is overlooked by the lovely restored Richmond Theatre and the early 18th-century Maids of Honour Row, which stands next to the last vestiges of an enormous Tudor Palace. For some history visit the local Museum, in the Old Town Hall, where the visitor information centre is based.

Restored façade of Richmond Theatre

◈ *Richmond, Surrey • Train to Richmond • Museum of Richmond: open 11am–5pm Tue–Sat*

Dulwich Picture Gallery

5 This wonderful gallery *(see p51)* is opposite the main entrance to Dulwich Park and is well worth the journey from Central London. Apart from the stunning collection, there are regular exhibitions, lectures and friends events, usually including music, food and wine, to which anyone is welcome. ◈ *Gallery Road SE21 • Train to North or West Dulwich • 020 8693 5254 • Open 10am–5pm Tue–Fri, 11am–5pm Sat–Sun • Admission charge*

Greenwich Palace

The ruins of this enormous royal riverside palace lie beneath the Old Royal Naval College green. Many of the Tudor monarchs lived here, including Henry VI, Henry VII and Henry VIII. Abandoned under the Commonwealth in 1652, it was eventually demolished for Wren's present buildings.

Chiswick House

6 This piece of Italy in London is a high spot of English 18th-century architecture. The villa, with its dome and portico, was built for Lord Burlington, with beautifully painted interiors by William Kent. Temples, statues and a lake complete the Italianate gardens. ◈ *Burlington Lane, Chiswick W4 • Tube Turnham Green • 020 8995 0508 • Open Apr: 10am–5pm daily; May–Oct: 10am–5pm Sun–Wed; Nov–Mar: closed • Admission charge (house) • www.chgt.org.uk*

Horniman Museum

7 This distinctive museum with displays on the cultural and natural world, appeals to both adults and children. A giant creepy crawly display sits alongside an interactive gallery devoted to music and world cultures. There is also a small aquarium. The café looks over the 16-acre garden. ◈ *London Road SE23 • Train to Forest Hill • Open 10:30am–5:30pm daily*

Left **Richmond alley** Right **Chiswick House**

Ham House

Syon House and Park
8 This sumptuous Neo-Classical villa is home to the Duke of Northumberland. It has fine Robert Adam interiors and a 16-ha (40-acre) garden landscaped by Capability Brown and dominated by a splendid conservatory.
Brentford, Middlesex • Train to Kew Bridge • 020 8560 0882 • Open Apr–Oct: 11am–5pm Wed, Thu & Sun (gardens open daily) • Admission charge • www. syonpark.co.uk

Ham House and Garden
9 This outstanding 17th-century house and garden was at the centre of court intrigue during Charles II's reign. Its interiors are richly furnished and there is a fine picture collection. The menu in the Orangery is inspired by 17th-century dishes. *Richmond, Surrey • Train to Richmond • 020 8940 1950 • House open Apr–Oct: noon–4pm Sat–Thu (garden 11am–5pm) • Admission charge*

Wimbledon Lawn Tennis Museum
10 With a view of the famous Centre Court, the museum tells the story of tennis, from its gentle, amateur beginnings to its exciting professional status today. The first tennis championship were held in Wimbledon in 1877. *Windmill Road, Wimbledon SW19 • Tube Southfields • 020 8946 6131 • Open 10am–5pm daily Admission charge • www.wimbledon.org*

A Day Exploring Maritime Greenwich

Morning

Start the day from Westminster Pier, because the best way to arrive at **Greenwich** *(see p147)* is by boat. The journey takes 50–60 minutes and there are terrific river sights on the way *(see pp70–71)*. The old tea clipper **Cutty Sark** *(see p71)* is undergoing restoration but the visitor centre is worth a visit. Step into the nearby Greenwich tourist information centre to get your bearings.

Behind is Greenwich Market, which is liveliest on weekends. Grab a coffee here, and then explore the surrounding streets, full of antique and other charming shops. Turn into Wren's Old Royal Naval College, walk around the Grand Square, and then down to the river. Take a break for some lunch and a pint at the old Trafalgar Tavern on the far side of the Naval College overlooking the river.

Afternoon

After lunch, make your way back up to the **National Maritime Museum** *(see p48)*, Queen's House and the **Royal Observatory Greenwich** *(see p147)*, which is on the hill behind. Spend a couple of hours exploring the fascinating museum, the largest of its kind in the world, then make your way to the Observatory. This is the home of world time, and stands on the Prime Meridian. You can be photographed with one foot in the eastern hemisphere and one in the west. Return to Central London by boat, DLR or rail from Greenwich.

Left **Battersea Park** Right **Brixton Market**

🔟 Best of the Rest

1 Brixton Market
This colourful market lies at the heart of London's Caribbean community. The atmosphere is lively, with music stalls pumping out sounds, and the scent of aromatic ethnic foods. Look for secondhand vinyl, fresh produce and bargain fabrics. Open 8am–5pm Mon–Sat. *Electric Avenue to Brixton Station Road SW9 • Tube Brixton*

2 Battersea Arts Centre (BAC)
One of the main fringe theatre venues in the capital, with a huge programme of activities. *Lavender Hill SW11 • Train to Clapham Junction • 020 7223 2223*

3 Battersea Park
Entertainments in this large park include a boating lake, a children's zoo, sports facilities, and a gallery. There is also a woodland walk, nature reserve and therapy garden. *Battersea Park SW11 • Train to Battersea Park • Open dawn to dusk daily*

4 The Bush
This off-West End theatre is one of London's premier showcases for new writers. *Shepherd's Bush Green W12 • Tube Shepherd's Bush • 020 8743 5050 • www.bushtheatre.co.uk*

5 Merton Abbey Mills
An arts and crafts village on the River Wandle, with a working Victorian watermill, a children's theatre and weekend craft market. *Merantum Way SW19 • Tube Colliers Wood • www.mertonabbeymills.org.uk*

6 WWT London Wetland Centre
This wetlands paradise for wildfowl is the best urban wildlife site in Europe (see p75). *Barnes SW13 • Train to Barnes • Open 9:30am–6pm daily (winter: 9:30am–5pm) • Admission charge • www.wwt.org.uk*

7 Wimbledon Common
Start with a visit to the windmill, and then try not to get lost roaming the 445 ha (1,100 acres). The Crooked Billet and the Hand in Hand on the south side are pubs to head for. *Wimbledon Common SW19 • Train to Wimbledon*

8 Stamford Bridge Stadium
Visit the home of Chelsea Football Club with a behind-the-scenes tour of this famous club. *Fulham Road SW6 • Tube Fulham Broadway • 0871 984 1955 • Tours from 11am–3pm daily • Admission charge*

9 Firepower
An exciting museum at the historic home of the Royal Artillery. Hundreds of exhibits as well as a spectacular multi-media display. *Royal Arsenal, Woolwich SE18 • Train to Woolwich Arsenal • Open 10:30am–5pm Wed–Sun • Admission charge • www.firepower.org.uk*

10 World Rugby Museum
At Twickenham Stadium, the national home of rugby. A visit includes a tour of the stadium. *Rugby Road • Train to Twickenham • Open 10am–5pm Tue–Sat, 11am–5pm Sun • Admission charge • www.rfu.com*

The River Café

Price Categories		
For a three-course meal for one with half a bottle of wine (or equivalent meal), taxes and extra charges.	£	under £15
	££	£15–£25
	£££	£25–£35
	££££	£35–£50
	£££££	over £50

🔟 Eating and Drinking

1 The River Café
The "best Italian restaurant outside Italy" is the long-standing reputation of this imaginative Hammersmith restaurant, housed in a converted warehouse with a river terrace. ◈ Thames Wharf, Rainville Road W6 • Tube Hammersmith • 020 7386 4200 • £££££

2 Thai Square Putney Bridge
A brilliant view of the river from this smart, innovative glass restaurant makes it a good spot year-round, and the Thai menu is excellent. ◈ 2–4 Lower Richmond Road SW15 • Tube Putney Bridge • 020 8780 1811 • £££

3 Chez Bruce
Stylish yet relaxed, Chez Bruce serves excellent modern European food. Service is impeccable and booking is essential. ◈ 2 Bellevue Road SW17 • Train to Wandsworth Common • 020 8672 0114 • £££££

4 The Glasshouse
The food is exciting, modern European at this relaxed restaurant. ◈ 14 Station Parade, Kew, Surrey • Tube Kew Gardens • 020 8940 6777 • No disabled access • £££££

5 The Gate
Probably the best vegetarian restaurant in London, The Gate is worth hunting out. The gourmet menu changes regularly, and the meals are hearty and inventive. Closed Sundays. ◈ 51 Queen Caroline Street W6 • Tube Hammersmith • 020 8748 6932 • No disabled access • £££

6 Carpenter's Arms
It may look like an old boozer but the food here is hearty fare made with well-sourced, seasonal ingredients. ◈ 89–91 Black Lion Lane W6 • Tube Stamford Brook • 020 8741 8386 • £££

7 Inn at Kew Gardens
A lovely hostelry with great pump ales and moreish gastro food. It's also perfectly located beside Kew Gardens. ◈ 292 Sandycombe Road, Kew TW9 • Tube Kew Gardens • 020 8940 2220 • £££

8 The Green Room
A thoroughly modern venue in an old fashioned part of town. Great cocktails at the stylish bar, simple but good Anglo-French food in the restaurant. ◈ 45A Goldhawk Road W12 • Tube Goldhawk Road • 020 8746 2111 • £££

9 Esarn Kheaw
Authentic Thai food, with all the usual favourites as well as more unusual dishes such as mud fish sweet and sour soup. Expect liberal use of chilli and spices. ◈ 314 Uxbridge Road W12 • Tube Shepherd's Bush • 020 8743 8930 • ££

10 Marco
Marco Pierre White's acclaimed restaurant at Chelsea Football Club offers a Modern take on classic English cuisine. The glamorous interior adds to the culinary experience. ◈ Stamford Bridge, Fulham Road SW6 • Tube Fulham Broadway • 020 7915 2929 • ££££

Note: Unless otherwise stated, all restaurants accept credit cards and serve vegetarian meals

Left **Columbia Road Market** Right **Bengali sweet factory**

Heading East

THE EAST END IS *booming. Always a vibrant, working-class area and home to London's dockworkers, the area has also prided itself on providing a refuge for successive generations of immigrants, from French silk weavers to Jews and Bangladeshi garment workers. Since the 1980s, the East End, where the murderous Jack the Ripper roamed, has under-gone a radical transformation. Today, the media and finance worlds occupy stylish Dockland developments, galleries and restaurants have sprouted in Hoxton and a host of Sunday markets, including trendy Spitalfields, draw newcomers who marvel at the area's unspoilt 18th- and 19th-century architecture.*

🔟 Sights

1. Canary Wharf
2. Museum of London Docklands
3. Hoxton
4. Whitechapel Gallery
5. V&A Museum of Childhood
6. Spitalfields
7. The Thames Barrier
8. Brick Lane
9. Columbia Road Market
10. Geffrye Museum

Fifty-storey-high Canada Tower at Canary Wharf

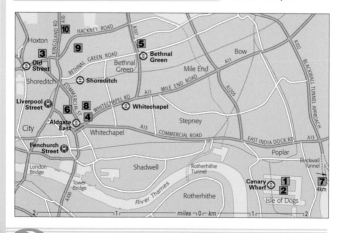

Vaulted glass roof, Canary Wharf DLR station

Canary Wharf

The centrepiece of the Docklands development is Canary Wharf and the 240-m (800-ft) -high, 50-storey Canada Tower designed by the US architect, Cesar Pelli. The tower is not open to the public but parts of the complex are, including the mall, with shops, restaurants and bars. The star of the area's exciting architecture is the stunning Canary Wharf station, designed by Norman Foster. *Tube & DLR Canary Wharf*

Museum of London Docklands

Set in a historic warehouse, this museum explores the history of London's river, port and people. A wealth of objects is on display, from whale bones to WWII gas masks, in state-of-the-art galleries. Don't miss *Mudlarks*, an interactive

area for kids; *Sailortown*, an atmospheric re-creation of 19th century riverside Wapping; and *London, Sugar & Slavery*, which reveals the city's involvement in the slave trade. *West India Quay E14 • Tube & DLR Canary Wharf, DLR West India Quay, Thames Clippers Canary Wharf Pier • 020 7001 9844 • Open 10am–6pm daily*

Hoxton

This is the place to see the latest in British contemporary art. Hoxton Square is home to the White Cube gallery, where many of the now established contemporary artists, known as the YBAs (Young British Artists), such as Damien Hirst, Sarah Lucas and Tracey Emin, first made their names. Cafés and eateries include the Hoxton Square Kitchen and Bar and the Real Greek *(see p157)*. *Tube Old Street*

Whitechapel Gallery

This excellent gallery has a reputation for showing cutting-edge contemporary art from around the world. The gallery has launched the careers of David Hockney, Gilbert and George and Anthony Caro. Behind the Arts and Crafts façade there is a bookshop, café and restaurant. *77–82 Whitechapel High Street E1 • Map H3 • 020 7522 7888 • Open 11am–6pm Tue–Sun (Thu 9pm) • www. whitechapelgallery.org*

Left **Museum of London Docklands** Right **Whitechapel Gallery's 1901 entrance**

5 V&A Museum of Childhood

Everyone will find something to delight them here: from dolls and teddy bears to train sets and games through the ages. There are special events and activities for kids of all ages, during weekends and holidays, as well as ones linked to current exhibitions. ◉ *Cambridge Heath Road E2 • Tube Bethnal Green • 020 8983 5200 • Open 10am–5:45pm daily • www.vam.ac.uk*

6 Spitalfields

Streets such as Fournier Street, lined with 18th-century Huguenot silk weavers' houses, are a reminder that this area, just east of the City, has provided a refuge for immigrant populations for centuries. London's oldest market, Old Spitalfields Market still has stalls selling food, with cafés and a large shopping complex around its edge. On Sundays the market draws hundreds, eager to find a bargain among the fashion, vintage clothing, and crafts stalls here. There are also free events such as lunchtime concerts. Opposite is one of Europe's great Baroque churches. Christ Church (1716) was designed by Wren's pupil, Nicholas Hawksmoor (1661–1736). ◉ *Commercial Street E1 • Map H2*

Christ Church Spitalfields

The Huguenots in London

Driven from France in 1685, the Huguenots were Protestants fleeing religious persecution by Catholics. They were mostly silk weavers, whose masters and merchants built the beautiful Georgian houses around Fournier, Princelet and Elder streets. Spitalfields silk was famous for its fine quality, but by the mid-19th century the industry had declined.

7 Thames Flood Barrier

Rising like shark fins from the river, this piece of engineering is an impressive sight *(see p71)*.

◉ *Visitors' Centre • Unity Way SE18 • Train to Charlton, tube North Greenwich • 020 8305 4188 • Open summer: 10:30am–4:30pm daily, winter: 11am–3:30pm daily • Admission charge*

8 Brick Lane

Once the centre of London's Jewish population, this street is now the heart of London's Bangladeshi community. Head here for inexpensive, Indian food at restaurants such as Preem and Shampan. Some of the city's best bagels are from the 24-hr Brick Lane Beigel Bake – a famous dawn haunt for late-night revellers. There are vintage and designer shops and, on Sundays, a lively flea market. ◉ *Brick Lane • Tube Aldgate East*

Left **Georgian terrace, Fournier Street** Right **Dining room, Geffrye Museum**

Columbia Road Market

Columbia Road Market

9 Londoners head east on Sunday mornings for the bustling street markets. In addition to Petticoat Lane in Middlesex Street, with its bargain clothes and household items, and Brick Lane's bric-à-brac, there is the teeming plant and flower market in Columbia Road. Ten minutes' walk from the north end of Brick Lane, Columbia Road is a delightful cornucopia of all things horticultural at bargain prices.
Ⓢ *Columbia Road E2 • Tube Old Street • Petticoat Lane • Tube Aldgate East*

Geffrye Museum

10 Devoted to the evolution of family life and interior design, this fascinating museum has a series of rooms decorated in distinct period style from 1600 to the present day. Originally a 1715 almshouse, the building has been transformed and you can wander through an oak-panelled 17th-century drawing room, a 1930s flat or a contemporary loft apartment. Period gardens are open from April to October. Ⓢ *Kingsland Road E2 • Map H2 • 020 7739 9893 Open 10am–5pm Tue–Sat, noon–5pm Sun*

A Day Around the East End

Morning

Start at **Old Spitalfields Market**, close to Liverpool Street station, where a mixture of stalls hold sway during the week, and many more, selling clothes, food and collectibles, fill the floor on Sundays. Have a delicious English breakfast at St John Bread & Wine opposite the market at 96 Commercial Street *(see p157)*.

Walk around the corner into Fournier Street, where the gallery at No. 5 retains the panelling of the 18th-century silk weavers' houses. Stroll along Princelet and Elder streets, just off Fournier, for a taste of historic London.

Head into **Brick Lane** to browse among the saree and Bangladeshi gift shops. Stop for lunch at one of the many authentic curry houses that line the street.

Afternoon

After lunch turn right into Whitechapel Road. Notice the distinctive Arts and Crafts façade of the **Whitechapel Gallery** *(see p153)* and pop into the gallery's stunning two-floor exhibition space dedicated to contemporary and modern art. Have a cup of tea in the café and stop by the bookshop.

Finally, take a ride on the driverless Docklands Light Railway (from Tower Gateway, a short walk from Whitechapel), for some of the best views of East London. Emerge at Canary Wharf to see some impressive architecture around Cabot Square, and finish the afternoon with a drink at **Via Fosse** *(see p157)* on West India Quay.

 For more on shopping **See p170**

Left **Folly, Victoria Park** Right **Sailing, Docklands Watersports Centre**

☰🔟 Best of the Rest

1 Theatre Royal Stratford East

A local theatre with an international reputation – established by the pioneering director Joan Littlewood in 1953 – where exciting new work can still be seen. Next door is an arts centre with a gallery and cinema. ✎ *Gerry Raffles Square E15 • Train, tube & DLR Stratford • 020 8534 0310*

2 Victoria Park

One of East London's largest and most pleasant parks. There are two lakes, where model boats are sailed at weekends, ornamental gardens, a children's zoo, tennis courts and a bowling green. ✎ *Bow E9 • Tube Bethnal Green*

3 Dennis Severs' House

This 18th-century silk-weaver's home *(see p154)* is kept perfectly in period and was created by the late Dennis Severs. Each room in this "still-life drama" appears as if the inhabitants have only just left it – dinner is half-eaten and cooking smells emanate from the kitchen. ✎ *18 Folgate Street E1 • Map H2 • 020 7247 4013 • Call to check opening times • Admission charge*

4 Sutton House

This Tudor merchant's house dates from 1535 and is one of the oldest in the East End. ✎ *2–4 Homerton High Street E9 • Tube Bethnal Green, then 253 bus • 020 8986 2264 • Open Sep–Jul: 10:30am–4:30pm Thu–Fri, noon–4:30pm Sat–Sun; Aug: 10:30am–4:30pm Mon–Wed*

5 Three Mills Museum

Built in 1776, this tidal mill complex was once the country's largest. Today it is a working museum with much of its original machinery on display. ✎ *Three Mill Lane E3 • Tube Bromley-by-Bow • 020 8980 4626 • Open Jun–Oct: 2–4pm Wed*

6 Cabot Hall

An events venue in Docklands with comedy clubs and public concerts. ✎ *Canary Wharf E14 • DLR Canary Wharf • 020 7418 2782*

7 Docklands Sailing & Watersports Centre

Enjoy sailing, rowing and canoeing facilities here. ✎ *Millwall Dock, Westferry Road E14 • DLR Crossharbour • 020 7537 2626 • www.dswc.org*

8 Mudchute Farm

Britain's largest city farm has a collection of livestock, plus a riding school. ✎ *Pier Street E14 • Open 9am–5pm daily • DLR Mudchute • 020 7515 5901*

8 ExCeL

An award-winning development beside the Royal Victoria Docks with shops, cafés and a vast exhibition space. ✎ *Victoria Dock Road E16 • DLR Custom House.*

10 Mile End Park

For skateboarders, BMX riders and rollerbladers. This park also has a go-kart track, an Ecology Park and Children's Play Park. ✎ *Mile End Road E3 • Tube Mile End • 020 7264 4660*

Price Categories

For a three-course	**£** under £15
meal for one with half	**££** £15–£25
a bottle of wine (or	**£££** £25–£35
equivalent meal), taxes	**££££** £35–£50
and extra charges.	**£££££** over £50

City bar and restaurant, Cantaloupe

🔟 Eating and Drinking

The Real Greek
Great restaurant serving Greek food like you've never tasted before. Start with *mezedes* (starters). The wine list has excellent Greek wines. ◈ *15 Hoxton Market N1 • Map H2 • 020 7739 8212 • £££*

Les Trois Garçons
Elaborate decor is all part of the dining experience at Les Trois Garçons. Happily, the food is consistently excellent and the service solicitous. Overall, this is not as pricey as you would think. ◈ *1 Club Row E1 • Map H2 • 020 7613 1024 • £££££*

St John Bread & Wine
This sister restaurant of St John *(p139)* is a much-loved local haunt, with its long opening hours (from 9am Mon–Fri, 10am Sat & Sun) and excellent British food. It has a great wine list, and the bakery sells amazing bread and cakes to go. Convenient for Old Spitalfields Market. ◈ *94–96 Commercial Street E1 • Map H2 • 020 3301 8069 • £££*

Canteen
Located in the complex next to Old Spitalfields Market, it serves traditional British food from 9am to 11pm. ◈ *Unit 2, Crispin Place, off Brushfield Street E1 • Map H2 • 0845 686 1122 • £££*

Cargo
Set in three railway arches, this large space is devoted to music, drink and food until 1am. Live music every night in the back-room club or the garden in summer, and a bargain priced lunch. ◈ *Kingsland Viaduct, 83 Rivington Street EC2 • Map H2 • 020 7739 3440 • ££*

Fox
Fine dining can be had upstairs in this lovely refurbished pub, which is frequented by City types looking for decent ales and wines. ◈ *28 Paul Street EC2 • Map H2 • 020 7729 5708 • £££*

Cantaloupe
A large warehouse bar serving chips and snacks at the bar and Mediterranean food in the restaurant. ◈ *35–42 Charlotte Road EC2 • Map H1 • 020 7729 5566 • £££*

Gun
This swish Docklands operation overlooking the Thames serves up quality pub food. ◈ *27 Cold Harbour E14 • DLR South Quay/Blackwell • 020 7515 5222 • ££££*

Café Spice Namaste
One of the best fine Indian restaurants in London, focusing on Goan and regional cooking. Closed Sundays. ◈ *16 Prescot Street E1 • Tube Tower Hill & Aldgate • 020 7488 9242 • ££££*

Prospect of Whitby
East London's finest pub, with rustic charm, dates to 1520, and has old beams and barrels, a pewter bar and great river views. ◈ *37 Wapping Wall E1 • Tube Wapping • 020 7481 1095 • £££*

 Note: *Unless otherwise stated, all restaurants accept credit cards and serve vegetarian meals*

STREETSMART

LONDON'S TOP 10

Umbrellas on a wet London day

TOP 10 Planning Your Trip

1 What to Pack
Be prepared for all weathers, and be sure to bring a waterproof jacket and umbrella, even in summer. In winter, you will need a warm coat and sweater. Formal dress is rarely obligatory, but people do dress up for the opera as well as for some theatrical shows and smart restaurants. If you are coming in summer bring sunscreen as London sun can be strong.

2 Currency
For security, bring a cash card or traveller's cheques. Check that your cash withdrawal card is acceptable in the UK – most are. Bring some British currency to pay for fares and immediate needs on arrival *(see Banking p165)*.

3 Passports and Visas
A valid passport is needed to enter the UK. Visitors from the EU, Commonwealth countries and the US do not need a visa. Always check with the British Embassy in your country. Contact your London-based embassy if you need to extend your stay beyond six months.

4 Customs Regulations
Firearms, offensive weapons, endangered species and some types of food and plants cannot be brought into the UK for personal use. If you need

regular medicine, bring adequate supplies and/or a prescription with you. For more information visit www.ukba.home office.gov.uk

5 Insurance
Take out an insurance policy that covers loss of baggage, theft and health. Although emergency treatment is usually free from the National Health Service, and there are reciprocal arrangements with other EU countries, specialist care, drugs and repatriation are costly.

6 Driving Licence
If you are planning to drive in the UK and you are an EU citizen, be sure to bring your licence as well as registration and insurance documents. Also inform your insurance company of the trip. Other foreign nationals require an international drivers licence.

7 Time Difference
Don't forget to set your watch to Greenwich Mean Time for the UK, which is one hour behind Continental European Time and five hours ahead of US Eastern Seaboard Time. From March to September clocks go forward an hour ("summer time").

8 Electrical Appliances
Throughout the UK, the electricity supply is 240 volts AC. Plugs are of a three-square-pin type, so

buy an adaptor before leaving home. Most hotels have two-pin sockets in their bathrooms for use with shavers only.

9 Children's Needs
Planning ahead when travelling with young children can make a trip more enjoyable. Avoid travelling on public transport during peak hours *(see p169)*. Book tickets in advance, and bring a fold-up stroller.

10 Membership Cards
Bring any membership cards for driving or heritage organizations with links to the UK, such as the Automobile Association or National Trust, that offer discounts at many attractions. A student ISIC card *(see p171)* is also useful.

Embassies

Australian High Commission
Australia House, Strand WC2 • Map M3 • 020 7379 4334 • www.australia.org.uk

Canadian High Commission
1 Grosvenor Square W1 • Map D3 • 020 7258 6600 • www. unitedkingdom.gc.ca

United States Embassy
24 Grosvenor Square W1 • Map D3 • 020 7499 9000 • www. usembassy.org.uk

Preceding pages **Piccadilly Arcade**

Left **Eurostar train** Right **Aeroplane, Heathrow Airport**

TOP 10 Arriving in London

1 Heathrow Airport

London's main airport is 15 miles (24 km) west of central London. The Heathrow Express train to Paddington is the quickest way into the centre, taking 15 to 20 minutes. Trains run from 5am until about 11pm daily. Taxis take an hour or more, depending on traffic, and are very expensive. Cheap options include the tube (Piccadilly line) or National Express coach into the centre. ◈ *Heathrow information: 0844 335 1801 • www.heathrowairport.com*

2 Gatwick Airport

London's second airport is 31 miles (50 km) south of the centre, on the Surrey-Sussex border. The Gatwick Express train runs every 15 minutes into Victoria Station, taking around 30 minutes. There are also train connections to London Bridge and St Pancras. The National Express coach is a little cheaper and takes an hour longer. ◈ *Gatwick information: 0844 3351 802 • www.gatwickairport.com*

3 Stansted Airport

The UK's third busiest airport is 35 miles (56 km) northeast of London. The Stansted Express train to Liverpool Street station takes 45 minutes. Coaches to various London locations take between 1 and 2 hours. ◈ *Stansted information: 0844 335 1803 • www.stanstedairport.com*

4 Luton Airport

This airport is 31 miles (50 km) north of London. A shuttle bus connects the airport to Luton Airport Parkway station, from which trains go to St Pancras taking around 20 minutes. Green Line operates a coach service to central London. ◈ *Luton information: 01582 405 100 • www.london-luton.co.uk*

5 London City Airport

Situated in Docklands, 9 miles (14 km) from the centre, this airport is best served by DLR from Bank tube station. A taxi to the centre takes about 35 minutes. ◈ *London City information: 020 7646 0088 • www.londoncityairport.com*

6 Other Airports

England's other main airports are Birmingham, Liverpool, Manchester, Newcastle and East Midlands. All have direct road, rail and bus connections to and from London.

7 Victoria Coach Station

Both national and international buses operate from here, London's main coach station. The terminal is a 10-minute walk from Victoria railway station. ◈ *Victoria Coach Station, 164 Buckingham Palace Road SW1 • Map D5 • Reservations: 0871 781 8178 • www.national express.com*

8 St Pancras International

Home to over 50 shops, bars and restaurants – including Europe's longest champagne bar – this is the place to arrive in London via Eurostar. Trains take under 2 hours from Brussels or 2 hours 15 minutes from Paris. ◈ *St Pancras International • Map E2 • Eurostar enquiries and reservations: 08432 186 186 • www.eurostar. com, www.stpancras.com*

9 Channel Crossings

Eurotunnel operates a drive-on-drive-off train service between Calais, in northern France, and Folkestone, in the south of England (35 minutes). Ferries from Calais to Dover, the shortest Channel crossing, take around 90 minutes. The drive to London on the M20 motorway takes around 1 and a half hours. ◈ *www. eurotunnel.com • Reservations: 0844 879 7379*

10 Other Sea Links

Car ferries sail from northern France to other Channel ports in the south of England, as well as from Bilbao and Santander in northern Spain to Portsmouth or Plymouth. Hoverspeed operates a fast catamaran service from Dieppe to Newhaven (summer only). Passenger and car-ferry services also run to other ports around the country from the Netherlands, Scandinavia and Ireland.

Left **Taxis** Centre **Bus line** Right **Walking**

Getting Around

1 The Underground

London's underground train network, or "tube", is the fastest way to get around town, but trains are crowded during rush-hour. Lines are colour-coded and easy to follow on the map on the back cover of this book. Trains run from around 5:30am to midnight, with fares based on the six zones into which the network is divided. Zone 1 covers Central London. ◊ *Transport for London: 0843 222 1234 • www.tfl.gov.uk*

2 London Buses

Slower than the tube but a cheaper way to travel, buses are also a good way of seeing the city as you go. To travel in the city between midnight and 6am, you will need a night bus. Most night buses may be picked up at bus stops around Trafalgar Square and the West End.

3 Docklands Light Railway (DLR)

The automated overland railway serving Docklands has two branches, one that heads south to Greenwich and Lewisham and the other to Woolwich, Arsenal. It is linked to the Underground network at Bank, Tower Gateway (near Tower Hill) and other points. Outside rush hour, it is a pleasant way of seeing this regenerated area of the East End. ◊ *Transport for London: www.tfl.gov.uk*

4 Pre-paid Travel Passes

One-day and weekend Travelcards are economical if you make more than two trips by public transport in a day. They can be bought at tube stations or newsagents, and are valid on the Underground, some overground trains, buses and the DLR, on weekdays after 9:30am. Oyster cards and weekly and monthly Travelcards are also available: for a monthly pass you need a passport-sized photo. You can buy a Visitor Oyster Card or Travelcard online before you arrive. ◊ *www.tfl.gov.uk*

5 Rail Travel

Suburban and intercity travel is served through the 10 main London termini. Rail travel is expensive and the fare structures complicated. Planning ahead for long journeys is advisable and may save money. ◊ *National Rail Enquiries: 08457 484950 • www. nationalrail.co.uk*

6 Taxis

London's black cabs can be hailed anywhere; their "For Hire" sign is lit up when they are free. You can also find them at railway stations, airports and taxi ranks. A 10 per cent tip is customary. Black cabs can be ordered in advance from Radio Taxis and Dial-a-Cab. ◊ *Dial-a-Cab: 020 7251 0581 • Radio Taxis: 020 7272 0272*

7 Minicabs

Only obtain a minicab by telephone or by visiting a firm's office. Never pick one up on the street, or from one of the unofficial offices in Soho, as they are likely to be uninsured. "Lady Minicabs" have only women drivers. ◊ *Lady Minicabs: 020 7272 3300 • www.ladyminicabs.co.uk*

8 Car Rental

Car rental is not cheap in the United Kingdom and the rates are similar among the larger companies. Europcar and Thrifty are most likely to offer deals. Drivers must show a valid licence and be aged 21 or even 24. ◊ *Europcar: 0871 384 9847 • Thrifty: 01494 751500*

9 Cycle Rental

You need a strong nerve to cycle in London's busy traffic, but it can be a great way to see the city. Barclays Cycle Hire has docking stations in central London. ◊ *• www. tfl.gov.uk/BarclaysCycleHire*

10 London on Foot

Walking is a rewarding option in London. The centre of the capital is not large, and you will be surprised at how short the distance usually is between two points that seem quite far apart when travelled by tube. Traffic drives on the left in the UK, so take care when crossing the road, and watch for light signals.

For information on guided tours **See pp168–9**

Left **Britain Visitor Centre sign** Right **Britain and London Visitor Centre interior**

🔟 Sources of Information

1 London Tourist Board

Visit London is the official tourist organisation for London and has a range of services for visitors to the capital, including a useful accommodation booking scheme. Their website gives a number of options. ✆ *Visit London: 020 7234 5800 • www. visitlondon.com*

2 Tourist Information Centres

Offering advice on anything and everything from day trips and guided tours to accommodation, you will find these Visitor Centres at 1 Lower Regent Street W1, on level 2 of Tate Modern and in Greenwich, at Pepys House SE10. They stock free leaflets on current events and attractions. The City of London Information Centre (opposite St Paul's Cathedral in EC4) is also useful.

3 Accommodation

Pre-paid hotel reservations booked through Visit London are guaranteed to be the lowest rate you can find. If paying by credit card, you can use their hotel booking service online. You can also book in person at centres in Victoria and Liverpool Street stations, and at Heathrow. ✆ *Visit London Accommodation Booking Service: 0871 222 3118 • www.visitlondon offers.com*

4 Restaurant Websites

There is a wide range of restaurant review sites that offer both unbiased professional appraisals and local diners' reviews of London establishments, complete with online reservation facilities. The most popular are London Eating and Top Table. ✆ *www.london-eating.co.uk; www.toptable.com*

5 Television

Apart from satellite and digital television, there are five terrestrial channels in the UK: two run as public service channels by the BBC (BBC1 and BBC2), and the three commercial channels (ITV, Channel 4 and Channel 5). Ceefax and Teletext are text programmes on these channels, giving travel and weather updates.

6 Radio

London radio stations bring constant news and travel updates for the capital. They include BBC London Live (94.9 FM), Capital FM (95.8 FM) and LBC (97.3 FM).

7 Publications

For current events in London, see the daily papers, particularly the *Evening Standard* (the capital's free evening paper), and *Time Out*, the weekly listings magazine, which includes activities for children. The *Evening Standard*'s website *www. thisislondon.co.uk* is also helpful. Visit London (London's Tourist Board) publishes useful guides on accommodation and activities in the capital.

8 Weather

London's weather is unpredictable, but if you want to check ahead phone Weathercall for an up-to-the-minute forecast. There are also regular weather forecasts for the capital and other regions on radio and television. ✆ *Weathercall: 0845 610 1800 • www. weathercall.co.uk*

9 Britain and London Visitor Centre (BLVC)

Here you will find a vast amount of information on London and the rest of the country, with advice on accommodation, travel, attractions and activities. As well as the Visitor Centre in Regent Street, there is a good website. ✆ *1 Lower Regent Street W1 • Map J2 • 0870 156 6366 • Open daily • www.visitbritain.com*

10 London Lesbian & Gay Switchboard

This telephone helpline provides information, support and a referral service for lesbians and gay men. They can give advice on services, organisations and entertainment venues. ✆ *020 7837 7324 • www. turingnetwork.org.uk*

Left **Low floor bus** Right **Wheelchair access ramp**

🔟 London for the Disabled

Accommodation
Most large, modern hotels have disabled access, but older or small hotels may not, so do check before booking. RADAR (Royal Association for Disability and Rehabilitation), the main organization for the disabled, publishes an annual guide, *Holidays in Britain and Ireland*, which lists recommended accommodation.
🕾 *RADAR: 020 7250 3222 • www.radar.org.uk; www.tourismforall.org.uk*

Public Transport
With long escalators, stairs, walkways and heaving rush hours, it is particularly difficult for the disabled to travel on the Underground. However, the total bus fleet is wheelchair accessible. A useful travel access leaflet called "Get on Board" is produced by Transport for London and available at Travel Information Centres at Heathrow airport, main tube and rail stations, and some suburban ones. For more information call Transport for London. 🕾 *Transport for London: 020 7222 1234 • www.tfl.gov.uk • www.accessproject-phsp.org*

Museums
Most of London's museums and galleries have ramps for wheelchair access and disabled toilets. Recorded "audio tours" can often be hired, which are useful to those with impaired vision.

Theatre and Cinema
Most theatres and cinemas in London have disabled access. Call in advance to find out what seating is allocated for disabled visitors – some offer good seats, others not so good. For more information on accessibility in arts venues, call Artsline.
🕾 *Artsline: 020 7388 2227 • www.artsline.org.uk*

Restaurants
Some restaurants are more accessible than others: even if they have wheelchair access, the dining areas may be on an upper or lower floor, so check when booking a table. Our Top 10 listings state if a restaurant does not have disabled access.

Guided Tours
Based in Kensington, London W8, Can Be Done specializes in holidays and tours for the disabled. They will put together a package to suit your requirements. The company offers accommodation, theatre packages and sightseeing trips around London. All the accommodation offered is wheelchair adapted while transfers and private sightseeing tours can be arranged in wheelchair adapted vehicles *(see p168)*.
🕾 *Can Be Done: 020 8907 2400 • www.canbedone.co.uk*

Students
SKILL, the National Bureau for Students with Disabilities, offers limited help and information, as does the UK Council for International Student Affairs (UKCISA).
🕾 *SKILL: 0800 328 5050. www.skill.org.uk • UKCISA: (1800 10 prefix for textphone) 020 7288 4330. www.ukcosa.org.uk*

Impaired Hearing
Many theatres have a sign-language interpreter on duty at all or some performances. Call in advance to check. The Royal National Institute for the Deaf (RNID) may be able to help with some enquiries. 🕾 *RNID: 0808 808 0123/9000 (textphone). www.rnid.org.uk*

Impaired Sight
The Royal National Institute for the Blind (RNIB) can provide information on holiday options. Braille maps of London's transport system are available from Transport for London's Access & Mobility unit.
🕾 *RNIB: 0303 123 9999 • www.rnib.org.com • Transport for London: 020 7222 1234. www.tfl.gov.uk*

Other sources
Organisations including Dial UK, Disability Now, Disabled Go and Enabled London offer a wide range of information and advice for people with disabilities. Information is available on the Internet.

For more information on getting around London See p162

Left **Bank** Right **Post box**

🔟 Banking and Communications

1 Money
The pound sterling (£) is divided into 100 pence (p). Paper notes are in denominations of £5, £10, £20 and £50. Coins are £1 and £2 (yellow-gold); 5p, 10p, 20p, 50p (silver); and 1p and 2p (copper).

2 Banks
Opening hours for banks are generally 9:30am–4:30pm Monday to Friday. Most banks and building societies have cash machines in an outside wall. Some also have lobbies with cash and payment machines – these can be accessed by your cash card at any time of night or day.

3 Bureaux de Change
Bureaux de Change are regulated, and their rates are displayed along with commission charges. These are either flat fees or percentage charges. Many offer exchange without a commission fee, but check their rates as these may be less favourable than those charging a fee. Travelex has many branches throughout London where money can be changed.

4 Credit Cards
Most establishments accept the major credit cards such as Visa and MasterCard (Access). American Express and Diners Club cards are less widely accepted in the UK. Credit cards are particularly useful for hotel and restaurant bills, shopping, car rental and reserving theatre or movie tickets by telephone. They can also be used to obtain cash advances, with a PIN number.

5 Postal Services
Post offices and sub-post offices are located throughout London. They are generally open from 9am–5:30pm Monday to Friday and until 12:30pm on Saturday. You can also buy stamps in shops, hotels and other outlets. The main West End post office is near Trafalgar Square. Mail sent *Poste Restante* to this address will be kept from two to four weeks. American Express also provides a *poste restante* service for its customers. Ⓢ *Post office: 24/28 William IV Street WC2. Map M3 • American Express: 30–31 Haymarket SW1. Map L4. www. americanexpress. com • Royal Mail Customer Services: 0845 774 0740. www.royal mail.com*

6 Telephones
Most phone boxes take coins (40p minimum) and credit cards. You will need at least £2 to make an international call. If you have difficulty contacting a number, call the Operator (100) or International Operator (155). In an emergency, dial 999 or 112.

7 Dialling Codes
The code for London is 020, which you omit when dialling within the city. When calling from abroad, dial the access code followed by 20, omitting the initial 0. To call abroad from London, dial 00 followed by the access code of the country you are dialling. To find a number call one of the directory services listed below. Ⓢ *Directory Enquiries: 118 500 • International Directory Enquiries: 118 505*

8 Faxes and Photocopies
There are fax and photocopying shops throughout London, and most of the larger hotels also offer these facilities.

9 Mobile Phones
London is awash with mobile (cellular) phones. Check before leaving home whether yours will work within the UK, which uses a 900 or 1800 GSM system.

10 Internet
There are a number of Internet bars and cafés throughout London with charges varying from free (if you're buying drinks at the bar) to £5 an hour. The worldwide chain Easy Internet Café has several branches in central London, including one at the Trafalgar Square end of the Strand. Ⓢ *Easy Internet Café: 456–59 Strand WC2 • Map M4*

Left **Bow Street police station, Covent Garden** Centre **Mounted police** Right **Boots pharmacy**

Security and Health

Emergency
For emergency police, fire or ambulance services dial 999 – the operator will ask which service you require. This number is free on any public telephone.

Personal Protection
London, like most metropolitan areas, has its share of bagsnatchers and pickpockets. You should be aware of this late at night and in outlying or poorly populated areas. Look after your possessions, keeping valuable items concealed. In pubs and other public places, keep hold of your bag – it is not unknown for bags to vanish from between their owners' feet in movie theatres and bars. Avoid poorly lit back streets, at night and if you are on your own.

Theft
Make sure that your possessions are insured before you arrive and, if possible, leave passports, tickets and travellers' cheques in the hotel safe. Report all thefts to the police, especially if you need to make an insurance claim. There is a police presence in such busy areas as Leicester Square and Oxford Street, as well as several central police stations. ✆ *West End Central Police: 27 Savile Row W1 • Map J3 • 0300 123 1212.*

Lost Property
Anything found on the tube, buses, trains or black cabs is sent to the Transport for London Lost Property Office. Allow three to five days for items to get there. ✆ *Transport for London Lost Property: 200 Baker Street NW1. Map C3. Open 8:30am–4pm Mon–Fri • 0845 330 9882 • www.tfl.gov.uk*

Hospitals
There are a number of hospitals in central London with 24-hour emergency services, including dental hospitals. Emergency accident treatment may be free for visitors *(see p160).*

Pharmacies
Pharmacies (known as chemists in England) are open during business hours, some until late, and can give advice on minor ailments. Boots is a large, respected chain with branches throughout London. ✆ *Boots, Piccadilly Circus W1. 020 7734 6126. Map K3. Open 8am–midnight Mon–Fri, 9am–midnight Sat, noon–6pm Sun • Bliss Pharmacy, 107–109 Gloucester Road SW7, 020 7373 4445. Map B5. 9am–midnight daily*

Dentists
Hotels can usually suggest local dentists, and many are listed in Yellow Pages. For emergency dental work, go to Guy's Hospital Dental Department, near London Bridge.

Embassies and Consulates
These are around Mayfair, Belgravia, Kensington and the West End if you lose your passport, need a visa or legal advice *(see p160).*

Women Travellers
If travelling alone, take sensible precautions. Use busy, well-lit streets at night, don't travel in empty carriages on trains and use licensed black cabs displaying an identification disc *(see p162).*

Sexual Health
St Mary's Hospital, Paddington, and St Thomas', Westminster have clinics for sexually transmitted diseases. ✆ *NHS Sexual Health Line: 0800 567 123*

London Hospitals

St Mary's
Praed Street W2 • Map B3 • 020 3312 6666

St Thomas'
Westminster Bridge Road SE1 • Map N6 • 020 7188 7188

University College
A&E (24 hrs), Euston Road NW1 • Map E2 • 0845 155 5000

Guy's Hospital Dental Department
St Thomas' Street SE1 • Map G4 • 020 7188 8006

NHS Direct
24-hour advice line • 0845 4647

Left **Punting, River Cam, Cambridge** Right **Palace Pier, Brighton beach**

🔟 Excursions from London

Windsor Castle
This ancient bastion of British royalty is well worth a day out. Its state apartments and the 15th-century St George's Chapel are glorious. As a working Royal residence, opening hours can change. Check website before visiting. ⊗ *Windsor, Berks • Train: 40 mins • 020 7766 7304 • Open Mar–Oct: 9:45am–5:15pm; Nov–Feb: 9:45am–4:15pm • Admission charge • www.royalcollection.org.uk*

Oxford
Britain's oldest university town is a fascinating place to visit, with ancient colleges, museums and galleries at every turn. For a short introduction to the city, start at The Oxford Story on Broad Street. The most magnificent colleges are Christ Church, Magdalen and Merton. ⊗ *Train: 1 hr • Tourist Information: 01865 252 200 • www.visitoxford.org*

Cambridge
Don't miss King's, Trinity, Queens' colleges, and Peterhouse, the oldest college (1284) in Cambridge. Relax on a punt on the river Cam, which runs along the backs of the colleges. ⊗ *Train: 45 mins • Tourist Information: 0871 226 8006 • www.visitcambridge.org*

Brighton
"London-on-Sea" is the nickname of this cosmopolitan city, established as a fashionable resort by the Prince Regent in the late 18th and early 19th centuries when he moved to the extravagant Royal Pavilion. Shop for antiques in The Lanes, have fish and chips on the pier and visit the beach. ⊗ *Train: 1 hr • Tourist Information: 01273 290 337 • www.visitbrighton.com*

Stratford-upon-Avon
William Shakespeare's birthplace (1564) is firmly on the tourist map. There are several buildings here associated with the great playwright, as well as the Royal Shakespeare Theatre if you want to catch a performance. ⊗ *Train: 2 hrs • Tourist Information: 0870 160 7930 • www.shakespeare-country.co.uk*

Canterbury
In AD 597, this pleasant market town southeast of London became the seat of the primate, the Archbishop of Canterbury. The magnificent cathedral includes the tomb of St Thomas Becket. ⊗ *Train: 1½ hrs • Tourist Information: 01227 378 100 • www.canterbury.co.uk*

Chessington World of Adventures
A vast amusement park that was originally a zoo (it still has jungle animals in its Animal Land section) will keep children happy all day. The rides include a terrifying upside-down rollercoaster. Tickets bought in advance are cheaper. ⊗ *Chessington, Surrey • Train: 30 mins • 0871 663 4477 • Open Mar–Dec: opening times vary • Admission charge • www.chessington.com*

Thorpe Park
The highest water ride in Europe is just one of the attractions at this theme park, which is popular with families. ⊗ *Chertsey, Surrey • Train to Staines: 30 mins • 0871 663 1673 • Open Mar–Oct: opening times vary • Admission charge • www.thorpepark.com*

Woburn Abbey
Home to the Dukes of Bedford, this outstanding 18th-century stately home with large grounds has a fine collection of paintings and furniture. There is a full events programme each year and a Safari Park 10 minutes away. ⊗ *Woburn, Bedfordshire • Train to Flitwick: 1 hr, then taxi • 01525 290 333 • See website for opening times • Admission charge • www.woburn.co.uk/abbey*

Leeds Castle
England's most romantic castle is built on two islands in a lake surrounded by 500 acres of Kent parkland. ⊗ *Maidstone, Kent • Train to Bearsted 1 hr, then coach transfer (all-inclusive ticket) • 01622 765 400 • Open all year; check website or call for details of times and events • Admission charge • www.leeds-castle.com*

Left **Walking tour** Right **London sightseeing bus**

🔟 Trips and Tours

1 Sightseeing Bus Tours

Open-top sightseeing buses provide one of the best ways of getting to know London. There are several operators and a number of tours with pick-up points around the city, so you can get on and off all day, wherever you want. Some companies include a cruise along the River Thames. ✎ *Original Tour: 020 8877 1722 • Big Bus Tours: 020 7233 9533*

2 River Trips

There is a choice of boat services on the Thames but they are run by different operators and tickets are not interchangeable. It is best to buy tickets at the piers so that you can find out exactly what is on offer. Westminster and Embankment are the principal central London piers. Boats from here go up river to Hampton Court and downriver to Tower Bridge and Greenwich. ✎ *Embankment Pier: Map M4 • Westminster Pier: Map M6*

3 Regent's Canal

This is a lovely backwater for idle cruising, between Camden Lock and Little Venice. Catch the boat at either end, and stop off at London Zoo *(see p68)*. ✎ *London Waterbus Co: 58 Camden Lock Place NW1 • Map B2 • 020 7482 2550 • www.londonwaterbus.com*

4 Themed Walks

Jack the Ripper Haunts, Ghosts of the Old City, Shakespeare's London, Hidden London – there are dozens of such walks on offer from both individuals and companies. The longest established operator, The Original London Walks, offers a wide choice of two-hour walks. ✎ *020 7624 3978 • www.walks.com*

5 City Jogging Tours

For a healthy and eco-friendly sightseeing tour, join a guided jogging tour around London. The daily tours are led by experienced runners and cater both to individuals and groups of all running abilities. The guides promise a fascinating journey through the streets of the city. ✎ *0845 544 0433 • www.cityjoggingtours.co.uk*

6 Backstage

Most of London's historic theatres offer daytime backstage tours. The National Theatre's tour of all three theatres (the Olivier, the Cottesloe and the Lyttelton), as well as of dressing rooms and workshops, lasts about 75 minutes. Call to reserve *(see p56)*. ✎ *National Theatre: 020 7452 3400*

7 Open House

On one weekend at the end of September, around 700 buildings in London, from city blocks to private homes, open their doors to the public, revealing some hidden architectural gems. The event is run by the organisation Open-City – check out their website. ✎ *http://open-city.org.uk • Free*

8 Air Tours

Several companies offer sightseeing tours by helicopter. Cabair offers a half-hour tour of London that follows the route of the Thames. The flight leaves from Elstree Aerodrome in north London. ✎ *Cabair: Borehamwood, Hertfordshire • Train to Elstree and Borehamwood, then taxi • 020 8953 4411 • www.cabairhelicopters.com*

9 Thames Barges

The magnificent Thames barges that used to fill the Pool of London can now be seen in St Katharine Docks *(see p71)*. Topsail Events hires out barges for the day or an overnight stay. Tower Bridge is opened to let them through. ✎ *Topsail Events: 020 7022 2201 • www.topsailevents.co.uk*

10 Out of Town

Several operators run bus trips to well-known sights within an hour or two's drive of London or further afield, including Paris. Golden Tours is one of London's leading sightseeing companies and offers a wide range of scheduled tours daily. ✎ *Golden tours: 020 7233 70 30 • www.goldentours.com*

➜ *For more on trips out of London* **See p167**

Liverpool Street Station, the City

TOP 10 Avoiding the Crowds

1 Rush Hour
Try to avoid travelling in the Monday to Friday morning (8–9:30am) and evening (5–6:30pm) rush hours when tube trains and buses are filled to bursting point and cabs are scarce. If you can, it is often more pleasant and quicker to walk.

2 Lunch Hour
Londoners generally have lunch between 1 and 2pm, when pubs, cafés and fast-food restaurants fill up and sandwich bars have long lines of people. On the other hand, this can be a good time to go to smarter restaurants which try to attract lunchtime crowds by offering cheap menus. Lunch in the City tends to be earlier: noon–1pm.

3 Dining Out
Although restaurants in the West End and the South Bank are generally packed with theatregoers taking advantage of the inexpensive pre- and post-theatre dinner menus, many of these become less crowded around 8pm once the curtain has gone up.

4 Early Start
Most sights in the capital – especially the major sights, such as the Tower of London and Madame Tussauds – are least crowded early in the day. You will have to fight the rush hour to get there, however.

5 School Holidays
During school holidays, London's museums and other sights in the capital are filled with families and groups of children. In general, school holidays last six weeks in summer from the end of July to the beginning of September, with additional two–three week breaks at Easter and Christmas. Sights are also crowded during half-terms: the last week in February, May and October.

6 Matinees
Some of the most popular shows and events in London theatres are heavily booked far in advance. However, they often have seats available for their midweek and Saturday matinees.

7 Booking Ahead
Popular exhibitions operate a system of pre-booked, timed entry tickets in order to prevent overcrowding. Try and reserve well in advance to secure an early morning or late admission to avoid the biggest crowds.

8 Late Evenings
Shops and galleries in the capital often have late-opening evenings when they are less crowded than during the day. The shops in Oxford Street, for example, open late on Thursday evenings. Major exhibitions at the Royal Academy (see p113) and elsewhere often stay open until late one night a week. The V&A (see p119) is open until 10pm on the last Friday of each month; Tate Modern (see pp18–19) is open until 10pm on Fridays and Saturdays.

9 Weekends
London is emptier on weekends, without the commuters who stream in to work here from Monday to Friday. The City, in particular, is deserted on weekends. This is a good time to wander around and see its sights, when it is relatively free from crowds and traffic.

10 Public Holidays
The capital is quieter during the holidays as many Londoners leave town over holiday weekends. Apart from New Year and Christmas, the main bank (public) holidays in the UK are at Easter, May Day, Whitsun (end of May) and at the end of August. Be aware that some sights may be closed and that museums and galleries tend to have shorter opening hours at these times. They are unlikely to be closed completely, except for Christmas and Boxing Day (26 Dec). It is becoming increasingly common for shops and supermarkets to remain open for some, if not all of the holidays.

Left **Westfield Shopping Centre** Centre **Harrods** Right **Covent Garden Central Market**

Shopping Tips

1 Shopping Areas
There are many great places to shop in London. Covent Garden has the most up-to-the-minute clothes, shoes, jewellery and gifts; Oxford Street is best for large department stores, music, and cheaper fashion; Bond Street and Knightsbridge are where you will find all the most expensive designer labels and goods; Mayfair and St James's have the best art and antiques dealers. One New Change in the city has 60 shops spread over three floors.

2 Shopping Hours
Shops generally open 9:30am–6pm Mon–Sat, with late-night shopping until 8pm in the West End on Thursdays, and in Kensington and Chelsea on Wednesdays. Sunday has limited trading hours.

3 Payment
Most shops accept major credit cards and personal cheques endorsed with guarantee cards. VAT (Value Added Tax) is charged at 20% and almost always included in the marked price. Stores offering tax-free shopping display a distinctive sign and (for non-EU residents) will provide you with a Global Refund form for customs to validate when you leave the country.

4 Consumer Rights
Shoppers have a right to expect that goods are not faulty or damaged (this isn't always the case with sale items). Always keep receipts so you can return any unsatisfactory items.

5 Sales
Large stores and many fashion outlets usually have end-of-season sales in January and July when there are enormous savings on many items, from furniture to fashions.

6 Fashion
Big-label fashion houses are in Bond Street, Knightsbridge and Sloane Street. Bespoke wear for men is in Savile Row and St James's. Oxford Street is good for mid-range clothes. For street fashion, try the markets: Camden (see p141), Portobello (see p120), Petticoat Lane and Spitalfields (see p154).

7 Music
London is one of the world's music capitals, and its big music stores, such as HMV Oxford Street, have huge selections of CDs and DVDs, including imports. Many specialist, second-hand and collectors' shops deal in vinyl, which remains popular. The main opera and concert houses also have music outlets. For sound systems, visit Tottenham Court Road.

8 Gifts and Souvenirs
Covent Garden is great for gifts. The big West End stores (Selfridges, John Lewis, Liberty, Harvey Nichols, Harrods see pp64–5) have gift departments with bright ideas. Elsewhere around the city, there are shops selling designer jewellery, pottery, ceramics and household goods, many of which are designed in the UK. The main museums, galleries and tourist sites all have interesting gift stores.

9 Art and Antiques
The major commercial galleries are in the West End, around Bond Street and Cork Street (see p116). Bonhams and Sotheby's (see p114) auction houses are here, too. You can find inexpensive art and craft throughout London. All kinds of antiques can be sought out in Portobello Road, Kensington Church Street and King's Road (Chelsea).

10 Out of Town
If you want to do a lot of shopping under one roof and avoid the city centre, there are several huge out-of-town shopping malls. Brent Cross in north London, calls itself "London's North West End". Bluewater is another option in Greenhithe, Kent, and Westfield, Europe's largest shopping complex, is in Shepherd's Bush. Shops are open until around 8pm, restaurants and entertainments stay open later.

Left **Covent Garden Piazza** Right **St John's, Smith Square**

TOP 10 London on a Budget

1 Accommodation

There are several youth hostels in London, and universities offer rooms from June to September. International Students House has year-round rooms. There are also many cheap bed and breakfasts *(see p170)*.

2 Travel

Buses are cheaper than the tube (Underground), but they do usually take longer. If you are making more than two tube journeys in a day, Travel Cards are good value. They are also valid on buses and the Docklands Light Railway. Pre-Pay Oyster cards also save you money *(see p162)*.

3 Eating

It's quite possible to eat a two-course meal with a drink and coffee for under £20 in many places in London. Chinese and Indian restaurants are often inexpensive, and many churches have cheap lunchtime cafés. Expensive restaurants can become affordable with set-lunch or pre-theatre menus.

4 Museums and Galleries

Some museums are free. Others have free late afternoon or evening entry. A London Pass gives access to over 55 major sights plus many other savings *(www.*

londonpass.com). An International Student Card (ISIC) offers reduced-price entry to many museums. Look out for free lunchtime lectures.

5 Street Entertainment

Covent Garden is the best place for day-long entertainment, and there's always someone to look at or listen to in Leicester Square. At weekends artists hang their work up on the railings in Piccadilly outside Green Park, and by Hyde Park on Bayswater Road.

6 Free Music

London is awash with free music. Free lunchtime concerts are held in churches and at the music colleges (in term time). Performances also take place at the Southbank Centre and at the National Theatre, the National Gallery, and in malls such as Hays Galleria and Canary Wharf.

7 Cheap Tickets

The best place for these is the half-price ticket booth called "Tkts", located on the southside of Leicester Square, which sells tickets for performances on that day only. "Fringe" theatres outside the West End (often in pubs) are considerably cheaper. On Mondays, all seats are £10 at the Royal Court. The Royal Opera House has

standing tickets from £4–£14. The Prince Charles cinema in Leicester Place is the cheapest one in central London.

8 Fashion

Pick up barely worn, designer clothes at a dress agency (try The Loft, 35 Monmouth St WC2; L'Homme Designer Exchange, 50 Blandford St W1).

9 Markets

London's markets have bargain antiques, fashions, jewellery and cheap food *(see pp64–5)*.

10 Parks

London's parks offer endless free entertainment, whether watching sports in Regent's Park or listening to bands at St James's Park bandstand *(see pp28–9)*.

Directory

London Hostel Assoc
54 Eccleston Square SW1 • 020 7727 5665

Youth Hostels Assoc
Trevelyan Hse, Dimple Rd, Matlock, Derbyshire DE4 3YH • 01629 592 700 • www.yha.org.uk

International Students House
229 Gt Portland Street W1 • 020 7631 8300

London Bed & Breakfast Agency
71 Fellows Road NW3 • 020 7586 2768 • www.londonbb.com

Left **Elizabeth Hotel** Right **Fielding Hotel**

⭐10 Inexpensive Hotels

1 Travel Inn London County Hall
London's best budget hotel has a memorable location in County Hall near the river and the London Eye. Facilities are more than adequate, with fold-out beds for children in each of the 313 rooms. Book well in advance. ⊗ *Belvedere Road SE1 • Map N6 • 0871 527 8648 • www. premierinn.com • £*

2 Columbia Hotel
The Columbia has a delightful leafy setting overlooking Kensington Gardens. Originally five mansions, and once used as a US military officers' club, it has magnificent rooms and is much more opulent than its prices suggest. ⊗ *95–9 Lancaster Gate W2 • Map B3 • 020 7402 0021 • www.columbia hotel.co.uk • ££*

3 Fielding Hotel
Ideally situated for Covent Garden, this quaint room-only hotel is a warren of oddly shaped rooms, with showers and basins tucked in corners. Outside there is all of Covent Garden to breakfast in. ⊗ *4 Broad Court, Bow St WC2 • Map M2 • 020 7836 8305 • £££ • www.the-fielding-hotel.co.uk*

4 Morgan Guest House
This stylish budget B&B in a Georgian terrace in fashionable Belgravia has light, modern decor.

It is close to Victoria station and all rooms are comfortably furnished, four with private bathrooms. ⊗ *120 Ebury Street SW1 • Map D5 • 020 7730 2384 • www. morganhouse.co.uk • ££*

5 Lancaster Court Hotel
Between Paddington station and Hyde Park, Sussex Gardens is a quiet, pleasant street lined with inexpensive hotels. Lancaster Court is just a few minutes walk from Hyde Park. ⊗ *202–4 Sussex Gardens W2 • Map B3 • 020 7402 8438 • www.lancaster-court-hotel.co.uk • ££*

6 Craven Gardens Hotel
Located in a quiet, upmarket part of town, this privately run hotel has 43 bedrooms and two executive suites, with 24-hour service, coffee- and tea-making facilities in the rooms and a bar. It has no restaurant but there is a good Greek taverna just a few yards away. ⊗ *16 Leinster Terrace W2 • Map B3 • 020 7262 3167 • www. smartbackpackers.com • £*

7 Brompton Hotel
Situated just by South Kensington tube station and handy for the museums, this typical west London hotel has comfortable rooms with bathrooms. Reception is on the first floor. On the

ground-floor is an American-style bar (not owned by the hotel) run by New Yorker Janet Evans, which serves great cocktails. ⊗ *30 Old Brompton Road SW7 • Map C5 • 020 7584 4517 • www.bromhotel.com • ££*

8 Morgan Hotel
This cheerful family-run hotel is long established. Several rooms overlook the British Museum and all have air conditioning. The cosy breakfast area has framed London memorabilia on the walls. ⊗ *24 Bloomsbury Street WC1 • Map L1 • 020 7636 3735 • www. morganhotel.co.uk • £££*

9 Elizabeth Hotel
This handsome town house overlooks a quiet, private square, which is available for guests' use. It is close to Victoria station, and has single, double, triples and family rooms. ⊗ *37 Eccleston Square SW1 • Map D5 • 020 7828 6812 • www. elizabethhotel.com • ££*

10 Arran House Hotel
This child-friendly family-run hotel is conveniently located a short walking distance from the British Museum, Oxford Street and the West End. 24-hour Internet facilities and a walled summer rose garden. ⊗ *77–79 Gower Street WC1 • Map E2 • 020 7636 2186 • www.arran hotel-london.com • £££*

Price Categories

For a standard,	**£**	under £70
double room per	**££**	£70–100
night (with breakfast	**£££**	£100–150
if included), taxes	**££££**	£150–200
and extra charges.	**£££££**	over £200

Royal Garden Hotel

TOP 10 Mid-price Hotels

1 Bedford Hotel
One of six large, good-value Bloomsbury hotels run by Imperial London Hotels, the Bedford's advantage is a good restaurant and a sunny lounge and garden. ⓢ 83 Southampton Row WC1 • Map M1 • 020 7636 7822 • www.imperialhotels.co.uk • £££

2 Zetter
Modern and fun, this laid-back option offers luxuries such as the latest in-room entertainment, walk-in rain showers and free espresso machines. Its Bistro Bruno Loubet restaurant is a must. ⓢ 86–88 Clerkenwell Road EC1 • Map F2 • 020 7324 4444 • www.thezetter.com • ££££

3 The Royal Trafalgar
The Thistle Group has 10 hotels in London, many in prime sites. This one is next door to the National Gallery, so staying here will save on transport costs. ⓢ Whitcomb Street WC2 • Map L4 • 0871 376 9037 • www.thistle.com • ££££

4 Hoxton Hotel
Set in trendy Shoreditch, the Hoxton offers rooms at low prices, (which increase on higher demand). Four times a year they do an incredible £1 per room deal. ⓢ 81 Great Eastern Street EC2 • Map H2 • 0207 550 1000 • www.hoxtonhotel.com • ££££

5 Cranley Gardens Hotel
Occuping four large Victorian mansions, this is one of the best of the many South Kensington town-house hotels. Overlooking a quiet square (some rooms have balconies), this is a relaxed and friendly place to stay. ⓢ 8 Cranley Gardens SW7 • Map B6 • 020 7373 3232 • www.cranleygardenhotel.com • ££

6 Grange Langham Court Hotel
Located in a quiet side street near Oxford Circus, this enticing hotel, with its attractive façade, is as friendly inside as its exterior promises. Rooms are comfortably furnished and there is a good restaurant serving mainly French food. ⓢ 31–35 Langham Street W1 • Map J1 • 020 7436 6622 • www.grangehotels.com • ££

7 Malmaison
Located in a lovely part of Smithfields, this chain hotel is both charming and reasonably priced. As well as comfortable rooms, it has a gym, a beautifully chic brasserie and a stylish subterranean bar. ⓢ Charterhouse Square EC1 • Map G2 • 020 7012 3700 • www.malmaison.com • £££££

8 Base2stay
This "luxury budget" hotel offers free Wi-Fi, aromatherapy toiletries and mini-kitchens with free Fairtrade tea and coffee in every room. Its 67 rooms, decorated in contemporary style, range from singles and luxury bunks to family rooms and adjoining suites. ⓢ 25 Courtfield Gardens SW5 • Map A5 • 020 7244 2255 • www.base2stay.com • £££

9 Royal Garden Hotel
This refurbished hotel squeezes into the mid-price category for its excellent weekend rate. It is a pleasantly airy modern hotel next to Kensington Gardens and Kensington Palace and close to the shops of Kensington High Street. Facilities include a health centre, spa and gym, 24-hour business centre and two restaurants. ⓢ 2–24 Kensington High Street W8 • Map B4 • 020 7937 8000 • www.royalgardenhotel.co.uk • ££££

10 Meliá White House
Close to Regent's Park, this classic hotel was built as a block of model apartments in 1936. Now refurbished as a comfortable 581-room hotel, it has spacious rooms, a restaurant and bar. Prices can vary by 100 per cent, the most expensive times being mid-summer and Christmas. ⓢ Albany Street NW1 • Map D2 • 020 7391 3000 • www.solmelia.com • £££

 Note: Unless otherwise stated, all hotels accept credit cards and have private bathrooms

Left **Halkin** Centre **One Aldwych** Right **St Martins Lane**

🔟 Designer Hotels

1 Sanderson
London's most stylish hotel is cool, minimalist and thrillingly expensive. Behind a 1950s office-block exterior, plain walls are punctuated by Dali-lips and Louis XV sofas, while wafting curtains and oil paintings decorate the ceilings of the sparse bedrooms. Facilities include a gym and spa. Try the special break deals. ◎ *50 Berners Street W1 • Map K1 • 020 7300 1400 • www.morganshotelgroup. com • £££££*

2 One Aldwych
In a former 1907 newspaper building, this is a relaxing designer hotel with art-filled lobby and corridors, two good restaurants and an 18-m (56-ft) pool with underwater music. ◎ *1 Aldwych WC2 • Map N2 • 020 7300 1000 • www.onealdwych.com • £££££*

3 St Martins Lane
The Sanderson's sister hotel was designed by Phillipe Starck. Rooms have floor-to-ceiling windows and even the bathrooms (all with big tubs) are 50 per cent glass. ◎ *45 St Martin's Lane WC2 • Map L3 • 020 7300 5500 • www.morgans hotelgroup.com • £££££*

4 myhotel Bloomsbury
Just off Tottenham Court Road, this hotel is an oasis of calm, with a mystical, Oriental style and attentive staff. The rooms are light and feng-shui assured, with white orchids, fishtanks and candles for decoration. ◎ *11–13 Bayley Street WC1 • Map L1 • 020 3004 6000 • www.myhotels. com • £££££*

5 Charlotte Street Hotel
One of the most tasteful and comfortable hotels in London, where leather armchairs and antiques mix with contemporary works of art, and log fires burn in the drawing room and library. The bustling Oscar bar and brasserie attract Charlotte Street diners. ◎ *15 Charlotte Street W1 • Map K1 • 020 7806 2000 • www.charlotte streethotel.com • £££££*

6 Mercure London City Bankside
Just a stone's throw from Tate Modern, this seven-storey hotel has pay TV and a four-star restaurant. ◎ *75 Southwark Street SE1 • Map R4 • 020 7902 0800 • www.mercure.com • £££*

7 No. 5 Maddox Street
Glass, steel and bamboo feature in these high-quality Japanese-style serviced apartments, with a restaurant delivery service, Green and Black's chocolate in the fridge and full Internet facilities. ◎ *5 Maddox Street W1 • Map J3 • 020 7647 0200 • www.no5maddoxstreet. com • £££££*

8 The Hempel
When you walk into this dazzling white, Zen-inspired hotel, you'll think you've reached Nirvana. Immaculate and stylish, it has a central atrium from which five floors radiate. Each room is individually designed in a minimal Japanese style. The restaurant serves European cuisine. ◎ *31–5 Craven Hill Gardens W2 • Map B3 • 020 7298 9000 • www.the-hempel.co.uk • £££*

9 Metropolitan
Contemporary and stylish, this was one of the first of the classy modern hotels in London, with black-clad staff, cool interiors and chic bedrooms. Go celebrity-spotting in the Met Bar or in Nobu, its fashionable Japanese restaurant (see p117). ◎ *Old Park Lane W1 • Map D4 • 020 7447 1000 • www.metropolitan.london. como.bz • £££££*

10 Halkin
A startlingly beautiful hotel in a Georgian town house, which has been given a thoroughly modern overhaul with marble, glass and dark woods and oriental details. The Michelin-starred restaurant overlooks the garden and the rooms are equipped for communications and sound. ◎ *Halkin Street SW1 • Map D4 • 020 7333 1000 • www.halkin.como.bz • £££££*

➤ ***Note:** Unless otherwise stated, all hotels accept credit cards and have private bathrooms*

Price Categories

For a standard,	**£**	under £70
double room per	**££**	£70–100
night (with breakfast	**£££**	£100–150
if included), taxes	**££££**	£150–200
and extra charges.	**£££££**	over £200

Left **Marriott** Right **Tower Hotel**

🔟 Business Hotels

1 Andaz Liverpool Street

Built in 1884 as the railway hotel serving Liverpool Street station, Andaz is the only hotel in the City of London. Andaz, meaning "personal style" in Hindi, is luxurious yet friendly with a great range of eating and drinking options. It fuses a five-star hotel with a boutique, design-driven atmosphere, and has five fabulous eateries. 🕲 40 Liverpool Street EC2 • Map H3 • 020 7961 1234 • www.andaz.com • £££££

2 The Bloomsbury Hotel

This beautiful Neo-Georgian building was designed by Edwin Lutyens for the YWCA in 1929. The Queen Mary Hall is now a conference centre and the former chapel provides a quiet meeting room. The rooms have been designed for a mainly business clientele, with Internet facilities and work desks. 🕲 16–22 Great Russell Street WC1 • Map L1 • 020 7347 1000 • www.doylecollection.com • ££££

3 Four Seasons Hotel

As smart and stylish as you would expect from a Canary Wharf hotel, the Four Seasons has a central atrium and good sense of space. Rooms are all well equipped for business needs and there is a good northern Italian restaurant. 🕲 46 Westferry Circus E14 • DLR Westferry • 020 7510 1999 • www.four seasons.com • ££££

4 London Bridge Hotel

Just over the river from the City, this handsome, modern, independently owned hotel is equipped for business guests. The Londinium restaurant serves classic British food. 🕲 8–18 London Bridge Street SE1 • Map H4 • 020 7855 2200 • www.londonbridgehotel. com • £££££

5 Marble Arch Marriott

A modern hotel near the western end of Oxford Street. Facilities include a bar and restaurant, gym, health club and swimming pool. There are full business facilities in the executive lounge. 🕲 134 George Street W1 • Map D3 • 020 7723 1277 • www.londonmarriott marblearch.co.uk • £££££

6 Paddington Court Hotel

Located in a quiet area of west London north of Kensington Gardens, this Best Western hotel has 200 comfortable, spacious rooms, an inexpensive restaurant for residents and a pleasant lounge bar. 🕲 27 Devonshire Terrace W2 • Map B3 • 020 7745 1200 • www.paddington court.com • £££

7 Sheraton Park Tower

This circular hotel is a Knightsbridge landmark – views get better and more expensive the higher you go. Business guests are well catered for. 🕲 101 Knightsbridge SW1 • Map C4 • 020 7235 8050 • www.luxurycollection.com/ parktowerlondon • £££££

8 The Tower Hotel

Many of the 800-plus rooms in this vast modern block near Tower Bridge and St Katharine's Dock have spectacular river views. 🕲 St Katharine's Way E1 • Map H4 • 0871 376 9036 • www.guoman. com • £££££

9 Express by Holiday Inn

One of a chain of 10, value-for-money London hotels, the London City hotel is not actually in the City, but backs onto fashionable Hoxton Square (see p153), an area known more for art than for business. 🕲 275 Old Street EC1 • Map H2 • 020 7300 4300 • www.holidayinn.co.uk • £££

10 City Hotel

Just off Whitechapel High Street, at the bottom of Brick Lane (see p154), this hotel is ideal for business travellers who wish to be close to the City. 🕲 12 Osborn Street E1 • Tube Aldgate East • 020 7247 3313 • www.cityhotel london.co.uk • £££

Left **The Academy** Right **Durrants Hotel**

🔟 Character Hotels

Hazlitt's
As much a literary event as a hotel, Hazlitt's is located in the former townhouse of essayist William Hazlitt (1778–1830). The hotel's literary feel is enhanced by its library of books signed by the many authors that have stayed here. ◎ 6 Frith Street W1 • Map L2 • 020 7434 1771 • www. hazlittshotel.com • £££££

Durrants Hotel
This Georgian hotel, close to Marylebone High Street and Oxford Street, has been in business since 1790. It has a comfortable, old-fashioned style, with oak-panelled rooms, paintings on the walls and comfy leather seats. ◎ George Street W1 • Map D3 • 020 7935 8131 • www.durrants hotel.co.uk • £££££

The Chesterfield
Set in the heart of Mayfair, just off Berkeley Square, this 4-star luxury hotel is full of British old-world charm. Rooms are decorated with fabrics from nearby Saville Row and florals from English Cottage Garden. The fine dining restaurant serves excellent British food. ◎ 35 Charles Street W1 • Map D4 • 020 7491 2622 • www.chesterfield mayfair.com • £££££

Miller's Residence
Miller's is crammed full of fabulous chandeliers, antiques and four-poster beds. Breakfasts are generous and there's a free bar. ◎ 111a Westbourne Grove W2 • Map A3 • 020 7243 1024 • www.millershotel. com • ££££

The Academy
This charming Bloomsbury hideaway occupies five Georgian houses. The rooms are individually designed and there is a library, a conservatory and pleasant gardens. ◎ 21 Gower Street WC1 • Map E2 • 020 7631 4115 • www.theetoncollection. co.uk • ££–£££

Blakes Hotel
A Victorian delight, with sumptuous cushions and drapes, bamboo and bird cages, each room is individually styled with exotica from all over the world. The Chinese Room bar and restaurant in the basement continues the theme with low seating and cushions. ◎ 33 Roland Gardens SW7 • Map B6 • 020 7370 6701 • www. blakeshotels.com • ££££

The Gore
Originally opened in 1892, this hotel retains a relaxed, fin-de-siècle feel. Persian rugs, potted palms and paintings are in keeping with the elegance of the building, and rooms are furnished with antiques. The restaurant is also recommended. ◎ 190 Queen's Gate SW7 • Map B5 • 020 7584 6601 • www. gorehotel.com • £££

Portobello Hotel
Full of character, full of junk, with each room individually and tastefully cluttered, this is the kind of hotel you would hope to find near London's great antiques market. Food in the restaurant is prepared by the nearby Julie's wine bar. ◎ 22 Stanley Gardens W11 • Map A4 • 020 7727 2777 • www.portobello-hotel. co.uk • £££££

The Rookery
A warren of rooms has been linked together to create a brilliant hotel that evokes Victorian London, with a Gothic touch. It takes its name from the gang of thieves who once haunted this area near Smithfield market. ◎ 12 Peter's Lane, Cowcross Street EC1 • Map Q1 • 020 7336 0931 • www.rookeryhotel.com • £££££

Dorset Square Hotel
Located in an elegant square near Regent's Park, this small boutique hotel is decorated in English country style. Its charming Potting Shed restaurant serves superb modern English cuisine with a fusion twist. Rooms are decorated with antiques (two have four-posters) and there is a pleasant garden. ◎ 39 Dorset Square NW1 • Map C2 • 020 7723 7874 • www. dorsetsquare.co.uk • ££££

Note: Unless otherwise stated, all hotels accept credit cards and have private bathrooms

Price Categories

For a standard, double room per night (with breakfast if included), taxes and extra charges.	£	under £70
	££	£70–100
	£££	£100–150
	££££	£150–200
	£££££	over £200

Palm Court, Ritz

1 The Lanesborough
In London's most luxurious hotel, the Regency decoration reaches a peak in Aspleys, a Heinz Beck restaurant, while all the rooms, with deep pile carpets and gleaming mahogany, are fitted with the latest entertainment and communications technology. There is also a spa and fitness centre. ⊗ 1 Hyde Park Corner SW1 • Map D4 • 020 7259 5599 • www. lanesborough. com • £££££

2 Kensington Hotel
Set in London's Regency quarter, this luxurious townhouse hotel has 150 stylish rooms and suites. There is also a vibrant cocktail bar, modern restaurant and full-service gym. ⊗ 109–113 Queen's Gate SW7 • Map B5 • 020 7589 6300 • www.doylecollection.com/kensington • £££££

3 Savoy
Fortunate in its riverside setting, the Savoy is London's top traditional hotel and has been restored to its original Art Deco splendour. Leisure facilities include a small rooftop pool. ⊗ 1 Savoy Hill, Strand WC2 • Map M4 • 020 7836 4343 • www. fairmont.com/savoy • £££££

4 Ritz
One of London's most glamorous hotels, the Ritz is decorated in cream and pink, with gold and silk trimmings, chandeliers and Louis XVI furniture. Afternoon tea in the Palm Court is popular and the restaurant has a garden terrace. ⊗ 150 Piccadilly W1 • Map K3 • 020 7493 8181 • www.theritzlondon.com • £££££

5 Covent Garden Hotel
London's most innovative hotel group is distinguished here by modern style and traditional elegance. Rooms are individually designed with luxurious marble bathrooms. A basement screening room is a nod to its showbiz guests. ⊗ 10 Monmouth Street WC2 • Map L2 • 020 7806 1000 • www.firmdalehotels.com • £££££

6 The Waldorf Hilton
This is one of London's great Edwardian hotels. Located in the heart of the West End, a stone's throw from theatres and shopping. Leisure facilities are excellent. ⊗ Aldwych WC2 • Map N3 • 020 7836 2400 • ££££ • www.hilton.co.uk/waldorf

7 The Dorchester
Part of the fabric of London, The Dorchester opened in 1931 and has been the pinnacle of glamorous London life ever since. Alain Ducasse at The Dorchester offers contemporary French fine dining and has three Michelin stars. Book a "superior executive" for a view over Hyde Park. ⊗ 53 Park Lane, W1 • Map D4 • 020 7629 8888 • £££££ • www.thedorchester.com

8 Brown's Hotel
This Mayfair hotel was founded in 1837 by James Brown, valet to Lord Byron, to accommodate country society staying in London. Made up of 11 Georgian town houses, it is decorated with antique and contemporary art, while retaining its intimacy and charm. It is also renowned for its restaurant and English teas. ⊗ Albemarle Street W1 • Map J4 • 020 7493 6020 • www.roccofortecollection.com • £££££

9 The Colonnade
Located in the exclusive residential area of Little Venice, this four-star luxury townhouse hotel has 43 individually designed rooms, most with four-poster beds and some with private terraces. ⊗ 2 Warrington Crescent W9 • Map B2 • 020 7286 1052 • www.theetoncollection.co.uk/colonnade • £££–££££

10 The Goring
Decorated throughout in delightful Edwardiana, this gracious, family-run, country-house-style hotel combines comfort with delightful nostalgia. ⊗ Beeston Place SW1 • Map D5 • 020 7396 9000 • www.thegoring.com • £££££

Left **Hampstead Village Guesthouse** Right **Richmond Hill Hotel pool**

🔟 Hotels Out of Town

1 Hampstead Village Guesthouse

This large double-fronted Victorian family house, located just off the bottom of Hampstead High Street – and still full of the family memorabilia and toys – is now run as a guesthouse. There is a pleasant garden in which guests can eat breakfast. ✪ *2 Kemplay Road NW3 • Tube Hampstead • 020 7435 8679 • www.hampstead guesthouse.com • ££*

2 Premier Inn Hampstead

Located between Camden and Hampstead, this modern 140-bedroom hotel has all the regular facilities of a chain hotel, including a bar and brasserie. It offers very good rates at weekends. ✪ *215 Haverstock Hill NW3 • Tube Belsize Park • 0870 242 8000 • www. premierinn.com • ££*

3 Richmond Hill Hotel

Dating from 1726, this Georgian mansion at the top of Richmond Hill, close to Richmond Park, has a modern wing. A few select rooms, which are not necessarily more expensive, have river views. Guests have use of such facilities as a pool, sauna and a beauty salon. ✪ *Richmond Hill, Surrey • Train & tube Richmond • 020 8940 2247 • www.richmondhill-hotel.co.uk • £££*

4 Riverside Hotel

Based in an attractive Victorian building, this hotel has a great position near the River Thames and is not far from Richmond Park or the shops of Richmond. Some of the rooms overlook the river and one has French windows on to the hotel garden. ✪ *23 Petersham Road, Richmond, Surrey • Train & tube Richmond • 020 8940 1339 • www.riverside richmond.co.uk • ££*

5 Mitre

Originally an 18th-century coffee house, this bustling pub-with-rooms (16 en suite) is close to Greenwich's sights and transport links. The traditional pub is popular with locals and market shoppers, and serves a good selection of pub food, including Sunday lunch. There is a conservatory and garden. Parking available. ✪ *291 Greenwich High Road SE10 • Train to Greenwich • 020 8293 0037 • www. mitregreenwich.com • ££*

6 Novotel London Greenwich

Located right next to the station as well as being in the heart of Greenwich, this stylish four-star hotel, part of a chain, has 151 rooms. ✪ *173–175 Greenwich High Road SE10 • Train to Greenwich • 020 8312 6800 • www.novotel.com • £££*

7 Ibis London Docklands

This inexpensive French chain's Docklands hotel is near the river on the east side of Canary Wharf, just off the main streets. Rooms are perfectly adequate, and a buffet breakfast is served. ✪ *1 Baffin Way E14 • DLR Blackwall • 020 7517 1100 • www.ibishotel.com • ££*

8 Renaissance London Heathrow

With a 24-hour fitness centre and well-appointed, soundproofed rooms, this hotel lets you recharge while enjoying views of Heathrow's runways. ✪ *Bath Road, Hounslow • Tube Hounslow West • 020 8897 6363 • www.marriott.co.uk/ LHRBRL • ££*

9 Sofitel London Gatwick

Walk directly from Gatwick's North Terminal to this elegant hotel, which has a full range of facilities. It is linked to London by the Gatwick Express train service. ✪ *Gatwick Airport • 01293 567070 • www.sofitel.com • £££*

🔟 Hilton London Stansted Airport

A modern hotel with standard facilities, this is just a 5-minute journey to the terminal at Stansted Airport via shuttle bus. Ideal for early flights. ✪ *Stansted Airport • 01279 680 800 • www.hilton.co.uk/ stansted • £*

➡ *Note: Unless otherwise stated, all hotels accept credit cards and have private bathrooms*

Price Categories

For a standard,	£	under £70
double room per	££	£70–100
night (with breakfast	£££	£100–150
if included), taxes	££££	£150–200
and extra charges.	£££££	over £200

Left **St Paul's Youth Hostel** Right **London City YMCA**

🔟 Budget Accommodation

1 Generator Hostel London

Somewhere between sci-fi and industrial chic, this youth-orientated hostel provides budget solutions for impecunious travellers. 24-hour Internet facilities, breakfast and walking tour available. ✎ *Compton Place, 37 Tavistock Pl WC1 • Map E2 • 020 7388 7666 • www.generatorhostels.com/london • £*

2 Arosfa

Set in a Georgian town house, Arosfa has a pleasant garden and en-suite rooms. ✎ *83 Gower Street WC1 • Map E2 • 020 7636 2115 • www.arosfalondon.com • ££*

3 Elysée Hotel

In a quiet street opposite one of west London's most attractive corners, Leinster Mews, this small hotel is one of the cheapest in the area. Basic but comfortable, there are various size rooms available, including a family room for up to five people. ✎ *25–26 Craven Terrace W2 • Map B3 • 020 7402 7633 • www.elyseehotel.co.uk • ££*

4 The Court Hotel

This is a favourite with Australian and South African backpackers. Basic accommodation is offered in single or shared rooms, and reduced weekly rates are available. Internet facilities. ✎ *194–196 Earl's Court Road SW5 • Map A5 • 020 7373 0027 • £*

5 St Christopher's, The Village

This is the largest of three hostels on this street run by St Christopher's Inns. Other branches are in Camden, Greenwich, Shepherd's Bush, London Bridge and Hammersmith. Double rooms or cheaper dormitories are available. There is a café and bar, roof terrace and female-only floor. ✎ *165 Borough High Street SE1 • Map G4 • 020 8600 7500 • www.bookbeds.com • £*

6 Dover Castle Hostel

A privately run hostel offering value-for-money accommodation for backpackers, with 60 beds in dormitory-style rooms ranging from 3 to 12 persons. Showers, breakfast and lock-up included in the price. Late licensed bar with DJs and bands at weekends. ✎ *6a Great Dover Street SE1 • Map G4 • 020 7403 7773 • www.dovercastlehostel.com • £*

7 Youth Hostels Association

There are seven youth hostels in London: London Central, Oxford Street, St Paul's (Fitzrovia), Holland Park, St Pancras, Earl's Court and Thameside (all en suite). Not all do breakfast and most have shared facilities. There are various rooms, including family rooms, and cheaper rates for under 18s.

✎ *Trevelyan House, Dimple Road, Matlock, Derbyshire DE4 3YH • Central booking: 01629 592 700 • www.yha.org.uk • £*

8 YMCA

There is some nightly accommodation at the London City YMCA (8 Errol Street EC1) and Barbican YMCA (2L Fann Street EC2). Otherwise try the German YMCA (35 Craven Terrace W2) or the Indian YMCA (41 Fitzroy Square W1). ✎ *City 020 7614 5000; Barbican 020 7382 5360; German 020 7723 9276; Indian 020 7387 0411 • www.ymca.org.uk • £*

9 Host and Guest Service

This agency specializes in inexpensive B&B accommodation in homes in London and elsewhere in the UK. A two-night minimum stay is preferred. ✎ *103 Dawes Road SW6 • Map A6 • 020 7385 9922 • www.host-guest.co.uk • £*

10 International Students House

In university holidays, some student rooms are available at reasonable rates. This house, though, has space all year. Dormitories, single and twin rooms are available at a range of prices. There is a bar, a gym, a restaurant and a common room. ✎ *229 Great Portland Street W1 • Map J2 • 020 7631 8300 • www.ish.org.uk • £*

General Index

Acknowledgments

The Author
Roger Williams is a London-born journalist and long-time Soho inhabitant. He has written and edited several dozen travel guides, including Dorling Kindersley's Eyewitness guides to Provence and Barcelona. He is also the author of *The Royal Albert Hall: A Masterpiece for the 21st century*, and his fictions include *Lunch With Elizabeth David and High Times at the Hotel Bristol*.

Project Editor Simon Hall
Art Editor Nicola Rodway
Senior Editor Marcus Hardy
Senior Art Editor Marisa Renzullo
Publishing Manager Kate Poole
Senior Publishing Manager Louise Bostock Lang
Director of Publishing Gillian Allan
Photographer Demetrio Carasco
Illustrator Chris Orr & Associates
Cartography Casper Morris
Maps Tom Coulson, Martin Darlison (Encompass Graphics Ltd)
Editors Michelle de Larrabeiti, Irene Lyford
Researcher Jessica Doyle
Picture Research Brigitte Arora
Proofreader Stewart J Wild
Indexer Hilary Bird
DTP Jason Little
Production Joanna Bull, Marie Ingledew

Design and Editorial Assistance
Emma Anacootee, Lydia Baillie, Emily Bevan, Sonal Bhatt, Julie Bowles, Mariana Evmolpidou, Emer Fitzgerald, Fay Franklin, Rhiannon Furbear, Janice Fuscoe, Camilla Gersh, James Hall, Laura Jones, Maite Lantaron, Carly Madden, Alison McGill, Caroline Mead, Catherine Palmi, Helen Partington, Helen Peters, Marianne Petrou, Mani Ramaswamy, David Saldanha, Lilly Sellar, Melanie Simmonds, Hayley Smith, Sadie Smith, Susana Smith, Rachel Symons, Sylvia Tombesi-Walton, Conrad Van Dyk, Karen Villabona.

Additional Photography Max Alexander, June Buck, Jo Cornish, Michael Dent, Mike Dunning, Philip Enticknap, John Heseltine, Roger Hilton, Ed Ironside, Colin Keates, Dave King, Bob Langrish, Robert O'Dea, Stephen Oliver, John Parker, Rob Reichenfeld, Kim Sayer, Susana Smith, Chris Stevens, James Strachan, Doug Traverso, Vincent Oliver, David Ward, Matthew Ward, Steven Wooster

Picture Credits
a-above; b-below/bottom; c-centre; f-far; l-left; r-right; t-top.

The publishers would like to thank the following individuals, companies and picture libraries for their kind permission to reproduce their photographs.
ALAMY IMAGES: Robert Harding Picture Library Ltd. 147bl; ARCAID: Richard Bryant. Architect: Foster & Partners 11c, 11b, 11t; ARCBLUE: Peter Durant 16l, 18cl; ARENAPAL: Elodie Negrinotti 61tl, Michael le Poer Trench 60-61b; Colin Willoughby 60tl; L'ATELIER DE JOEL ROBUCHON: 76cra; BAR 101: Poorang Shahabi 93tl; BENJAMIN POLLOCK'S TOY-SHOP: 100cl, 103tl; STEPHEN BERE: 93tl; BRIDGEMAN ART LIBRARY, LONDON / NEW YORK: Guildhall Library, Corporation of London 43c; Kenwood House 51t; BRITISH LIBRARY: 107bl; BRITISH MUSEUM: 6tr, 8b, 9tl, 9cb, 9bl, 9cra, 10tr, 10bl; Peter Hayman 8cr; Liz McAulay 10c; CAFE DES AMIS 104tr; CAMERA PRESS: Cecil Beaton 39b; CAMINO: Ed Reeves 145tc; CARLUCCIO'S: 111tl; CHRIS CHRISTODOULOU: 57cr; COLLEC-TIONS: James Bartholomew 7crb; John D. Beldom 55br, 66cr, 119br; Oliver Benn 150tr; Nigel Hawkins 129tl; David McGill 80tl, 130cl; Keith Pritchard; Brian Shuel 66tr; Liz

Stares 17bl; BILL COOPER: 56c; CORBIS: S. Carmona 160t; Jeremy Horner 147tl; Robbie Jack 99br; Pawel Libera 50tl; London Aerial Photo Library 6cl, 16-17c; Kim Sayer 154bl; Grant Smith 17r; Adam Woolfitt 34cb. CUTTY SARK TRUST: 71tr; DEAN AND CHAPTER OF WESTMINSTER: 33tl. THE ENGLISH HERITAGE PHOTO LIBRARY: 148br. EPO ONLINE: Walt Disney Theatrical Productions/ Catherine Ashmore 60cl; FIELDING HOTEL: 172tr; FERNANDEZ AND WELLS: 94tl; FINANCIAL TIMES: 72c; FREEDOM BREWERY COMPANY: 63cr; FREUD MUSEUM, LONDON: 52b; FRIENDS OF HIGHGATE CEMETERY: Doug Traverso 75bl, 143tl. GETTY IMAGES: Hideo Kurihara 1; Jo Cornish 30-31; SALLY & RICHARD GREENHILL: Sally Greenhill 164tr; HAYWARD GALLERY ARTS COUNCIL COLLECTION: Richard Haughton 82br; HEALS: 110tl; HISTORIC ROYAL PALACES: 36tr; KOKO: 58bl; LEIGHTON HOUSE MUSEUM: 53bl; THE LONDON AQUARIUM: 68bl; LONDON TRANSPORT MUSEUM: 49cb; MADAME TUSSAUD'S, LONDON: 128tl, GARRY SAMUELS 129bl; MANGO Pr.: The Eton Collection 176tl; MARINEPICS LTD: Mark Pepper 156tr; MARY EVANS PICTURE LIBRARY: 52c, 72tl, 72tc, 72bl; MBC MANAGEMENT 61tl; MEADOWCROFT GRIFFIN ARCHITECTS: David Grandorge 145t; MORGANS HOTEL GROUP: 174tr; MUSEUM IN DOCKLANDS: 153bl; MUSEUM OF LONDON: 44c, 44b, 44t, 45tl, 48bc; 136cl; NATIONAL GALLERY, LONDON: 12b, 12t, 13cr, 13cb, 13bl, 13t, 50c, 50cl; NATIONAL MARITIME MUSEUM: James Stevenson 149cr; NATIONAL PORTRAIT GALLERY, LONDON: 6c, 14cl, 14bl, 14-15c, 14br, 15tl, 15cl, 15cr, 15b; NATIONAL TRUST PHOTOGRAPHIC LIBRARY: Bill Batten 149tl; Michael Boys 52tr; NATURAL HISTORY MUSEUM, LONDON: 22cr, 22b, 23tl, 23tr, 23ca, 23b, 119bl. THE O2: 58tr; NETWORK LONDON P R & MARKETING: 95tl; PERETTI COMMUNICATIONS: Chris Gascoigne & Lifeschutz Davidson 77tr; PHILIP WAY PHOTOGRAPHY: 40bl, 40-41c, 41t, 42c, 42bl, 43b, 80bl, PHOTOFUSION: Paul Bigland 153tl, 155br; Paul Doyle 152cr; Ray Roberts 67tr; PICTURES COLOUR LIBRARY: David Noble 4-5; POINT 101: 93tl; POPPERFOTO: Reuters/ Greg Bos 72tr; PREMIER PR: Tristram Kenton 60tr; 144tl; PRESS ASSOCIATION PICTURE LIBRARY: Toby Melville 28br; PRIVATE COLLECTION: 43tr; REX FEATURES: 27b; Tim Rooke 26br, 54tl; Ray Tang 73bl; Andy Watts 67br; RICHMOND HILL HOTEL: 178tr; THE RITZ, LONDON: 177tl; ROBERT HARDING PICTURE LIBRARY: 66tl, 66cl, 107br; Nigel Francis 28-29c; Simon Harris 36-37c; D. Hughes 137tl; M.P.H. 26bl; Walter Rawlings 130br; R. Richardson 34-35c; Ellen Rooney 54tr, 67bl; A. Tovy 126-127; Adam Woolfitt 67cr; THE ROYAL COLLECTION © 2001 HER MAJESTY QUEEN ELIZABETH II: A. C. Cooper Ltd. 27tl; Crown © HMSO 39cl, 39tr; Derry Moore 27tr; ROYAL BOTANIC GARDENS, KEW: 147br; ROYAL GARDEN HOTEL: 173tl; SADLER'S WELLS

Acknowledgments

THEATRE: Hugo Glendinning 56tr; SCIENCE MUSEUM: 24tr, 24c, 24br, 25cr, Justin Sutcliffe 7tl, 25 bl; IMAX Cinema 25cra; National Railway Museum/Science & Society 25tl; RONNIE SCOTT'S: Redferns 93tc; SHAKESPEARE'S GLOBE: 86tr; SMITHS OF SMITHFIELD: 139tl; SMITHY'S RESTAURANT & WINE BAR: 111tc; ST PAUL'S CATHEDRAL: Produced with permission of the Dean & Chapter, St Paul's Cathedral. The work illustrated on page 41cr has been reproduced by permission of the Henry Moore Foundation: *Mother and Child* (1983) Henry Moore © DACS, London 2011 41cr; Sampson Lloyd 40bl, 40-41c; ST PETER'S BREWERY CO. LTD: 63crb; STRINGFELLOWS: 59r. TAMARIND RESTAURANT: 117t; © TATE, LONDON 2011: 6bl, 20cl, 20br, 20-21c, 21tl, 21c, 21bl, 21r, 21br, 50tr; *Girl with White Dog* (1950–1) Lucian Freud 21c; *Three Studies for Figures at the Base of a Crucifixion* (one of three panels) (c. 1944), Francis Bacon © Estate of Francis Bacon/DACS, London 2011 21cr. © THE TATE MODERN: *Fish* (1926) Constantin Brancusi © ADAGP, Paris and DACS, London 2008 19cb; *Spatial Concept "Waiting"* (1960) Lucio Fontana ©

Fondazione Lucio Fontana 19cr; *The Acrobat and His Partner* (1948) Fernand Leger © ADAGP, Paris and DACS, London 2008 18–19; *Whaam!* (1963) Roy Lichtenstein © The Estate of Roy Lichtenstein/DACS, London 2008 18cb; *The Reckless Sleeper* (1928) Rene Magritte ADAGP, Paris and DACS, London 2008 19ca; *The Three Dancers* (1925) Pablo Picasso © Succession Picasso/ DACS, London 2011 18tr; *Summertime No. 9A* (1948) Jackson Pollock © ARS, New York and DACS, London 2008 18–19b. THYME: 76cr, 95tl; TRANSPORT FOR LONDON: 164tl; THE TROUBADOUR: 59clb; V&A IMAGES: 48tl 119c; V&A MUSEUM OF CHILDHOOD 69t; THE WALLACE COLLECTION: 50b; WHITE STAR LINE RESTAURANTS: 125tl; WOODMAN-STERNE PICTURE LIBRARY: 40b; YELLOW DOOR PR: Dafydd Jones 170tl.

All other images are © Dorling Kindersley. For further information see *www.dkimages.com*
